OLD GARDEN
NEW GARDENER

Gay Search and Geoff Hamilton

BBC BOOKS

PICTURE ACKNOWLEDGEMENTS

T = top, B = below, C = centre, R = right, L = left

A–Z Botanical Collection: 71, 74T.
Brian Carter/The Garden Picture Library: 67.
Liz Eddison: 70, 135.
Liz Eddison/The Chelsea Flower Show: 30B, 55T, 98B.
John Glover: 22B, 30T, 147, 171T, 178.
Mark Kershaw: 7, 11T, 14T,B, 38, 39, 50, 86T,C,B, 106, 110T,B, 119T, 127L, 162T,BL,BR.
Andrew Lawson: 23T,B, 63, 98C, 102, 119B, 146, 151, 163B,T.
Peter McHoy: 58R, 74B, 94, 122, 134, 158, 171B, 175, 179.
Clay Perry: 22T, 31, 55B.
Harry Smith Collection: 66, 91, 98T.
Ron Sutherland/The Garden Picture Library: 155.
Brigitte Thomas/The Garden Picture Library: 138.
John Vigurs: 10, 11B, 15, 58L, 114T,B, 115L,R, 127R, 130, 155B.
Andrew Wearing: 123T,B.

Published by BBC Books,
a division of BBC Enterprises Limited,
Woodlands, 80 Wood Lane, London W12 0TT
First published 1992
Reprinted 1992 (twice)

ISBN 0 563 36280 4

Illustrations by Gill Tomblin

Set in Itek Meridien by Ace Filmsetting, Frome
Printed and bound in Great Britain by Clays Ltd, St Ives plc
Colour separations by Technik, Berkhamsted
Jacket printed by Belmont Press, Northampton

CONTENTS

Acknowledgements

We would like to thank the following people and companies who all helped in the transformation of the gardens:

Robin Williams, for garden designs, Kathleen Brown, for container planting schemes, Neil Cleaton of Midshires (Rugby) Landscapes, Oscar Lawson of Bernhard's Garden Centre, Robert Kennedy of Midland Tree Surgeons, Creteprint Ltd, Lotus Water Gardens, Alan Sargent of Town and Country Gardens (Sussex), Bradstone Garden Products for paving and walling, Border Stone for boulders, pebbles and gravel, Hickson Leisure Developments for architectural trellis and fencing, Larch Lap for garden trellis and arches, Forest Fencing for *trompe-l'œil* trellis, Frolics of Winchester for 'Trellix' trees, Sadolin (UK) for wood stains and preservatives, Dulux for paints, Whichford Pottery, Grosfillex and Woodlodge Products for containers, Unique Garden Furniture Ltd for the seat table, Quigley Plastics for drain planters, Netlon Ltd for lawn path, David Austin for roses, Highfield Nurseries for fruit trees, Johnson's of Oxford for water plants and Bressingham Gardens for trees, shrubs and herbaceous plants.

As well as the owners of the three main gardens, the Bunyard family, Steve Cutner and Mandy Williams, Steve Hartwell and Jackie Mitchell, we would also like to thank Maureen and Joe Leeming, Olivia Kane and Venetia and Bill Chase for allowing us to tackle a particular problem feature in their gardens.

For a complete list of products and suppliers please send a large stamped addressed envelope to Catalyst Television, Brook Green Studios, 186 Shepherds Bush Road, London W6 7LL.

CHAPTER 1

Introduction

The chances are that your first garden will not be a bare and muddy patch behind a brand-new house, but an existing garden. If you are very lucky, it will have been well planned, well planted, and well maintained and just the sort of garden you'd have wanted anyway. All you need to do then is find out about the plants growing in it, and how to look after them, to keep the garden in good shape.

But, of course, most people aren't that lucky. The garden you inherit may have been well laid out once, with some nice plants in it, but may have become neglected over a period of years. The lawn isn't really a lawn any more – it's a mixture of tussocky coarse grasses, weeds and moss, and the borders are now so overgrown both with weeds and with the plants growing into each other that they're in need of a fairly radical sort-out.

On the other hand, you may take on a garden that is just plain boring – the classic suburban strip, for instance, with narrow flower beds on either side and a narrow concrete path straight down the middle, all emphasising its long, thin shape, with maybe an overgrown apple or cherry tree casting half the garden into shade on a summer's day.

Your new garden may also have some features that were once attractive, but are now in urgent need of restoration or repair. There may be a concrete pond that leaks, for instance, leaving you with just a few inches of water in the bottom, a few expiring plants, and even a couple of fish. Or you may find an old rockery which is structurally sound but overgrown with couch grass or, worse, ground elder, against which the few surviving rock plants are fighting a losing battle. You might have a wonky pergola, a shed or greenhouse that has seen better days. Hedges may have become thin and leggy, with such large gaps in them that they no longer perform a useful function. On the other hand, conifer hedges planted fifteen or twenty years ago to provide a quick screen and never pruned may now be taller than the house, depriving it of much needed light.

If you're really unlucky, you might inherit a wilderness, a garden neglected for so many years that it's now overrun with brambles, docks and ground elder, that have smothered most of the smaller shrubs and herbaceous plants, while the larger shrubs and trees are so overgrown that you almost expect to discover Sleeping Beauty's castle in the middle.

If the house you've bought is in the centre of a town or city, then you might find yourself taking on a small back yard covered with cracked, stained concrete, perhaps with a broken-down lean-to or maybe even an air-raid shelter and piles of rubbish, while the only plant life is likely to be a straggly self-sown buddleia or rosebay willow herb growing out of the wall.

However, it is worth saying that any old garden, no matter how badly neglected it may be, has points in its favour. It will almost certainly have some mature trees and shrubs which are worth saving, it may already have 'bones' – paths, retaining walls and so on – that are basically sound, and it will have some kind of boundary – all things that no brand-new garden has. And since it has plants growing in it, the soil will have been cultivated over the years, and while it will almost certainly benefit from digging over and feeding you won't be faced with the backbreaking task of digging over a mud heap, full of builders' rubble and compacted by weeks of mechanical diggers going back and forth across it!

When you look at the garden for the first time, your heart may well sink, and you'll wonder where on earth to start. But don't despair! In *Old Garden, New Gardener* we will show you how to overcome a whole range of problems that you might find yourself facing when you move house, especially if you're a new, or, at least, not very experienced gardener. We're also working on the assumption that, like most people when they buy a house, you have spent most of your money on the bricks and mortar and any essential jobs that need doing, so that, even with a very sympathetic bank manager, there's not a lot left to spend on the garden. There is certainly no question of simply calling in the professionals, handing over a large cheque and letting them do all the work, although sometimes you may need professional help for particular jobs.

We've chosen to concentrate on three real gardens with a range of fairly typical problems, although we'll also be looking at other gardens that each have one particular common problem and we'll show you how surprisingly quick, easy, inexpensive and – yes – exciting it can be to transform even the most unpromising patch into a beautiful garden that you can be proud of, and enjoy!

The Gardens

The over-mature garden

This garden, behind a small 1930s semi, faced southeast and was a good size – just over 28 m (92 ft) long and tapering from 12.6 m (41 ft) wide by the house to 9.2 m (30 ft) wide at the far end since it was on a bend in the road. There were wooden fences in good condition on both sides – one put up within the last year. There was some wooden fencing at the bottom of the garden, plus a bit of chain-link fencing, although the fact that there were trees in both gardens meant that there was plenty of privacy even there.

When we started work on it there were quite narrow borders down both sides, and on the northeast side of the garden another long narrow bed between the concrete path and the lawn area. Across the middle of the garden, just over halfway down, was a large bed, edged with stones and with a couple of wires stretched across it fixed to a piece of rusty angle iron at one end and a concrete post at the other.

The over-mature garden before we started – too many trees casting too much shade were a major cause of problems.

This garden was clearly well looked after at one time. There were lots of plants in it, but many of them were over-mature, and the garden had clearly been neglected for a few years.

One of the main problems here was the trees. There were too many of them, some of them were just too big, others were in the wrong place, some were growing into their neighbours (the trees' neighbours, not the people next door), while others were diseased. The net result was that what should have been quite a sunny garden was, in fact, very shady – witness the moss growing on the smaller trees. It was clear that some would have to go.

Right outside the kitchen window was the classic example of the wrong tree in the wrong place. A thuja, planted twenty-one years ago (we counted the rings of the trunk after it had been felled!), no doubt as a 'dwarf' conifer, had done a Topsy, and just growed and growed until it was taller than the house, with some of its branches only a few feet away from the back wall. It not only blocked most of the light from the kitchen window but also obscured the view of the garden. That one clearly had to come down.

On the southwest-facing border was a huge old apple tree that had been so badly hacked about that it was just an ugly tangle of twiggy branches, many of them dead or dying, which produced no fruit. The fact that it had a *Clematis montana* growing all over it only added to the problem. Planting a vigorous clematis *can* often be an answer to the question of what to do with an old tree but, in this instance, the tree itself was so unattractive that the clematis didn't help, so really the only answer was to take it out. Next to it was a large holly, a pyramid of glossy dark green that was well worth keeping, although it needed something planted in front of it, or even through it, to brighten it up a bit.

On the opposite side of the garden there was a large, although by no means fully grown, copper beech tree. It was already about 15 m (45 ft) high and, once it was in leaf, cast the area of the garden below it into deep shade. Clearly it was a tree that belonged in a forest or in rolling acres, not in a suburban garden, but it was attractive and did provide some privacy, so that one was to stay. In a few years' time a tree surgeon could reduce its size – either by reducing the height, or thinning out the crown, or both – and doing so again at four- or five-yearly intervals.

Halfway down the garden was a huge pear tree, a bit neglected, but an attractive shape and a useful focal point, while at the bottom of the garden there was a rather scruffy larch and a sorbus which provided some kind of screen and a little privacy.

Dotted around the rest of the garden were a number of small trees and large shrubs. Some of them had to go – some spindly planted-out Christmas trees, a misshapen small apple tree, a couple of leggy old brooms, some unhappy-looking, elderly roses, and rhododendrons, whose state suggested that the soil really wasn't acid enough for their needs. But quite a few trees and shrubs could stay. Right outside the kitchen window, conspiring with the thuja to block the view of the garden, there was a lovely large camellia which would have masses of deep pink semi-double flowers in March and

April. That could be dug up, put in a pot while we worked on the garden, and replanted somewhere else later on. There was also another smaller camellia in the southwest-facing border. The fact that its leaves, like the rhododendrons', were very slightly yellow was another indication that the soil was too limey for acid-loving plants. But camellias are not quite as sensitive to lime as rhododendrons, so, while the rhododendrons that were still struggling on would eventually have died if we had left them, giving the camellias a watering with Sequestrene or a special feed for acid-loving plants like Miracid increased the acidity of the soil enough for them to thrive. There were some clumps of *Kerria japonica*, with its arching sprays of bright-yellow, dandelion-like flowers in April and May, a large forsythia, and a couple of overgrown lilacs, all of which would respond well to being cut hard back.

At the bottom of the garden, in the southwest-facing border was a huge, overgrown dogwood (*Cornus alba*). These are usually grown for the bright red bark of their new stems in winter, and so are pruned back hard every spring to produce those new stems. This one clearly hadn't been pruned for years, and to cut it back really hard might have proved too much of a shock to its system, so the answer was probably to prune it moderately in the first year, and use the prunings to take hardwood cuttings. These root very easily, and in a couple of years will provide some vigorous new young plants to replace the old one altogether.

In the long narrow bed under the pear tree there was a nicely shaped young *Magnolia stellata*, which would display white starry flowers on its bare branches in spring, before the pear tree came into leaf, taking most of the light. Over by one fence a vigorous honeysuckle was sprawling untidily but that could be cut back after flowering and tied in to keep it neat.

Apart from the apple and the pear, there were some old fruit bushes – blackcurrant and gooseberry – which were worth keeping for this summer anyway. The large bed in the centre of the garden was full of old strawberry plants which were not worth saving. They were past their best and were quite likely to be suffering from virus diseases and so would produce little or no fruit. Growing in among them were bulbs, daffodils mainly, as well as aquilegias, and even a couple of large clumps of peonies. There were also quite a few peonies, primulas and aquilegias dotted around the garden, as well as a patch of lungwort (*Pulmonaria saccharata*), with its speckled green and white leaves and pink and blue spring flowers. There were a couple of large hostas, too, both in the wrong place, but well worth digging up, dividing (see p. 87) and replanting.

As for the lawns, 'grassy areas' would have been a more accurate description. There were lots of tussocks of coarse grass, bare patches and a fine crop of plantains and speedwell as well as moss, but it wasn't too bumpy, and there were still some fine lawn grasses, so it was worth trying to save.

Steve Hartwell and Jackie Mitchell – the couple who had just bought the house – were both beginners but keen to get into gardening. They wanted an attractive garden in which to relax, and also a vegetable garden.

Six months later the trees in the over-mature garden are under control.

The blank garden

This garden, behind a small 1950s semi, was a long, thin rectangle – 21.5 m (70 ft) by 8.3 m (27 ft) facing north-northeast and surrounded by weathered six-foot-high fences in good condition. All it contained was a couple of small apple trees halfway down the garden, a large old apple tree near the bottom, and a small Victoria plum on a dwarfing rootstock to restrict its growth, planted behind it in the bottom, south-facing corner. Right next to the west-facing fence, there was a small birch tree which looked as though it had grown through from next door, and in the southwest-facing corner a mahonia. The borders, all of which were overgrown with grass and weeds like couch grass and brambles, contained very few plants, mainly primulas, wallflowers, a clump of irises, and two old neglected roses.

There was a long, thin, straight concrete path running the length of the garden and four other concrete paths (some of which were completely hidden under grass and weeds) crossing the garden. By the house was a large old shed in need of renovation, and at the far end of the garden an old wooden greenhouse which had fallen down of its own accord just after the new owners moved in, leaving low brick walls and a concrete base.

Between the kitchen extension which was just under 2 m (6ft) deep and the new, deeper extension the next door neighbours had built, there was a door opening out from the dining room on to a concrete patio area. Unfortunately, because the back of the house faced just slightly east of north, this area lost the sun by mid-morning and was in shade for the rest of the day.

The blank garden had just a few apple trees, a bumpy lawn, the remains of a greenhouse and lots of bare fence.

In six months' time there's no comparison.

The couple who bought the house, Sian and Robin Bunyard, had three young children, aged nine, seven and three, and wanted to create a garden they could all enjoy, with attractive plants to look at, somewhere for the adults to sit, somewhere for the children to play in safety, and somewhere to grow some fruit and vegetables. Their previous garden was basically all grass so they considered themselves beginners, and while they were keen to learn they wanted a garden that would be easy to look after.

As for its style, Sian was keen on cottage gardens, with lots of different plants all growing together, but she also wanted the garden to be attractive in winter too. She liked soft colours, although in the shady patio area by the house they both agreed that warm colours were needed to cheer it up.

The city backyard

The estate agent's details had described this small terraced Victorian house as having 'a well-stocked garden', and it certainly was well-stocked – with all manner of debris. This long, very narrow yard – 23 m (75 ft) by 5.5 m (18 ft) – was what you could only describe as a real challenge! It faced north, backed on to both an oil storage depot and the railway sidings, with most of the area covered by a large old shed that backed on to the extension housing the bathroom, the remains of what had clearly once been a home-made garage, and a very strange raised area, covered (once a foot or so of rubbish had been removed) with paving slabs. On the east-facing side, there was a brick wall, just under 2 m (6ft) high sloping down to about 1 m (3 ft) opposite the end of the extension. It was in need of rebuilding at the far end and of repointing all the way along.

Along a section of the low part of the wall, there was some flimsy, broken-down diamond trellis, with a grape vine growing through it, although it was hard to say now which was supporting which. In the same narrow bed there was also a *Viburnum tinus*, a holly, and a deutzia, all too large for the space, plus a clump of lily-of-the-valley by the wall. Opposite them, by the shed, there was one large, leggy, neglected lavender bush.

On the west-facing side, the shed formed the boundary for part of the way, and then there was an old privet hedge about 3.5 m (11 ft) high, bare and twiggy at the base, and spreading about 2 m (6 ft) into the garden. At the end there was a large old apple tree, and, behind that, a hazel. At the bottom of the garden were two wooden gates, giving access to what had been the garage from the narrow entry behind the houses.

The new owners, Steve Cutner and Mandy Williams, had concentrated in the past on indoor plants but they were keen to expand outside. They wanted to create a garden that was reasonably private where they could eat out, relax and catch the sun, and, although there was neither the space nor the amount of sunshine needed to grow many vegetables, they did want to grow some culinary herbs. They both also liked the idea of fragrant plants, especially around the sitting-out area.

First things first

When it comes to the garden *you* have taken on, there are a number of questions you should ask yourself before you cut so much as a blade of grass. Perhaps the most important question to ask is what do you want the garden for? Do you want to work in it because gardening is your hobby or you'd like it to be? Do you want it to produce enough fruit and vegetables to feed the family? Do you want it to be somewhere where the children can play football or race their BMX bikes without giving you heart failure every time they crash into a border? Do you want it to be somewhere in which you can relax and entertain, that's attractive to look at but doesn't take up most of every weekend to keep it that way?

Be realistic – just how much time can you devote to the garden? If it's just a couple of hours a week, then you'd be mad to opt for a large vegetable garden, or borders filled with bedding plants. It would be much better to go for permanent planting – a mixture of shrubs, herbaceous plants and bulbs that more or less look after themselves once they're established.

You need to look critically at the garden itself as well. Is it sunny or shady? The answer will depend on which way it faces, and on whether it's surrounded by buildings or large trees. It would be pointless to put the patio next to the house if it's going to be in shade for best part of the day. Find the sunniest spot in the garden and think about creating a sitting-out area there. What kind of views do you have? Are they worth exploiting, building in to your design for the garden, or are they best hidden? What kind of features do you have, and are they worth keeping? Is that overgrown rockery properly built with large pieces of rock, or is it just a bank with lumps of hardcore dotted about on top of it? Do you really need a shed? If not, where are you going to keep the mower, the fertiliser and so on? If so, is *that* shed worth saving? Is it in the right place? Or are you better off starting again with a new shed somewhere else in the garden?

You must also think about any additional features you want in the garden. Perhaps you'd hardly call a washing line, or the dustbins 'features', but you must have them and they have to go somewhere. Do you want a herb garden? If so, you'll need to choose an area that gets plenty of sun, but is as close as possible to the kitchen. If it has to be right down the end of the garden, then you'll need a path leading to it. If picking a handful of rosemary for the Sunday joint becomes an expedition that involves wellies, then you'll soon find you're not bothering! If you are really keen to learn about gardening and want a greenhouse, you'll need to find a sunny spot for it but one that doesn't dominate the whole garden. Maybe you'd like a pond, but if you have small children that really isn't a good idea. Instead, why not build a sandpit for them which can be turned into a pond later on when they've outgrown the sandpit and are old enough for a pond not to be a danger any longer?

Take a good look at the garden's existing plants, trees and large shrubs, in

The first glimpse of our city backyard from outside the back door is hardly encouraging, and there's worse to follow.

The estate agent's details described our city backyard as a 'well-stocked garden'. From the far end, it's clear that it is indeed well-stocked – with hardcore, bits of broken wood, tin cans and debris of all kinds.

particular. Which ones are you going to keep, and which need to come out? The best advice is don't rush in and start digging everything up right away, especially if you take over the garden in winter. Ideally, wait a year to see what comes up, but if you can't bear to wait that long, hang on at least until early summer by which time you'll know what shrubs and herbaceous plants you've got. With trees, however, it will be pretty obvious right away which, if any, need to go (see p. 8). The one thing you do need to think about, though, is the purpose the tree serves. If it screens an ugly view or is the one thing that prevents your neighbours at the bottom of the garden from looking straight at your sunbathing area, it's worth thinking twice before you have it taken down. Alternatively, it may be worth keeping a particular tree for a few years to allow one you plant to mature and take its place eventually.

The city backyard has been transformed in just six months.

If you've got a side access to your garden, you don't have to make all the major decisions right away. If you've moved into a terraced house, though, and your only access to and from the garden is through the house itself, then it makes sense to get rid of the old lean-to, the old apple tree, the straggly old shrubs that are past redemption, and to carry in the bags of sand, the sacks of composted straw, the paving slabs, and whatever else you need *before* you've finished decorating and put the pale beige carpets down! Of course, you can do it afterwards, provided you cover the walls and carpet with sheets of heavy-duty polythene, but it's much simpler to do it first. Incidentally, if you've got so much debris to clear that you're going to need a skip, it's better to get it all together in piles before the skip arrives. While that does mean you have to move it all twice – once into a pile, the second time into the skip – it also means that you'll only need the skip for a day which will obviously reduce the costs, and will stop everyone else in the area filling it up to the brim with their rubbish before you can throw away so much as a sackful of your own!

Planning ahead

It's highly unlikely that you'll be able to afford to do everything you'd like to do in the garden right away, but it is well worth thinking long term, so that you have an overall plan for your garden. Even if you can only afford to do Phase One now, know before you start what Phase Two and Phase Three are going to be, when money permits. The mistake so many people make is to tackle the garden piecemeal, and then realise in two years' time that the place where they built the rockery is actually the perfect place for the conservatory, and so all the time and money they spent on the rockery is wasted.

You might feel overwhelmed by the thought of planning a garden, but there are all kinds of help at hand. For a start you can go and look at other people's gardens – the 'Yellow Books' or, to give them their full titles, *Gardens in England and Wales Open to the Public* and *Scotland's Gardens*, are a wonderful source of information on small, private gardens which open to the public for charity a few days a year. There are also lots of books on garden design available now, and some of the gardening magazines are beginning to feature design ideas too.

Or you could seek professional help. The Royal Horticultural Society offers the services of a garden designer to members at a surprisingly reasonable cost. The designer will come and look at your garden, suggest which plants are worth keeping, and which aren't, and make suggestions about the design. They may even give you a detailed planting plan too.

Some of the larger garden centres offer a design service now, as do some magazines – you return their detailed questionnaire on your garden and what you want from it, along with its measurements, aspect (which way it faces), soil type and a rough sketch of its shape, and they send you a computer-drawn plan and a plant list. That costs about £100. You could, of course, employ a garden designer yourself, but that could be expensive – £300–£500 depending on the designer, and how far he or she has to travel. It seems an awful lot when you don't have much money to spare but if you really aren't sure what to do, and can take the long-term view, it's worth it. Just a couple of really good ideas can make all the difference in the world.

Surveying the scene

If you are going to have a go at designing your garden yourself, the first thing you need to do is make a plan. To do that, you need to measure your garden accurately. You can't rely on the dimensions given in the estate agents' details, and, besides, very few gardens are perfectly regular shapes. Perhaps the easiest scale to work to is 1 cm to 50 cm (or .5 m), or if you are still happier working in imperial measurements, ⅛ in to 1 ft.

Start by measuring the back of the house, then, using the corners of the house as fixed points, measure first from the right-hand corner (A) to the bottom right-hand corner of the garden (Y), then to the bottom left-hand corner (Z). Do the same from the other corner of the house (B). Scale down the measurements, and then set a pair of compasses to the first scaled-down measurement A–Y. Put the point on A, and draw an arc roughly where you expect Y to be. Then set the compasses to the second scaled-down measurement B–Y, and draw another arc. The point where they cross is Y. Do the same with the other two measurements. Mark in any fixed features – trees, paths, sheds and so on, by measuring their position in relation to boundary walls or fences. Find out where north is and mark it on the plan. That will help you work out where the sun is going to be at different times of day.

When you've got a plan of your garden, either make lots of photocopies, so you can keep on trying different design ideas without having to draw the plan each time or transfer it to a piece of stiff card and cover it with plastic film, so that you can use chinagraph pencils or special marking pens which you can simply rub off if you don't like what you've done. Incidentally, you might find it helpful to take some black and white photographs of the garden (they'll give you a better idea of the bones of your garden than colour would) from different positions, and sketch in your ideas on those with a felt-tipped pen.

What matters most is that you create a garden you're happy with, and it doesn't matter if it's not what is currently in vogue. But there are a few simple guidelines, which are worth following. The first, and most important, especially for beginners, is keep it simple. The big mistake people often make is to try and cram in too much – the pool, the rockery, the herb garden, the patio, the pergola – with the result that they all cancel each other out and the overall result is a mess.

Keep the shapes bold and simple, whether they are squares, rectangles or curves. Fussy, elaborate shapes are not only 'busy' visually, they'll keep *you* busy too, for a lawn with lots of nooks and crannies takes much longer to mow and keep trimmed than one without. Don't use too many different materials in the garden, either. If you're going to build low walls in the garden, either use the same material as the house, or one that matches the patio or path.

The design ideas that follow are simple, easy to execute and don't cost a fortune.

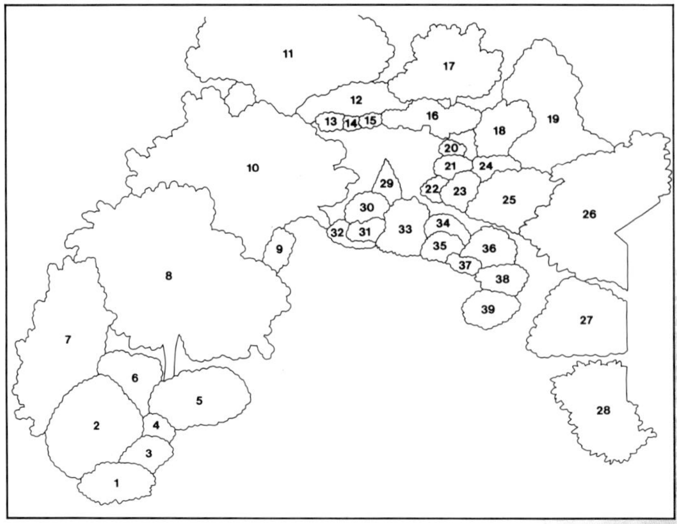

The Blank Garden – in Five Years' Time
We had to take down the apple tree to open up a new vista

1 Sage **2** Rosemary **3** Golden marjoram **4** Chives **5** *Geranium wallichianum* 'Buxton's Blue' **6** Japanese anemones **7** Fan-trained cherry 'Stella' **8** *Malus floribunda* (on dwarfing rootstock) **9** *Lamium maculatum* 'Beacon Silver' **10** Existing apple tree **11** Existing Bramley apple tree **12** Climbing roses – 'Zéphirine Drouhin' and 'Kathleen Harrop' (both thornless) **13** *Crocosmia* 'Solfatare' **14** *Agapanthus* 'Headbourne Hybrid' **15** *Anthemis tinctoria* 'E.C. Buxton' **16** Rose 'Margaret Merril' **17** *Acer platanoides* 'Crimson King' **18** *Lavatera thuringiaca* 'Barnsley' **19** Existing birch tree **20** Impatiens **21** *Aster × frikartii* 'Mönch' **22** *Campanula carpatica* **23** *Fuchsia magellanica* 'Versicolor' **24** Rose 'Jayne Austin' **25** Rose 'Heritage' **26** *Sorbus vilmorinii* **27** *Bergenia* 'Silberlicht' **28** *Helleborus orientalis* **29** *Chamaecyparis lawsoniana* 'Minima Aurea' **30** *Achillea filipendulina* 'Gold Plate' **31 & 32** Pansies – yellow and purple **33 & 36** Crocosmia **34** *Sedum spectabile* 'Autumn Joy' **35** *Osteospermum* 'Whirligig' **37** Pansies **38** Rudbeckia **39** *Coreopsis verticillata*

Changing shapes

One of the simplest and most dramatic ways of improving the look of a very small or dull rectangular garden is by changing the shapes of the lawn and borders. (For how to do it, see p. 49.) All too often, the planting simply follows the boundaries, just emphasising the rather boring shape, and making small gardens look smaller. Since the whole garden is laid out in front of you, there is no sense of mystery, no reason why you would want to walk into it and explore.

Our blank garden was a case in point, with narrow borders each side and a narrow concrete path running the length of the garden. One plus was that two small apple trees had been planted about halfway down to form a screen, so that you wouldn't see the whole of the garden the moment you walked out into it. In five years' time, though, they would be too close together, so one would have to come out and be replaced by something smaller – a conifer, perhaps. Building on that idea, we decided to make the lawns a very gentle serpentine shape, emphasised by a new path along the edge, following its contours. We decided to use a method called Creteprint, in which concrete is tinted in one of a range of colours and then imprinted with a pattern just before it dries – brick or crazy paving or, the one we chose for this path, stable setts. At the end of the garden the path will end at a circular patio done in the same way, in the sunny southwest-facing corner which will catch the sun from midday until late into the evening. Curving the lawn means that the borders curve too, and become much wider, with a couple of new trees planted at strategic points to provide the reason for a curve at that particular point.

As creating curves is such an excellent way of disguising the rectangular shape of a garden, another good solution would be to make the curve much more dramatic, bringing a bed close to the house right out, almost to the centre of the garden, and then bringing another bed further down the garden and on the opposite side almost out into the centre too, so that the lawn forms an 'S' shape. By planting something dramatic – a small tree, for example, or a tall conifer – at the broadest point of each bed, there will be a visual incentive to walk around the garden and see what lies beyond. The fact that there is very little or nothing beyond doesn't matter. After all, it is better to travel hopefully than to arrive!

Creating a 'set square'-shaped or, if you like curves, a P-shaped lawn is another very simple but effective way of making a rectangular garden more interesting. Making a large, oblong bed close to the house and planting it with fairly tall shrubs or herbaceous plants means that you have created a small hidden corner of the garden not visible from the house.

Another way of coping with small or dull rectangular gardens is to shift the axis, so that the eye doesn't travel straight down the garden to the back fence, but is drawn across it. One simple way of doing it is to shift the whole axis through 45°, so that the patio area becomes a triangle, and the lawn a diamond shape. This can be particularly dramatic if you have an existing path running down the centre of the garden. If you prefer curves to straight lines, you could make the patio a quadrant shape, the lawn a circle or an oval. In either case, you want some kind of focal point in the far corner to draw the eye across the longest axis.

With small, square gardens, one option is to create wide borders on each side and at the end of the garden, planted with tall plants, with gaps in the centre of each, in which you can put a bench or an arbour or even a specimen tree. As you first look at the garden, the gaps on either side, particularly, suggest paths leading off in different directions, which makes it more intriguing and interesting.

You can also cheat with perspective to make it work to your advantage. If you taper the lawn, so that it is narrower at the far end of the garden and the borders are subsequently wider, you will make the garden look longer. You can also add to that impression in a number of ways. Plant taller plants near the house and smaller ones further away, and do the same with large- and small-leaved plants. Colour can help here too. Bright colours have the effect of foreshortening distances, so only use them close to the house. Pale colours have the opposite effect, so use them at the far end of the garden.

Another classic way of making a garden look bigger is by making the boundaries seem to disappear. The easiest way to do that is by covering walls and fences with climbing plants and by planting tall shrubs in front of them. 'Borrowing' scenery from your surroundings helps, too. If a neighbour has a spectacular tree, plant a couple of small trees or shrubs to frame it, so that the group looks as though it belongs in your garden.

Disguising fences

One of the problems with our blank garden was that it was surrounded on all sides by bare wooden fences with nothing growing against them, so that you felt you were inside a rectangular wooden box. Fortunately the wood had weathered to a neutral, light greyish-brown, and wasn't that aggressive ginger colour that most new fencing seems to come in these days, or it would have been infinitely worse! Staining the fence a different colour can make a huge difference. If it's already a pale colour then you can choose from a much wider range of colours than you can if it's a strong colour where you will have to go for something darker to cover it effectively. That's no problem, though, since dark colours seem to disappear into the background much more, which is just the effect you want. In our overmature garden, for example, we could have painted the fence at the bottom of the garden a dark green so that it would seem to disappear, and form the perfect background for the focal point at the end of the vista we created.

Another simple answer is to cover fences with climbing plants as quickly as possible (see the illustration on pages 18–19) – a mixture of deciduous

This picture, taken square-on from the back of the house, shows how, by swinging the axis of the garden, it can appear larger than it really is.

Hiding the fences can make your garden look larger. A backbone of evergreens like Elaeagnus × ebbingei *'Gilt Edge', the variegated Persian ivy, and* Senecio greyi *keep the fence largely hidden in winter, too.*

The annual cup and saucer vine (Cobaea scandens) *can grow 3 m (10 ft) or more in one season (left).*

Crambe cordifolia *with its dramatic sprays of small white flowers reaching 2 m (6 ft 6 in) or more, is an excellent plant to give instant height in a new border (below).*

flowering ones and evergreens to give you interest in the winter too. Obviously permanent climbing plants like roses, clematis, ivy and jasmine take a year or two to get established, so, in the meanwhile, make use of quick-growing annual climbers like Canary creeper (*Tropaeolum peregrinum*), the cup and saucer vine (*Cobaea scandens*), good old-fashioned sweet peas, the variegated Japanese hop (*Humulus japonicus* 'Variegatus') with white speckled, maple-like leaves, or even runner beans – good foliage, pretty flowers in red or white and an edible bonus!

Borders running parallel to the fence, particularly if they're very narrow, only draw attention to it, too, and so do shrubs planted in a straight line along its length. So curve your borders and plant the shrubs in groups rather than in rows. It also helps to divert the eye if you choose a few plants that will quickly grow taller than the fence, to break up its line. Since most shrubs that are very quick-growing never know when to stop, and so will create different problems for you in a few years, go for something like *Lavatera thuringiaca* 'Barnsley' which grows about 2 m (6 ft 6 in) in a season, but needs to be cut back hard (if the frost doesn't do it for you) each spring. Alternatively, go for tall-growing herbaceous plants, which die down in winter and so never get any taller than the growth they can make in one season. For a sunny fence, try the pink-flowered plume poppy (*Macleaya microcarpa* 'Coral Plume' or *M. cordata* 'Flamingo'), the foxtail lily (*Eremurus robustus* which has pale pink flowers or the white flowered *E. himalaicus*) or the ornamental rhubarb (*Rheum palmatum* 'Atrosanguineum'). In our blank garden, we chose *Crambe cordifolia* – the flowers reach 2 m (6ft 6in) or more. For a shadier spot, try *Filipendula rubra* which has deep rose-pink flowers and attractive vine-like leaves. Tall plants like these do tend to have a broad spread as well, so think of them as a short-term measure in the border while the shrubs are getting established. You could grow biennials of course, like hollyhocks (*Althaea*), or even annuals like sunflowers (*Helianthus*) which reach 2.3 m (7 ft) or more, and die after they have flowered.

Alternatively, you could try one of the perennial ornamental grasses like *Miscanthus sinensis* 'Silver Feather' or the evergreen golden oats (*Stipa gigantea*) which both reach over 2.2 m (7 ft). The former doesn't spread more than 60 cm (2 ft) and the latter no more than 90 cm (3 ft). (Incidentally, avoid *Miscanthus sacchariflorus* which grows up to 3 m (10 ft) and just keeps on spreading indefinitely.) Cut the miscanthus down to the ground in spring, and remove any dead leaves of the golden oats.

The problems of the long, thin garden

When it comes to designing gardens, this is one of the most common and difficult problems to solve. The usual layout in gardens like these consists of long, narrow borders down each side and a long, narrow path down the centre, all of which emphasise its narrowness. Once we had cleared away most of the debris, and got rid of the shed, this was one of the problems we faced in our city back yard which is 23 m (75 ft) long by 5.5 m (18 ft) wide.

The last thing you want is to reinforce this narrowness, so the path running down the length of the garden had to go. Anything that emphasises its width was to be welcomed, so we created two square sitting-out areas, one next to the house to catch the early morning sun, and one right at the end of the garden, the sunniest spot, to catch the afternoon and evening sun (see illustration overleaf).

Between the side of the kitchen extension and the 1.8 m (6 ft) grey-painted garden wall was a dark, narrow strip. Originally the owner planned to sand-blast the bricks to get rid of the paint, but, given the expense, the rather poor state of the bricks, and the fact that the area was so dark, he decided to repaint it a light sandstone colour instead. Since it was so narrow, there wasn't space for pots or troughs large enough for permanent climbers so we cheated with trellis trees!

At the end of the extension, we considered creating an entrance to the garden, with an arch – again emphasising the width and dividing up the length. But the change between the narrow passage and the first patio area was already so dramatic that, in the end, an arch seemed an unnecessary complication.

There is also trellis across the garden on the far side of the patio, again breaking up the length, with a gap in the centre, where a new path begins. As you step on to the first patio, you don't see the rest of the garden beyond the trellis, although the trellis lets enough light through for this 'room' we've created not to feel claustrophobic and you can see enough of the tall shrubs and the apple tree beyond to make you want to venture further. In this area, the morning sitting-out area, we chose to use matching dark blue Chinese pots in a range of sizes and planted with bright colours – the golden *Choisya ternata* 'Sundance', for example, and the multi-coloured foliage of *Houttuynia cordata* 'Chameleon', the flame nettle (*Coleus*), the lime-green *Helichrysum petiolare* 'Limelight', and white nicotiana for its wonderful evening scent.

The new central path is bounded on both sides by raised beds, the east-facing one backed by the existing shrubs – holly, *Viburnum tinus*, and deutzia – all pruned back, and the west-facing one by the old privet hedge, cut hard back to head height, reduced considerably in width and given a good feed, no doubt for the first time in years. For the bed immediately in front of the privet, we chose plants that would be happy in poor soil and some shade – Lady's Mantle (*Alchemilla mollis*), foxgloves (*Digitalis grandiflora*), bugle (*Ajuga reptans* 'Rainbow'), elephant's ears (*Bergenia* 'Silberlicht') and bamboo (*Arundinaria variegata*) while we dug plenty of organic matter into one area of the border a good metre away from the hedge to allow hostas to thrive. We also trained a honeysuckle (*Lonicera periclymenum* 'Serotina') up the apple tree to scent the afternoon sitting area. We mulched the bed with small pebbles, which blend with the grouping of boulders and large pebbles at the point where the path makes a 90° turn to join up with the original path on the east-facing side of the garden. That leads into the second square patio, right at the end of the garden, where, apart from the apple tree, now pruned to let through a lot more light, and a very narrow bed on the east-facing side, all the planting is in containers – terracotta pots in various shapes and sizes, planted with cottage garden favourites like salmon-pink geraniums, white marguerites, golden feverfew, and lobelia. Between the new wall and the old one on the east-facing side, we planted *Potentilla fruticosa* 'Katherine Dykes', with soft yellow flowers, and underplanted with the dwarf artemisia, *A. schmidtiana* 'Nana'.

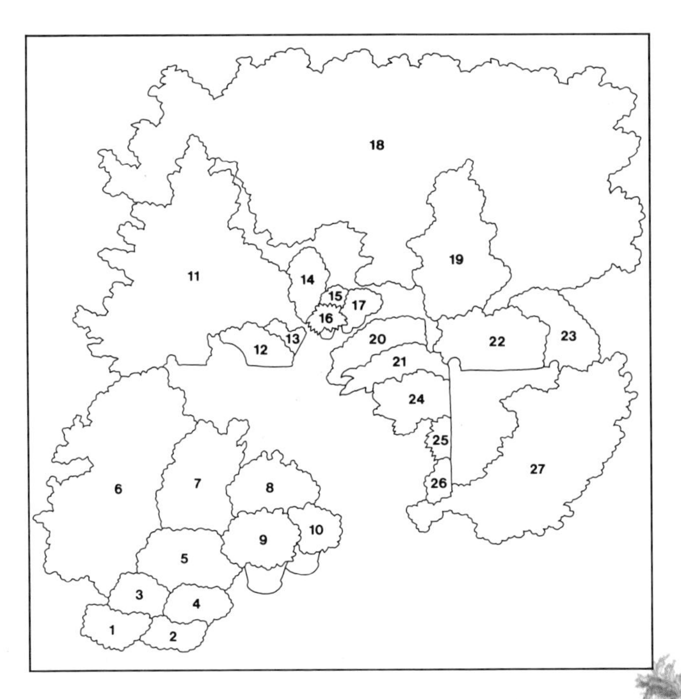

The City Backyard – in Five Years' Time

1–5 assorted herbs – thyme, sage, marjoram **6** Existing grape vine **7** Rosemary **8** Blue pot with tobacco plants and *Helichrysum petiolare* 'Limelight' **9** Blue pot with *Choisya ternata* 'Sundance' with *Houttuynia cordata* 'Chameleon' **10** Blue pot with mixed tuberous begonias, lobelias etc. **11** Existing holly **12** Existing *Viburnum tinus* **13** *Artemisia schmidtiana* 'Nana' **14** *Potentilla fruticosa* 'Katherine Dykes' **15** Terracotta pot with salmon pelargoniums, white marguerites, white petunias, blue lobelia **16** Terracotta pot with *Agave americana* 'Variegata' and echeverias **17** Terracotta pot with *Fuchsia* 'Thalia' and golden feverfew **18** Existing apple tree **19** *Lonicera periclymenum* 'Serotina' **20** *Bergenia* 'Abendglut' **21** *Hosta sieboldiana* 'Elegans' **22** *Arundinaria variegata* **23** Existing privet hedge **24** *Dryopteris filix-mas* **25** *Liriope muscari* **26** *Alchemilla mollis* **27** *Lonicera japonica* 'Aureoreticulata'

The new layout of the garden means that you can no longer walk straight down it. You are forced to walk across it as well, so that you see different angles that you might not have seen before. The fact that our city yard was so narrow, and mostly covered with hard surfaces, meant that squares, rectangles, straight lines suited it best.

If you do use angular shapes it's best to use asymmetrical ones, rather than divide the garden up into areas all the same shape and size. If one area is wider than it's long, align the next one the other way. It's the same with the borders and surfaces, whether they're grass, paving, brick or gravel – if you have a narrow bed on the left-hand side in one area, for instance, either make the bed much wider in the next area, or put it on the other side. In a slightly wider garden, or one with a lawn, then it's possible to achieve the same effect with curves, or circles. Make sure that you don't make your garden a series of circles – round patio, round lawn, round pool possibly – all in a straight line since you will only succeed in making it look like a very slightly wider tunnel.

Although we wanted to divide up the length of the city yard to emphasise the width, using too many different materials would have looked messy. So, we used Bradstone's 'Old Weatherdale' paving throughout and also used it to cap the low walls in the garden, built from easy-to-lay 'Aztec' bricks.

You can also break up a long, thin garden very simply by using what you might call 'eye-stoppers' – a striking tree or shrub, or a garden ornament such as a particularly beautiful pot, a sundial, or even a statue, placed in the foreground, to one side, or even in the centre of the garden. What this does is catch your eye and stop it whizzing straight down to the far end. In one very long and thin town garden – 37 m (120 ft) by 5 m (16 ft) – divided up into a number of 'rooms', a huge black pot planted with the wine-red *Heuchera* 'Palace Purple' in the centre of a circular paved area performed this function to perfection.

Creating different areas in your garden, giving each one a different feel, can help accentuate the differences. To a large extent, what you plant will be dictated by how much sun a particular area gets. In our city backyard, the first patio area will be in shade for part of the day, so the planting in bright colours reflects that, while the sunnier second sitting-out area has softer colours, and fragrance from the honeysuckle growing up the old apple tree. Since it's unlikely that the owners will spend much time on the second patio in winter, we've made the planting there more seasonal, while on the patio closest to the house we have used some evergreens so they have something attractive to look at all year round.

In a sunnier situation, you could create a small formal herb garden in one area, while another had a more informal planting, or you could go for a Japanese effect with pebbles or sand and plants like small Japanese maples and bamboos, so that you actually wind up with a series of little gardens, instead of just one.

Focal points

Every garden needs a focal point, whether it's to distract your eye from a less than attractive view, to change the axis of the garden and make it look bigger, or just to give the whole garden a focus, something on which to base the design. The latter was the case with our large, over-mature garden. Once we had cleared away some of the trees, we had a large amount of space to play with, all of it much like the rest. We already had one focal point in the large pear tree, just under two thirds of the way down the garden, and though the wires stretched across the bed underneath it would have to go, the idea of putting a screen across there seemed a very good one. It would divide the garden into two areas, and that made practical sense since the owner wanted a vegetable garden, which could now be at the far end of the garden, behind the screen.

Although we thought about using evergreen hedging, possibly yew, or laurel for the screen, we decided on stout trellis instead, partly because it is instant, whereas the hedge would take five or six years at least to reach the required height, and partly because it allows light through, and so doesn't foreshorten the garden in the way that a solid barrier might. At the same time it provides support for decorative climbers like roses and clematis on one side, and possibly cordon, or espalier fruit trees on the other. Since the trellis and arch we chose were in the garish orange colour that most mass-produced trellis comes in, we decided to paint it with a dark green wood stain, a much more attractive colour, and the ideal foil for the pink and white roses, and white and purple clematis, we grew up it.

Right in the centre of the trellis is an arch through which a new grass path leads, with two formal vegetable beds on either side, ending at the bottom of the garden in a focal point. Since there are already trees and a fence at the bottom of the garden, making a rather dark background, it needs to be something bright to stand out, and catch your eye as you sit on the patio next to the house. We considered a tree with golden foliage – an Indian bean tree (*Catalpa bignonioides* 'Aurea', or the golden honey locust (*Gleditsia triacanthos* 'Sunburst') rather than the golden robinia (*Robinia pseudoacacia* 'Frisia') which would eventually grow too large. We also considered a statue, but a good enough, large enough, statue for this purpose would have used up the entire budget for the garden. A large urn on a plinth, even a reconstituted stone one, would have cost almost as much and a sundial seemed a bit insignificant. In the end we settled for an evergreen shrub in a pot.

Since the design was rather formal, with the central arch, the grass paths and the rectangular vegetable beds, we decided to make the top of the lawn and the two ornamental borders each side of the arch, rather formal too, coming out straight from the long borders on each side for about 60 cm (2 ft), then curving round to the start of the central grass path (see the illustration on pages 34–5).

Too many circles give this garden a fussy, cluttered feel (left).

This group of empty terracotta pots makes a very simple, inexpensive focal point (below).

A garden can have more than one focal point, of course, although not in the same general direction. Your eye needs to have a clear lead as to where to look. It shouldn't be pulled in two directions at once. In our over-mature garden, we had a concrete path on the northeast-facing side of the garden right up to the bottom right-hand corner of the garden where the compost heap was going to be. Walking up there was a pleasure because you had the ornamental garden and then the fruit and vegetable garden to look at. Coming back was not such a pleasant walk, though, because the path led directly to the back of a cement-panelled garage – not a pretty sight! We decided to make that into another focal point, painting the garage wall a soft green, putting up trellis, growing climbers like ivy and honeysuckle, and placing a wooden bench in front of them, directly facing the path. Given the sunniest part of the garden was the southwest-facing border, we also decided to put a dark green seat halfway down, set back from the shrubs, to create a secluded suntrap.

Perhaps the most exciting thing about the over-mature garden was how quickly it began to look very different indeed and how little it cost. The biggest expenses were the tree surgeon (worth every penny) and the trellis. The plants cost less than £50. Even so, we decided to leave extending and resurfacing the patio, as well as building a pergola over it, to Phase Two. For the moment, we simply covered it with gravel to make it look more attractive.

A perfect, if expensive, example of a focal point. The elegant statue draws your eye through the lush foliage on either side of the path and contrasts beautifully with it.

CHAPTER 2

Hacking back the Wilderness

The next steps depend entirely on what sort of state your garden is in. If it really is a wilderness, neglected for years with waist-high grass, full of docks, nettles, brambles, ground elder, bindweed and so on, with no plants worth saving, or even visible, then the only answer is to kill the whole lot off and start again. There really is no point in starting to garden unless the ground is as weed-free as you can possibly make it. And it's not just a question of killing off the top growth. Some perennial weeds, like bindweed, can regrow from even the smallest piece of root left in the soil, and, once the garden in planted, it will be almost impossible to get rid of.

Don't think, incidentally, that since you're planning to put a patio or even a conservatory on a weed-infested patch that you needn't bother to kill off all the weeds. Some of them, like horse tail and docks, can find their way up through the narrowest of cracks, and others, like Japanese knotweed, can even force their way up through hard surfaces.

So how do you clear the wilderness? The best way is to spray the whole lot with glyphosate weedkiller (sold as *Tumbleweed*). Even if you want to garden organically, our advice would still be to spray once, and then never use chemicals again.

The weeds absorb glyphosate through their leaves and pass it right down into their roots so that the whole plant is killed off over five or six weeks, and not just the top growth. For that reason the best time to spray is between April and July when the weeds are growing strongly.

Other weedkillers, based on paraquat, only kill off the top growth so that many persistent weeds, like docks, will regrow and will need further applications of weedkiller. Besides, paraquat is extremely dangerous to have around. If it's swallowed it can be fatal and there is no antidote. Glyphosate doesn't persist in the soil, like some other 'total' weedkillers, so that as soon as the ground has been cleared, you can start to replant. There are some weeds that can survive a spraying with glyphosate – Japanese knotweed and horse tail, for example. In fact, the advice usually offered to people with horse tail in their gardens is 'Move'! The reason why horse tail is so difficult to get rid of is that its leaves are covered with a waxy coating, and weedkiller just runs straight off it. You can help by bruising the leaves first and damaging that coating. Give patches of the weed a good beating with a stiff broom before you spray. It makes you feel better, too! You won't kill it all off in one go, but if you persevere you will eventually weaken the plant, although you will have to accept that it's going to be with you for some time.

Since glyphosate isn't selective in the vegetation it kills, it makes sense to spray on a still day when there's no breeze. Wiping out half the shrubs in your new neighbour's garden by accident isn't the best of starts to a long and happy relationship with them.

Although you can apply weedkiller with a watering can, a sprayer is far more effective. In order to work, the weedkiller needs to stay on the foliage for long enough to be absorbed and taken down to the roots. The tiny droplets produced by a sprayer are much more likely to stay on the foliage than the much larger ones produced by a watering can. If you've only got a relatively small area to spray, then you can buy a large pressure sprayer from the garden centre. If you've got a large area to cover, you're better off hiring a knapsack sprayer from the local hire shop, but do make sure that you give it a thorough wash before *and* after you've used it. You don't know what was in it the last time it was used, and it would be bad news if the person who has it after you forgets to wash it out and then uses it to spray their entire garden with a liquid feed . . .

While glyphosate is one of the safer weedkillers as far as people and pets are concerned, it makes sense to treat all chemicals as potentially dangerous and always to wear gloves, some form of eye protection (goggles or protective glasses with side pieces) and a face mask. It's also important to keep the container, along with all other garden chemicals, under lock and key. The comparatively few accidents that happen each year usually occur when a child or pet gets hold of the packet or bottle, not from the normal use of a product in the garden.

If you don't like the idea of using weedkiller even once, you may be tempted to hire a flame thrower and burn off the weeds. Our advice would be, don't. Not only are they potentially dangerous, it also takes a long time to set green vegetation alight and anyway, as you are only killing off the top growth, many of the really persistent weeds will simply regrow. The only option if you really don't want to use chemicals is to dig out the weeds, or, if that's just too daunting, hack off as much of the top growth as you can and cover what's left with black polythene, or an old carpet even, for at least one whole season. That deprives the weeds of light, essential for their growth so that they become weak and spindly and either die or are very easily pulled up.

You could grow potatoes in weed-free patches of soil underneath the black polythene. Plant them through slits in the polythene so that the foliage can grow up through the slits, but you must keep on pulling up any weeds that appear either through the slits or around the edges of the polythene. Remove the polythene after a season and dig over the ground, removing as many of the weeds – and their roots – as you possibly can. Then keep on hoeing, cutting off the young weeds at the surface of the soil, or, if you can, just below it. Eventually they will become so weak that they'll die.

Alternatively, if you want your garden to start being productive in its first year, you could try a method called Permaculture. What you do is hack

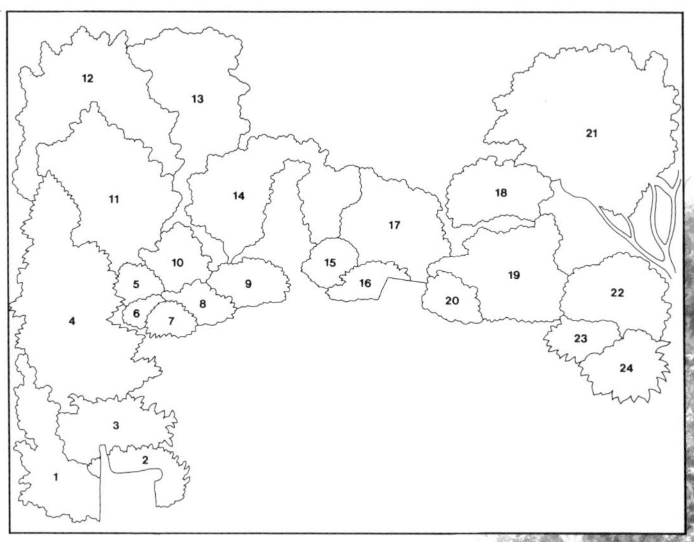

The Over-mature Garden – in Five Years' Time

1 Rose 'Compassion' 2 Lavender
3 Existing symphoricarpos
4 Existing conifer 5 *Spiraea* × *bumalda* 'Goldflame' 6 *Pulmonaria saccharata* 7 Bowles' golden grass
8 Bergenia 9 Paeony 10 *Photinia* × *fraseri* 'Red Robin' 11 *Clematis viticella* 'Little Nell' 12 Existing holly 13 Existing lilac 14 Rose 'Zéphirine Drouhin' with *Clematis* 'Henryi' 15 Astrantia 16 Existing paeony 17 Existing camellia (moved from bed by kitchen)
18 Rose 'New Dawn' with *Clematis* 'Jackmanii Superba' 19 Existing *Magnolia stellata* 20 Bergenia
21 Existing *Prunus cerasifera* 'Nigra'
22 Japanese anemones 23 *Hosta fortunei* 'Aureomarginata' 24 *Hosta* 'Halcyon'

down the weeds – brambles, docks, bindweed – in a small area of the garden, and trample them flat. Then spread a layer of newspaper over the top, at least a dozen sheets thick, wet it thoroughly and then pile 10–12 cm (4–5 in) of well-rotted stable manure on top of that. To grow vegetables, scrape aside the manure, fill the pocket you've created with garden soil and plant into that. If you want to plant trees or shrubs, then make a hole in the newspaper membrane and plant through it into the soil beneath. Weeds will almost certainly reappear the first year, so repeat the process the following year with another layer of newspapers and manure, and if one or two weeds reappear in the third year, do it again. By the fourth year, though, the weeds should have given up the ghost and rotted down, along with the newspapers and manure, to give you really good, rich, deep soil.

If you have used weedkiller, though, after six weeks or so, you will be left with a patch covered in dead vegetation. What you need to do then is slice it off with a spade and dig it in.

It may be tempting to get a mechanical digger in to scrape the whole lot off for you, but they are not precision tools, and you could lose three or four inches of your precious topsoil that way. While you could certainly buy a load of topsoil to replace it, you can't be sure that what you're buying is completely weed-free, and, having just cleared the ground, you would not be pleased to discover that you had re-imported bindweed into your garden. Incidentally, if you do find you have to buy a load of topsoil, do buy it from a reputable source, and, if humanly possible, go and look at it before it's delivered. While clearly you can't inspect it all, by getting your gloved hands into it and scooping out a few handfuls at random here and there, you'll at least know whether or not it's full of bits of rubble and weed roots. Once it's been delivered and dumped in your garden, it's too late.

Getting rid of rubbish

Once the vegetation has been cleared, you might find all sorts of other horrors are suddenly revealed – tree stumps, old fence posts, the concrete base of what had once been a greenhouse or shed. We will deal with tree stumps in detail in Chapter 6 , but if there are several of them, as well as some old fence posts, then it might be worth hiring a digger and driver for a few hours to dig them all out, assuming, of course, you have sufficiently wide access at the side of the house, to get the digger into the garden. When you speak to your local plant hire company, tell them exactly what you want done, so thay can bring any specialist equipment they need. To hire a man and a machine for a day would cost between £100 and £140 depending on where you live, but if you happen to come across a digger and a driver working on a building site in your area, you may find he'd be happy to do a few hours for you unofficially after work, or at the weekend, for a good bit less.

To get rid of an old concrete base you'll need a pick axe, a sledge hammer and someone to help you, plus a pair of safety goggles for each of you. If possible, one of you should get the point of the pick axe under the concrete base and lever it upwards while the other one hits the concrete with the sledge hammer. It doesn't matter if you can only lift the slab a little bit – it will break more easily than it would if you couldn't lift it at all. If that's just not possible, then you'll just have to pound away harder with the sledge hammer and break it up that way. If you're planning any building work in the garden – a patio, a path or a wall – then break the concrete into smallish pieces and use it later as hard core. If you won't need it, then either barrow it out to a skip or, if you're hiring a man with a digger, ask him to do it for you.

The weed-infested border

If your garden isn't a total wilderness and you've found some plants in reasonable condition that you'd like to keep, albeit in a pretty weed-infested border, then you need a slightly different approach.

If the weed is mainly couch grass, you're in luck. There is a weedkiller specifically for it, *Weedout*, which will only kill grasses and won't damage other plants at all. Obviously you can't use it if you have any ornamental grasses in the border, unless you protect them or dig them out temporarily while you spray.

If you've got a mixture of perennial weeds, you can use glyphosate. If you haven't got too many perennial weeds, then paint them with glyphosate gel (or, alternatively, mix up ordinary glyphosate with a few squirts of washing-up liquid, a cheaper way of achieving the same end) which is much less likely than the liquid to splash onto other foliage by accident. With something like ground elder, you might have to keep on painting the new growth as it appears for a couple of summers, but eventually you will kill it off. Brambles are even more resistant, so the only way of dealing with them is to dig them out, taking as much of the roots as you can, and then to keep a close eye on the area and pull out any new growth.

If you've got a lot of perennial weeds in among the shrubs, then you can still spray with glyphosate providing you take a few precautions. Choose a very still day, and, if there are two of you, one holds a large piece of hardboard in front of each shrub while the other one sprays. If you're working on your own, put a big plastic rubbish sack, or garden waste bag, over each of the shrubs you want to keep and tie the neck round the stem of the shrub close to ground level. These bags are large enough to cover most small and medium-sized shrubs; with larger shrubs, cut the bottom of the sack open and slide it over the shrub to cover the foliage low down. At least it will be protected at spraying level where accidents are most likely to happen. Then spray the weeds carefully, avoiding getting any of the weedkiller on the plastic sacks if you can and leave the sacks in place until the weedkiller has completely dried on the leaves – in warm, dry weather, a few hours.

If you really don't want to use chemicals at all, you'll have to dig out all the shrubs or herbaceous plants you want to keep, and carefully, by hand, remove any weed roots that are entangled with the roots of the shrubs or plants. In most cases it will be easy to see which is which. Either plant them in a temporary home somewhere else in the garden ('heel them in' by digging a trench deep enough for their roots, laying them in it and throwing soil forward to cover them), or put them in pots. Then dig the ground over, removing as many of the weeds and their roots as you can, and then be prepared to keep hoeing as soon as young weeds appear. When the ground seems pretty free from weeds, replant anything you've kept in containers, and any herbaceous plants that have been growing in another part of the garden. (Give them a bucketful of water before you move them, and afterwards as well.) Wait until the autumn to replant any shrubs that have been growing in the soil.

You might find that you have an infestation of, say, bindweed in one small part of a border, or underneath a hedge. If you don't want to use weedkiller there, you can use the black polythene treatment. Dig a narrow trench 20–30 cm in front of where the bindweed emerges from the soil. Put one long edge of a strip of black polythene into the trench which you then refill with soil to hold the polythene in place. Lay the black polythene over the bindweed and weight it down along the other long side, either with bricks, or stones, or soil. Leave it for a season, and when you lift it you'll find some very pale and sickly-looking, if not dead, weeds.

The border that has everything – docks, brambles, nettles, couch grass, ground elder.

You may find that if your neighbours have a neglected garden, weeds are coming under the fence into your garden. While both gardens were in much the same state, that didn't matter, but now that you're trying to get yours back into shape, it does. You could offer to kill off the weeds on their side of the fence, but if that doesn't work, or they are allowed to regrow afterwards, you may need to install a *cordon sanitaire*. What you do is dig a narrow trench as close to the fence as you can, down to the subsoil. Then tack a strip of strong polythene about 35 cm (14 in) deep along the bottom of your fence so that it hangs down into the trench, then replace the soil to hold it in place. You've then got a polythene wall under the soil between you and the neighbours' weeds, which should keep the vast majority of them – the weeds that is, not the neighbours – at bay.

Breaking up concrete is much easier if one of you can lift it just a little with a pick axe, while the other hits it with a sledge hammer.

To burn or not to burn

In the past, most people got rid of their garden rubbish by burning it, but since we now know that bonfires aren't environmentally friendly (nor very neighbour-friendly either) that's no longer an option. The best way to deal with old vegetation (dead plants, prunings, the leaves of weeds, though *never* their roots because they can regrow from the smallest piece of root) is to put it through a shredder. You could buy one yourself – they start at around £120 – or maybe jointly with your neighbours since it's a very useful piece of equipment to have two or three times a year. Alternatively, you could hire one from the hire shop for a day. If you compost the shreddings simply by piling them in a heap for a few months, they can be very useful in the garden as bulky organic matter to improve the soil (see p. 41). Alternatively, you can spread them over the surface of the soil, after you've planted your borders, as a mulch to conserve moisture and help prevent annual weeds from growing. The only time you really must burn garden rubbish is if you need to dispose of diseased wood, especially if it is suffering from a serious disease that is easily spread, like honey fungus, coral spot, fireblight or phytophthora (see p. 72).

Getting the soil back into shape

The first thing you need to know, once you've hacked back the wilderness, is what type of soil you have got. The easiest way to find out is to pick up a handful of moist soil and squeeze it in the palm of your hand. If it sticks together and you can mould it easily into a ball, you've got a clay soil. If it feels silky between your fingers, you've got a silt soil, which has many of the same problems as clay, and is treated in much the same way. If it feels very gritty and won't stick together no matter how hard you squeeze, you've got a sandy soil. If it looks dry, greyish and crumbly, and may have pieces of chalk in it, then you have a chalky soil. If you can squeeze it into a ball which crumbles apart again as soon as you touch it, then you have the ideal soil type – a medium loam, which doesn't dry out too quickly, but is never waterlogged, and is easy to work. The chances are that the soil in your garden was once well cultivated and will be in reasonably good shape – better than the muddy morass that so often passes for a brand-new garden, anyway! Although it's not strictly relevant at this point in the renovation of your garden, it is also vital to know whether your soil is acid or alkaline because that will dictate which plants will thrive in it, and which will simply become sickly and die. And since you're learning about your soil at this point, you might as well test for that now, too.

Of course, you will get some clues from looking at what's already growing in it. If you've got a few rhododendrons or camellias that look happy enough, for example, then you've got an acid soil, in that part of the garden anyway. The best way of finding out, though, is to use a cheap, simple soil-testing kit that you buy from the garden centre. (To be absolutely correct, what you're buying is a 'lime-testing kit' since it's testing the amount of lime in the soil, but since even some of the people who make them call them 'soil-testing kits' who are we to argue?)

Take a sample of soil, using an old teaspoon, from a couple of inches below the surface, and leave it to dry. then put it into the test tube that comes with the kit, add the chemical provided and top it up with distilled water. (Don't use tap water. It could actually affect the result.) Shake the test tube and then leave it to settle for a while. The soil will eventually settle at the bottom of the tube, and you are left with a coloured liquid on the top which you then compare with the chart provided. The more orange the liquid, the more acid your soil is. A neutral soil is mid-green while dark green indicates an alkaline soil. Incidentally, don't expect the colour of the liquid to be as bright or distinctive as the ones printed on the chart. But don't worry, it should be clear enough which your sample is closest to.

Clay soils

Clay is certainly the most difficult soil initially because when it is wet it's a sticky, boggy morass, and when it's dry it's as hard as concrete, and plants don't thrive in either of those conditions. But take heart, because once you've worked on it a bit, a clay soil is more fertile and will grow far better plants than a very light, sandy soil ever can.

If you have a really wet, sticky clay soil, you might be advised to install a drainage system, but that won't necessarily solve your problems. The water has to drain away somewhere, and, while you could dig a soakaway, where does the water go when the soakaway is full?

The best way to improve a sticky clay or silt soil is to open up the soil by mixing in plenty of coarse grit – about one barrowload to every two or three square metres. Different areas need different treatment. Where the lawn is going to be, for example, will only need single digging (digging to one spade's depth) since grass roots don't go very deep. You can rotavate it if it's a big area (hire a rotavator from the local hire shop) or dig it over with a spade. (Incidentally, you shouldn't cultivate too deeply areas where you're planning to put a conservatory or even a patio, since it could cause problems with subsidence later on.)

As well as digging in the grit, add plenty of organic matter too. This helps to open up the soil as well, and, in the case of well-made garden compost or well-rotted animal manure, it provides essential plant nutrients and a home for the millions of soil organisms that are vital to plant growth. You probably won't have any garden compost at this stage, and if you don't have a ready source of animal manure you can use spent mushroom compost. This is a mixture of well-rotted horse manure and peat, but it also contains a small amount of lime. That's fine if your soil is already limey or if you want to use it on the vegetable patch, but don't use it if you want to grow acid-loving plants. It doesn't contain many plant nutrients by the time you get it, either, so you will have to add those in the form of fertilisers.

In the past, peat used to be recommended as a soil conditioner, but given the growing awareness of how rapidly our peat bogs, which are unique wildlife habitats, are disappearing, it seems irresponsible to use it for this purpose when there are perfectly good substitutes available. One of the newer ones which is becoming more widely available all the time is composted straw. With the areas that are going to be your borders, it's a good idea to double-dig (see *First Time Garden*) if you can. It's really only essential if there is a 'hard pan' – a layer of compacted soil – below the topsoil, which won't allow the roots of shrubs and trees to penetrate unless it's broken up, but if you don't mind a couple of afternoons' hard work it will pay dividends. Once the borders are planted, you will never again get the chance to cultivate the soil so deeply or to work in organic matter and plant nutrients from which the trees and shrubs you plant will really benefit in future years.

On really heavy soil, as you double dig, mix in not only a layer of organic matter with the broken-up subsoil in the bottom of each trench, but a good thick layer of coarse grit as well. Then mix yet more of both with the soil you use to refill the trench. By adding all this organic matter and grit to the soil, you are raising your borders above the level of the lawn, and this will help them drain more freely as well. It is very important to dig heavy clay soils at the right time – not when it is dry and hard as a rock, nor when it's thoroughly waterlogged and sticky. The best plan is to dig it over roughly in the autumn – ideally when it's drying out but still moist – and leave it for the winter frosts to work on and break down into smaller and smaller clods. With a bit of luck and a few good hard frosts, you'll find that in the spring you only need to rake it down. Incidentally, you should *never* walk on heavy soils when they are wet since you are simply compounding the problem. If, for some reason, you simply must walk on it, you should always put down wide scaffolding planks to spread the weight.

Planting as much as you possibly can also helps, because the plants' roots also open up the soil as they grow, and even after the plants have been removed, in the case of annuals, or indeed vegetable crops, the remaining roots still perform that service. So aim to keep the soil covered with plants all the time.

Sand

At first glance, and certainly in comparison to heavy clay soils, sandy soils are a doddle to cultivate. Because they're so free-draining you can work them when other types of soil are still waterlogged, they warm up quickly in spring, ideal for raising early crops, and they are very easy to dig over in preparation for planting. But there is no such thing as a free lunch, and in the case of sandy soils the price you pay is that they dry out very quickly, losing not only moisture but valuable plant nutrients too.

For that reason they need both huge quantities of organic matter to help retain moisture in the soil, and additional plant nutrients in the form of fertilisers every year. But since the organic matter will work its way through the thin topsoil very quickly and into the subsoil, it is a waste of time – and compost – to dig it in too deeply. Either dig it in to the top few centimetres of soil only or simply spread it over the surface and allow the elements and the worms to work it in for you. There's another good reason for applying organic matter this way – as a mulch. Sandy soils lose moisture through surface evaporation as well as through free drainage, so by covering the surface with a mulch you can help prevent that happening.

Chalk

Chalky soils share many of the same advantages and problems as sandy ones. They're very free-draining and are rarely too wet to work, but they lose water and nutrients very rapidly. They have an additional problem in that the layer of topsoil is usually shallow and chalky soils are always very alkaline, which limits the range of plants that you can grow successfully in them. Don't despair, though. There are still lots of beautiful trees and shrubs, like lilac, mock orange (*Philadelphus*) and all the viburnums, that will thrive on chalk. The way to improve a chalky soil is much the same as for a sandy one.

If you are lucky enough to have 'medium loam', then, even though it won't need lots of work to improve it, it will still benefit from an annual dose of organic matter. It's really very simple – the more you put into the soil, the more productive it will be.

Rose sickness

Rose sickness is the soil disease you're most likely to encounter in a neglected garden. If you have inherited a bed of very weedy, sick-looking rose bushes, it's impossible to tell, without very expensive soil analysis, whether they are simply suffering from neglect, or old age, or whether there is rose sickness (thought to be a combination of viral disease, mineral imbalance, and microscopic pests) in the soil. It's not worth taking the gamble.

If the bushes are beyond salvation, then dig them up and dispose of them. As for the soil, you have two choices. You can either dig out all the topsoil from that bed, and replace it with fresh. Or, since rose sickness only affects roses and their close relatives, like cherries, you can simply plant the bed with other shrubs or herbaceous plants.

Lawns

When it comes to the grass in a neglected garden what you need to do will depend on just how bad it is. If it's waist- or even knee-high, you need to cut it back to see what you've actually got before you can make any decisions.

The best way to cope with really long grass is to cut it down with a petrol-driven brush cutter. These usually come with a nylon cord 'strimmer'-type head or sometimes with a metal attachment, although most reputable hire shops won't let you hire the latter because it really is a potentially very dangerous piece of equipment. Even if your hire shop is willing to let you have one, in our view they are best left well alone unless you're very experienced in their use, and, besides, the nylon cord version cuts down long grass just as well.

Make sure you wear stout shoes, tough gloves, long trousers and eye protection when you use it. Alternatively, you can cut down long grass by hand with a sickle. A scythe looks very romantic, but it takes quite a lot of practice to get the swing of it, and you may find your arm muscles, not to mention your shoulders, are complaining bitterly long before you've finished.

Don't choose a day when the grass is sopping wet, nor should you tackle the job in a period of prolonged drought. The grass simply won't have the strength to fight back. In the initial hack back, cut the grass down to about 12 to 15 cm (5 to 6 in) and leave it to green up for a week or two before you start to use an ordinary electric or petrol-driven mower on it. In this situation, a powerful rotary or hover mower is a much better bet than a cylinder one, so if the latter is all you have, hire one of the former for the day.

It may seem a bit excessive, but for the first cut wear eye protection and gloves. You just don't know what might be lurking in the long grass that the mower blade might catch and fling up. In our blank garden, for instance, there was half the glass from the old greenhouse, broken into small pieces and it's infinitely better to be safe than sorry.

Once it's cut back, you'll be able to see what you're actually dealing with. Chances are that you'll find plenty of coarse, broad-leaved grasses, growing in tussocks, taking over from the much finer lawn grasses, not to mention a fair old sprinkling of lawn weeds. If you've got predominantly coarse grasses, you have two choices. The first is to kill the whole lot off and start again from scratch (see p. 48). The second is to try and get it back to fine grasses by lavishing lots of attention on it.

Regular frequent mowing kills coarse grasses, but at this stage, when it's 12 to 15 cm (5 to 6 in) high, you should reduce the height gradually by no more than half each time and give the grass a chance to 'green up' – at least a week when it's growing strongly – before you cut it again. Once you've got it down to about 1.5 cm (a good half inch), then you should mow it twice a week if possible. Once a week will do, but the more often you mow it, the better it will be.

You should also scarify it, which means going over it with a spring-tine lawn rake, scratching out as much of the 'thatch' – dead grass and moss – as you can. It's hard work, so if you have a very large area of grass, it might be worth hiring an electric lawn rake which does the job effortlessly in a fraction of the time. The best time to scarify is in spring.

Hiring equipment

We've mentioned hiring equipment from a local hire shop several times already, and since, in the process of bringing a neglected garden back into good heart, you will be using your local hire shop quite a lot, it's worth making sure that it is reputable. Like any other trade, equipment hire has had its fair share of cowboys, which in recent years has resulted in it getting a pretty bad press about safety standards and so on. As a response to that, a number of the more reputable hire shops have got together and formed a professional body, the Hire Association of Europe. Its members have to conform to certain standards of safety, both in the servicing of the equipment they hire out, and in making customers aware of safety equipment – goggles, face masks, ear defenders, gloves and so on – and its importance. Some shops, for instance, offer a safety pack of the above items, on sale or return, and if customers don't want to take one they are asked to sign a form to that effect. It's worth checking if your local shop is a member and, if it's not, and you don't get a satisfactory explanation why not, then you're probably better off finding one that is.

Feeding and watering

Given that your grass is being cut and scarified, it'll need feeding in early spring, and again in early summer, to get the fine lawn grasses growing strongly enough to colonise the areas where the coarse grass is being slowly killed off. (Incidentally, if you do feed in spring and summer, don't bother with an autumn feed. It's a waste of money.)

If you want to garden organically, then use either a slow-release fertiliser like blood, fish and bonemeal, applied at a rate of 90 g (3½ oz) per square metre, or for the sort of instant 'greening up' effect that many chemical fertilisers produce, use a liquid manure diluted according to the manufacturer's instructions on the bottle. If you're not bothered about being organic, then use one of the reputable lawn fertilisers, either in the form of granules or liquid. Do be careful, though, to apply it at the exact rate recommended on the pack. The notion that, if a little does a lot of good, then a lot will produce miracles, does not apply, and in fact, too much fertiliser can scorch the grass badly. Some brands of granules come with their own spreader now, or if you choose a brand that doesn't, you may find that you can borrow – or even hire – one from the garden centre. They not only make the job much easier, they also control the rate of application, so you'd have to try very hard indeed to exceed it!

Keep the grass well watered, and pray we don't have another hosepipe ban.

Bald patches

As your regime starts to work, and the coarse grasses start to die off, you will almost certainly find a few bald patches appearing. The answer there is to re-seed them. Prick over the top inch of soil with a garden fork, or alternatively score the surface with an old kitchen knife to break up the surface. Then mix up some grass seed (about 1.5 oz for every square metre) with some soil and spread it over the patch. Cut a piece of clear polythene, slightly larger all round than the patch, prick a few holes in it and then fix it over the patch with a few large nails or hairpins pushed into the soil. Not only will it keep the birds off, it will also speed germination, though admittedly if you have several of these patches, your lawn will look like the face of a man who has shaved with a hangover! Remove the polythene (and all the nails) as soon as the first blades of grass appear and leave them until they're at least 7.5 cm (3 in) long before you mow them.

Broken edges

You may find that the straight edge of the lawn is broken in several places. The answer is to cut a rectangle of turf around each broken part, lift it carefully off, turn it round through 180°, and put it back. Now you've got a clean, unbroken edge again, and a hole in the lawn. You simply treat the hole as you would a bald patch and fill it with the compost and grass seed mixture.

Weeds

How large a proportion of weeds you are prepared to tolerate in your lawn is very much a matter of personal taste. The lawns at Barnsdale, for example, are about 30 per cent weeds, but they look fine, and from an organic point of view, better a few buttercups and daisies than lots of chemical weedkillers.

Obviously, at the early stages of renovation, you'll want to get rid of as many weeds as you can. The organic way is either to cut them out with an old kitchen knife, or, with 'rosette'-forming weeds like dandelions, to sprinkle a pinch of ordinary table salt in the centre of the rosette, on the growing point. Don't get any salt on the grass, though, or it will kill that, too.

If you're not gardening organically, then there is a wide range of specific lawn weedkillers on the market. There are 'spot' weedkillers, products which you apply to individual weeds and there are products that weed and feed at the same time. The idea is that as the weeds are killed off, the feed helps the fine lawn grasses to colonise the bare patches that result. Whatever method you use to get rid of the weeds, though, you may need to reseed larger patches.

Moss

Moss loves shady places, badly drained, poorly fed soil, small patches of soil where the grass is very thin, or where it has been cut too closely and virtually scalped. Healthy grass that is growing strongly doesn't allow moss much chance to get established.

If you're not an organic gardener, then the answer is relatively simple - use a moss killer in the spring and rake out the dead moss after it's turned black. You may have thought you only had a little moss when you applied the treatment, but you'll be astonished at how much dead stuff you'll rake out, and also at how, suddenly, your lawn looks less green than it did before! But be warned. Unless you do something to improve your lawn - by improving the drainage, spiking it all over with a fork, for example and getting the grass growing more strongly - the moss will be back.

If you are an organic gardener, then you'll just have to learn to live with the moss. There are no organic mosskillers and you can't rake it out without killing it first. If you try, you'll simply spread it all over the lawn and make the problem ten times worse.

All you can do in a very shady area is forget about having grass at all (see p. 54). As for the rest of the lawn area, get the grass growing as strongly as possible, so it can compete on more equal terms with the moss, and don't cut it too short.

Bumps and hollows

Many neglected lawns, or those that were badly laid in the first place, almost always have a few lumps and bumps. If it's like a ploughed field the only option is to start again. If you have just a few bumps or hollows then you can deal with them individually. With bumps, the best way is to cut a rectangle of turf around the bump and slice it off with the spade. Then level the soil underneath and replace the piece of turf. Some books recommend cutting a cross in the turf on top of the bump, then peeling back the four corners, removing the excess soil and putting the turf back. It's a perfectly acceptable way of doing it, although cutting out a rectangle is quicker.

The easiest way to get rid of individual hollows is to put no more than 2.5 cm (1 in) of top dressing (soil and sharp sand in equal parts) in the bottom of the dip and wait for the grass underneath to grow through. When it's growing strongly, add a little more compost, wait again, and so on, until the hollow has disappeared. If you've got an all-over slightly bumpy lawn, it's a good idea to cover the whole lawn with top dressing, so that all the hollows are filled in, then drag something heavy over the top of it, like a doormat, to make sure it's level and wait for the grass to grow through.

Worms

Once the lawn is reasonably short and is on the road to recovery, wormcasts can become a real nuisance. The mower just squashes them, to create marvellously fertile little seed beds which will get any airborne weed seeds off to a flying start. Some people deal with the problem by using a wormkiller which seems not merely brutal, but plain daft, given the enormous amount of good worms do in aerating the soil and pulling decaying organic matter down into it. Much simpler, surely, just to spread the wormcasts around the lawn with a stiff brush before you mow.

Starting from scratch

If the grass you inherit is really dreadful, then your best bet is to get rid of it, and start again. You can't just dig it over, scatter some lawn seed and hope for the best. Coarse grass will grow through again as sure as night follows day. You must kill it all off first. You could spray with glyphosate, or with dalapon, another weedkiller which doesn't stay in the soil. If you don't want to use chemicals, the only option open to you is to cover the area with black polythene, and leave it for three months. Once all the grass is dead, rotavate the area, or dig it over by hand.

It may be that you're happy with the shape of the old lawn in which case stick with it, but if you're redesigning the whole layout of the garden, you may want to change it. The shape is very much a matter of personal taste, but it's worth bearing in mind that curves help to break up the rather boring rectangular shape of many town and suburban gardens, and can make them seem wider. If you do go for curves, though, make them long, flowing ones. Lots of fiddly little curves not only look a bit of a mess, but they're also a lot more work.

Turf or seed?

When you're laying a new lawn, you can either turf it, or sow seed. Turf has the advantage of being immediate – it looks like a lawn from Day One, and you can use it after six weeks, although family parties and games of football should wait for some months. The drawback is that it is much more expensive. If you do decide on turf, though, and you can afford it, go for cultivated turf. It costs almost three times as much as the ordinary kind but the quality is superb with not a weed in sight. You can even choose whether you want bowling green stuff or a more hardwearing workaday turf. Unfortunately, the turf business has its fair share of cowboys and the 'turf' you buy may be just a bit of old pasture full of coarse grass and weeds – just like the stuff you've just got rid of. If you can't afford cultivated turf, then make sure you actually see what you're buying before you part with your money. It's also worth checking a few turves at random when the lorry arrives to deliver them and before they are unloaded. The driver may well get indignant, but at least you won't find after he's driven away that he's sold you the turf equivalent of a pup!

Seed is much slower than turf. It takes up to three weeks to germinate during which time you bite your nails and curse every sparrow which not only eats your seed, but has a dust bath in the soil, and once the grass is through it's ten weeks or more before you can use it. But it has the huge advantage of being much cheaper and of course you can choose exactly the kind of lawn you want, since there are now mixtures of seed for very fine lawns, everyday lawns, lawns that can stand up to a bashing from dogs and children, and even mixtures, based on woodland grasses, for shady places under trees.

Preparing the site

Whether you choose to lay turf or sow seed, the preparation of the soil is much the same.

Once you've dug it or rotavated it, removing any stones or bits of debris that you find, level the ground roughly with the back of a fork. At this stage. you're more concerned with getting the general level right than with every little bump and hollow.

Now is the time to mark out the exact shape of the new lawn. If it's going to be square or rectangular, that's very easy to mark, using the scale plan you've drawn (see p. 17), bamboo canes, and a builder's tape measure and square. Just measure from fixed points – the fences, or the back walls of the house – and mark the two corners nearest to them with bamboo canes. Then, with the tape measure, locate the other two corners using the builder's square to check that the corners are right angles.

With a circular lawn, measure from two fixed points to locate the centre of the circle. Mark it with a stout cane, and then cut a piece of twine the radius of the circle in length, plus a bit extra to attach to the central cane at one end and a marking stick at the other. Tie it to the central cane, and then with the twine pulled tight, walk round, scratching a circle in the soil with the marking stick. Mark the circle with bamboo canes pushed into the soil every metre or so. The mark on the soil could well be obliterated as you work on the area.

The simplest way to sow a lawn adjoining a curved hard surface is to edge it with turf first.

Oval lawns aren't that difficult to mark out either. Find the top of the oval by measuring from two fixed points, and knock in a peg. Measure the length it's going to be, and knock in another peg. Cut a piece of twine three times as long as the distance between the two pegs, and tie one end to each of them. With a sharp stick, pull the twine out to one side, taking up all the slack. Keeping the twine tight all the time, move the stick round from one peg to the other, and you'll find that it's marking half an oval on the ground. Do the same on the other side, and mark the line with canes. If you want a slightly narrower oval, don't make the string quite so long. If you want a fatter one, make it a bit longer.

Irregular curves are slightly more difficult to lay out. Undoubtedly, the safest way is to measure the distance on the plan between, say, the fence or the house wall and the curve at regular intervals, then scale it up and transfer it to the ground. Alternatively, you could chance it by eye, using the hose, or a trail of sharp sand to form the shape.

When you're reasonably satisfied with the way it looks in the garden, go into the house and look at it from all the windows you'll be viewing the garden from. Any section that's not quite right will be obvious. You might find, even if you've transferred the curve exactly from the plan, that it doesn't look quite right. Don't be afraid to change it. What works on paper doesn't always work in practice. The golden rule here is, if it *looks* right, then it *is* right. After all, it's the garden you'll be enjoying for years to come, not the plan.

Preparing the soil

Once you've marked out the lawn area, spread a 5-cm (2-in) layer of organic matter (and grit, if you've got a heavy clay soil) over the surface. The next stage is to consolidate it all over. Choose a day when the soil is dry enough not to stick to your boots (though clearly the middle of a drought is not the ideal time). And the boots are relevant because they're what you need to consolidate the soil. With your weight on your heels, tread systematically up and down the soil, making sure you cover every single inch. You may feel a bit silly, but all you can do about that is hope that the neighbours are either on holiday or are keen gardeners themselves, in which case you'll get approving nods. It's hard work too, but it really is the only way. If you don't do it all, your lawn will be full of bumps and hollows. Using a roller isn't an option, either, because it will simply push down the bumps a bit and skate over the hollows.

If the lawn area adjoins a hard surface – a patio or path, for instance – do make sure that the soil right up against the edge is really well consolidated, since it has a tendency to sink. If necessary, add some additional soil and firm it down really well.

Before you do the final raking, sprinkle fertiliser over the surface – two handfuls of blood, fish and bonemeal to the square metre if you're an organic gardener, or one handful of Growmore if you're not.

The final raking is critical. Don't reach a long way in front of you with the rake, otherwise you'll pull the soil up into ridges. Work close to your feet keeping the head of the rake almost horizontal. Every now and then, crouch down, and with your head as low as possible, look across the area you have raked. You should be able to spot any bumps and hollows that way.

Laying turf

Turf can be laid at any time of year, provided the ground isn't frozen or waterlogged, but, given that one of the keys to success is never allowing the young turf to dry out, you're better off avoiding July and August too. Decide when you're going to lay the turf, and arrange to collect it, or have it delivered, on the day itself, or the day before. The less time turves have to sit about, especially in warm weather, the better.

Obviously, before you order it, you must work out how much you need. With a square or rectangular lawn, it's very easy – length times breadth will give you the square metres or yards and if you're not using cultivated turf add on 10 per cent for wastage. Circular lawns aren't a problem either – for the first time in your life, probably, πr^2 will have a practical use. Measure the radius of the circle and your pocket calculator (or a teenage child) will do the rest.

Gently curved lawns are more of a problem. Probably the easiest way to calculate how much you need is to get your plan and draw a rectangle (or a square) around the lawn area, touching it at its extremities. That will give you a rough idea of how much of the rectangle won't be covered by lawn. If it is only a bit – 10 per cent or so – then work out the area of the rectangle and order that number of square metres. If it looks as though roughly a third of the rectangle or even a half won't be covered by lawn, adjust your order accordingly.

If you're planning to lay the turf during a dry spell, then a day or two beforehand put the sprinkler on and make sure that the whole area gets a good couple of hours' watering. There's a detailed description of how to lay a rectangular or circular lawn in *First Time Garden*.

When you've finished, put the lawn sprinkler on, and make sure every part gets half an hour's watering every day or two in dry weather. It really is vital to keep new turf well watered because, if you don't, cracks will appear between the turves and you've got a real job filling them in.

It'll take between three days and three weeks for the turf to start rooting into the soil, and until it does it looks a bit sorry for itself – flat and faded in colour. You can soon tell when it has rooted, though, because the grass stands up and begins to look a fresh green again.

Island beds

You might find, as we did in our over-mature garden, that there is a small island bed in the middle of the lawn that doesn't fit in with your new design. The answer is to remove all the plants that are worth keeping, and then fill it in with turf. Ideally, if you are redesigning your garden, there will be areas of grass that you're planning to dig up anyway, which would be ideal for the job. Not only is it much cheaper than buying turf, as it's the same grass it will match perfectly, and you'll find very quickly that you can no longer see the joins. Obviously, if you don't have any turf you can use, you'll have to buy some.

The first thing to do is clean up the edges with a spade, to make them square. Over the years people will have walked too close to the edge of the island bed, with the result that the edges have become bevelled and so if you just left them as they are and filled in the gap with turf you'd have a dip all the way round. If you have a round bed, as we did, or an oval one, then it makes life much easier if you convert it into a square or rectangle while you're straightening up the edges. Simply pile the pieces you've cut into the centre and chop them up a bit with the spade. As the grass rots down, it will help improve the fertility of the soil. Then treat it as you would treat any area to be turfed.

When it comes to cutting the turf from your own garden, remember that it will be much less fibrous than commercially grown turf, and so will break more easily if you try to cut too large a piece. About 30 cm by 40 cm (1 ft by 1 ft 4 in) is about right. Cut the four sides with a sharp spade, to a depth of just over 2.5 cm (1 in) and then slice carefully underneath and lift it free. Turn it face down on to a hard surface, and check the level. You may find the soil is thicker at one end than at the other, in which case, carefully slice off the excess with the spade.

Lay the turf a row at a time, cutting the end pieces to fit where necessary. As you first lay it, it should be higher than the surrounding lawn, but banging it down hard with the back of the rake will soon make it level. It will marry in very quickly with the rest of the lawn, so it's easy to forget that it's there, but do try to avoid walking on it for three weeks or so, to give its roots a chance to grow into the soil.

Seed

Traditionally, the best time to sow a lawn is spring or autumn. In fact, you can sow at any time from April until October, but you will have to be very vigilant with the sprinkler if your lawn is going to survive. Incidentally, if your new lawn is going to butt up against a patio or a path, you need to ensure that the grass is above the hard surface and that it has a firm edge. One answer is to use a strip of turf there and seed the rest. Certainly, if the hard surface is curved as it was in our blank garden, that's probably the only answer. If it is a straight line, you can put a scaffolding plank on the hard surface, right up against the edge, then rake some soil up against it, and firm it down with your heel. Do it two or three times more, until the soil is up to the top of the board and really well consolidated. Weight the board with bricks or slabs to stop it moving and leave it until three weeks after the seed has germinated. When you take it away, you'll have a good firm edge.

If the area isn't confined by hard edges, sow a slightly larger area than you want the finished lawn to be. That way, when the grass is growing strongly, about two months after germination, you can trim it to size and get a good, firm edge.

Once you've sown the seed, rake it lightly in with a spring-tine rake. You should aim to cover about half the seed with soil. Don't roll it or water it. Rolling it simply isn't necessary, while watering could form a hard crust which would prevent germination, or can make the surface of the soil uneven, and wash the seed into the hollows.

It's a fact of life that birds like grass seed. Although it may seem that the entire bird population of the area is out on your newly sown lawn, filling their beaks, the fact is that they rarely take enough to affect the quality of the lawn. More serious is the fact that they churn up the soil in the process, even bathing in it sometimes, which does mean you can wind up with bare patches. The best way to deter them, and speed up germination at the same time, is to lay a floating cloche over the area. This is clear polythene sheeting with hundreds of little perforations in it. You could use ordinary clear polythene, but be sure to take it off the moment the first blade of grass appears. Don't use fine polypropylene pea netting or black cotton stretched between sticks. Birds can get trapped in it and die.

Taking care of a new lawn

Whether your lawn was turfed or seeded, it will need much the same treatment for a while. Neither should be cut until the grass is at least 5 cm (2 in) tall. A couple of days before you mow your new seeded lawn, go over it and remove any stones that may have worked their way up to the surface. Not only could they damage your mower if you left them, they could fly up and cause you an injury.

The next step, with lawns of both types, is to roll them lightly, either with the roller on your mower if it has one, making sure you keep the blades well clear of the grass, or a hired roller.

When you first mow the grass a couple of days after rolling, set the mower blades to their highest setting. If you cut it too short, you will damage the young grass and if you scalp it, of course you're providing moss and weeds with an opportunity to get established. Gradually reduce the height a setting at a time over the next few mowings until the grass is being left 1.3 cm (½ in) long.

Despite all your sterling efforts in clearing the ground before you started, you may well find a few weeds germinating along with the grass. Most of them aren't a problem. Regular mowing will soon kill off annual weeds like chickweed and lesser yellow trefoil and even some perennial weeds. Those like dandelions and daisies, which form ground-hugging rosettes, almost always escape death by mowing but will succumb to the old kitchen knife or salt treatment (see p. 46).

A new lawn shouldn't need feeding in its first year. In the following year give it a feed in the spring (see p. 45).

Dealing with shade

If you've got a shady spot under an old cherry or plum tree, say, where moss thrives and lawn struggles in vain to compete, then the best bet is to forget about trying to make it a lawn. Instead, turn it into a patch of long, rough grass in which you naturalise bulbs, and even plant wild flowers, which makes a very attractive contrast with the rest of the lawn. If the tree is deciduous, there will be enough light for spring-flowering bulbs to flourish underneath it in the spring, before its new leaves are out. You could naturalise snowdrops, the golden winter aconites, crocuses, daffodils (the miniature ones are best unless it's a very large area), even something more unusual like the beautiful snakeshead fritillary (*Fritillaria meleagris*). Plant them in late summer.

Naturalised bulbs obviously look much better in informal groupings. You shouldn't cut the foliage of bulbs for at least six weeks after flowering has finished, but since you're planting them in long grass which will only be cut every two or three times a season, that's not a problem.

It is possible to create a wildflower meadow in a small garden, as John Chamber's gold-medal winning display at Chelsea proves categorically (right).

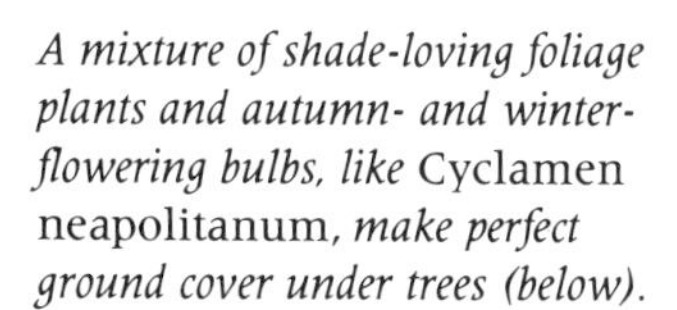

A mixture of shade-loving foliage plants and autumn- and winter-flowering bulbs, like Cyclamen neapolitanum, *make perfect ground cover under trees (below).*

If you plant wild flowers, obviously you can't take them from the wild – it's illegal as well as anti-social – and it's now very easy to buy them either as seed or as small plants from specialist growers.* Make sure you choose woodland mixtures, with plants like woodruff, bugle, and yellow archangel, which will thrive in shady conditions. Most woodland plants are spring- or autumn-flowering because in summer when trees are in full leaf there isn't enough light.

In the wild, seeds are just scattered and some of them germinate. But the fact is that an awful lot of them don't and you can't afford to scatter huge quantities of seed in order to get the comparatively small number of plants you want. You can either treat your patch of rough grass like a new lawn – clear the ground, prepare the soil and then sow a special wild flower and grass mixture, designed for shady areas. Alternatively, you can raise individual plants from seed in pots or trays, or buy collections of young plants, and then plant them out in spring. Once flowering is over, towards the end of May, you can give the grass its first cut of the season. A rotary mower with its blades at the highest setting is ideal because it will keep the grass a reasonable length, and leave most of the flowering plants' foliage. Next best is a cylinder mower, again at the highest setting, but not a hover mower because you have no control over the height.

Another solution to the problem of what to do with very shady places where grass won't grow is to go for ground-cover plants – low-growing species that will tolerate the damp conditions you often find in town gardens where the shade is cast by buildings, and the dry conditions under trees. Once they're established, they form a dense, weed-proof carpet and have the added advantage of needing practically no looking after.

Good ground-cover plants

All the following plants will grow in both moist and dry shade, although in practically every case they won't grow as well, or flower as freely in dry conditions as they do where there's a bit more moisture.

Bugle (*Ajuga reptans*) has spikes of vivid gentian blue in early summer carried above attractive variegated leaves. The green and buff *A. r.* 'Variegata' keeps its colour better in deep shade than the purple varieties, like 'Atropurpurea' and the well-named 'Burgundy Glow'.

Lady's mantle (*Alchemilla mollis*) has stunning fresh green scalloped leaves and sprays of tiny yellow-green flowers from June to August.

Elephant's ears (*Bergenia*) has large leathery rounded leaves and spikes of white, pink or red flowers in late spring. Look out for *B.* 'Abendglut' with

* For example, John Chambers, 15 Westleigh Road, Baron Seagrave, Kettering, Northants NN15 5AJ. Suffolk Herbs, Sawyers Farm, Little Cornard, Sudbury, Suffolk CO10 0NY.

vivid rosy-red flowers and deep red foliage in winter, *B.* 'Bressingham White' and the largest of all, *B.* 'Ballawley'.

Cranesbill (*Geranium*), particularly the *G. macrorrhizum* varieties, thrives in dry shade. These have aromatic, semi-evergreen leaves which often turn red in autumn, and stems of flowers in shades of pink. *G. m.* 'Album' has blush-white flowers, 'Ingwersen's Variety' has pinky-mauve flowers and 'Bevan's Variety' has taller stems of flowers in a vivid magenta pink.

Dead nettle (*Lamium maculatum*) spreads quickly and the variegated green and silver leaves of *L. m.* 'Beacon Silver' and 'White Nancy' can really brighten up a dark corner. They also have attractive flowers, the former clear pink, and the latter ivory white.

Lungwort (*Pulmonaria*) has sprays of very pretty flowers in pink, white and a range of blues, followed by clumps of very attractive silver-spotted or silver-frosted leaves. Look out for *P. officinalis* 'Cambridge Blue' which has pink buds which open into blue flowers, *P. saccharata* 'Sissinghurst White' with very large leaves and flowers, and *P. s.* 'Highdown'.

Viola labradorica seeds itself so freely where it's happy that, if it weren't so pretty, it could be a menace. A very low-growing plant, no more than 15 cm (6 in) in height, it has small round green leaves, flushed purple, which make the perfect background for its small clear mauve flowers in spring.

Alternatives to lawns

In some gardens, like very small gardens and city back yards behind terraced houses, lawn isn't really a sensible option. For one thing, tiny patches of grass never really look very good, and for another it's a great deal of bother for very little reward. For a start, where are you going to keep the lawnmower? You could cut it with shears, but it would look pretty awful. If you want to spend what little free time you do have sitting in your garden, not working on it, then lawn isn't a good idea either. Lawns are not low maintenance.

In these circumstances you're much better off going for a hard surface – brick, stone slabs (real or imitation), tiles, cobbles, setts, pebbles, gravel. But that doesn't mean the garden has to look 'hard', the sort of monument to the bricklayer's art that has become very fashionable lately, as long as you make sure there's plenty of greenery in it by creating wide beds for low-maintenance shrubs and by leaving planting holes for low-growing alpines, annuals or herbs in the hard surface itself.

There is a wide range of materials on offer these days to suit all kinds of pockets and situations. But, remember, whatever hard surface you choose will be a prominent feature in your garden, and ought to be attractive in its own right.

Combinations of hard materials, like brick and gravel or slabs and setts, bring out the best in each other and are more attractive than they would have been used on their own.

Perhaps the first factor to bear in mind when you're making your choice is the house and existing walls. While you're free to choose absolutely anything you like, it often looks better if the hard materials in the garden match or at least blend with the house. Brash new red bricks won't look very good behind a house built of old, yellow London stocks. In that situation, you'd be much better off visiting the local demolition contractor and buying weathered second-hand London stocks.

The next factor is how much it will cost. Old York stone slabs might be the perfect material for your garden, but they cost a fortune these days, so maybe one of the very good imitations on the market now would be a more realistic proposition. A few years ago, most concrete slabs came in bright, unnatural custard-cream yellows, vanilla-ice creams and garish terracottas. But they've come on in leaps and bounds and there are some really attractive, subtle colours available now. Before you buy, ask if you can see a slab wet to see how the colour changes. It may be a colour you loathe and, bearing in mind the nature of our climate, that's the colour it will be for quite a large proportion of the time. Texture is important too. Smooth slabs can be very slippery when wet, while textured surfaces give a better grip, and those with a 'riven' surface do look very like the real thing although it does mean your garden furniture might wobble a bit.

Bricks can look very attractive. You can lay them in all sorts of different patterns – herringbone, basketweave and so on – but do make sure you buy engineering bricks, or special paving bricks, since the ones used for building houses will flake when they freeze.

Gravel is probably the cheapest surface you can have, and it's relatively straightforward to lay. Go to the local builders' merchants and have a look at what's on offer, for the colours can vary quite significantly. Gravel is, after all, son of stone – literally the chip off the old block – and gravel from a limestone area will be quite different in colour to gravel from a sandstone, or ironstone area. Go for a large grade. It gives a more solid feel and, just as important, doesn't stick to your shoes like the smaller stuff does. It's a good idea, anyway, with gravel to make sure you have some sort of paving just outside the back door to minimise the chance of carting gravel into the house.

Perhaps the most attractive of all hard surfaces are those that combine materials – riven slabs and brick, brick and cobbles, slabs and gravel, pebbles and slabs. This way you can enjoy the beauty of expensive materials because you're using them sparingly – a few York stone slabs, say, laid as stepping stones among gravel and plants, or some lovely old bricks used to frame plain concrete slabs.

Using contrasting materials can also be an important design element. In an area that was mainly slabs, for example, you could use a couple of rows of bricks here and there to divide it up into 'rooms'. Bricks laid widthwise can actually help make a thin garden look wider, while laying them lengthwise will only emphasise its narrowness.

Do remember, though, that in a small garden, particularly, too many different materials can look a bit of a mess. You'd be better off just sticking to a couple, and repeating them. If your patio is a combination of bricks and slabs, say, then use the same bricks to edge the lawn.

Once you've decided which materials you're going to use, the next step is to work out how much you need. With slabs, bricks, setts and so on, you need to calculate the area to be covered – easy enough to work out from your plan – and since most suppliers use the metric system these days, work it out in square metres. Some ranges of paving include slabs of varying size to give an attractive, less uniform look. Either the manufacturers provide a brochure which will help you work out the number of each size that you'll need, or their stockist will do that for you. Unless you are extremely confident, it's not advisable just to buy an assortment of each and simply make it up as you go along. Chances are you'll wind up at the end having to use a number of slabs all the same size.

If you are going to use a combination of different materials – slabs and bricks, say, work out the number of bricks you'll need, the area they will cover, and subtract it from the total area. That will give you the quantity of slabs you need in square metres.

Materials like gravel are usually sold in cubic metres. Multiply the length of the area by the breadth and the depth. If you find your supplier sells it by weight instead, remember, as a rough guide, that one cubic metre of gravel weighs 2.3 tonnes.

Laying paving

The secret of laying paving successfully is getting the levels right, and that means absolutely spot on. In the case of a patio, or paving right up to the house, it must have a slight 'fall', so that rainwater runs away from the house walls, and doesn't just lie on the surface, or worse still, run down on to the base of the wall and into the foundations.

In one respect, laying a hard surface in an old garden is likely to be easier than tackling the same operation in a brand-new garden. There, where mechanical diggers have been used to dig out the foundations, and the soil has been pushed back into the trenches after the walls have been built, it will take a long time for the soil to settle again. If you try and lay a hard surface on it without making sure you lay really solid foundations first, you will get subsidence and your paving will soon start to look like a tank trap, with slabs at all angles, and you'll have all the expense and aggravation of digging up and starting again. (Laying a brand-new patio in a new garden was dealt with in detail in the book and television series, *First Time Garden*.) With an old garden, the soil is likely to be well compacted and if it is you won't need to worry about laying foundations.

If you already have some sort of hard surface – concrete most likely if it's an older house – outside the back door, then you might be able to use that as a base for slabs or bricks. The only proviso is that when you lay your chosen new surface, plus mortar, on top of it, it must still be at least 15 to 17 cm (6 to 7 in), or two courses of bricks, *below* the damp-proof course. This is a waterproof membrane built into the house walls to stop damp rising. Almost all houses built this century will have a DPC. In modern houses, it's usually marked by a wide course of mortar between two courses of bricks. In some older houses, it's sometimes a row of blue engineering bricks, and in some even older houses which didn't have DPCs originally, it appears as a line of small circles, about 2.5 cm (1 in) in diameter, and about 30 cm (1 ft) apart, through which a damp-proofing chemical has been injected. Some treatments are injected horizontally, others are at a downward angle, and since the damp-proof course starts at the lowest point, you need to know which yours is. Locate one of the circles, scrape out any infill and push something like a knitting needle carefully in. You'll soon feel whether it goes in horizontally or at a downward angle.

If your new patio will be too high in relation to the DPC, you'll have to break up the concrete with a sledge hammer and start again, although, if you're lucky, not quite from scratch. Once you've got rid of the concrete, you'll probably find either a layer of well-compacted hardcore, or even a layer of well-compacted soil. You can set levels in the same way as you would working on virgin soil, by hammering wooden pegs into the ground starting with the first 30 cm (1 ft) from the house walls, so that its top is level with the bottom of the second course of bricks below the DPC. Using that peg, plus a straight edge and spirit level, put in a line of pegs also 30 cm (1 ft) from the house walls and 1.2 m (4 ft) apart, and all level with the first peg. Obviously it will be more difficult to hammer them into well-compacted soil or hardcore than into ordinary soil, so you may need to make a hole with a metal spike and a club hammer first.

To make sure any water that falls on to the patio runs away from the house, set the second row of pegs, at a distance of 1.2 m (4 ft) from the first, about 13 mm (½ in) lower than the first. The easiest way to do it is to cut a small piece of wood 13 mm (½ in) and put it on each of the second row pegs before you use the straight edge and the spirit level to check the levels. When the level is exactly right you know that when you take away your small piece of wood the second peg is exactly 13 mm (½ in) lower than the first. Carry on until the whole area is marked out.

If it's absolutely impossible to put in any pegs, take a piece of paving (or use a whole slab if you haven't got a broken bit) and set it on a bit of mortar within straight-edge distance of the house walls, make sure it's absolutely level, then take your levels from that. You can easily knock your guide piece of paving out of the way when you come to lay that part of the patio.

Once you've set the levels and the falls then you can start laying the slabs as you would for a new patio. In addition to the straight edge and spirit level you used to set the levels, you'll need builder's sand and cement in the ratio 3:1, a board on which to mix it, a trowel, a bricklayer's nylon line and a club hammer. The slabs will be laid on five little mounds of mortar, about 10 cm (4 in) high, one at each corner, and one in the centre. Since the mortar has to bear the weight of the slab, it needs to be a fairly dry, stiff mixture, so add the water carefully.

Start at one end of the area to be paved, closest to the house. Without wishing to be too alarmist, it's worth pointing out that the first slab you lay will set the pattern for all the rest. You might think that the first slab being just a few millimetres out of true with the wall won't make much difference, but you'd be wrong. Ten slabs later, it'll be a few centimetres out of true, and looking a real mess.

Put down your five mounds of mortar and gently place the first paving slab on top 2.5 cm (1 in) away from the wall. Using the handle of the club hammer (never the metal head, or you could crack the slabs) tap it down until it's roughly level with the top of the peg.

To make sure it's straight, take your bricklayer's line and wrap it round a brick. Put the brick on the outside edge of the slab, at the back, so that the line, feeding from the bottom of the brick, runs along the back of the slab. Hold it in place with another brick, up against the first. Then take the free end of the line to the far side of the area to be paved, and, using a metal tape measure, hold it exactly 2.5 cm (1 in) from the wall. If the line runs straight along the back edge of the first slab you've laid, then the slab is straight. If it doesn't, it isn't, so tap the slab into line and check again. Ideally, you need someone to help you, either by holding the line while you tap, or vice versa.

Once it's absolutely true to the wall, check the level by putting your straight edge on to the slab and the nearest peg. If the straight edge doesn't lie flush along the surface of the slab, tap the slab down until it does. Double check with the spirit level. Using all the other pegs you can reach, check that the slab is level all round. Finally, just make sure that all the tapping hasn't skewed the slab slightly out of line with the wall, by checking again with the bricklayer's line.

You will be delighted to hear that once the first slab is perfectly positioned, laying the rest is a doddle by comparison. You simply put down five more little mounds of mortar, butt the next slab up against its neighbour, tap it down and check the level, with the straight edge and the spirit level, in both directions. If you plan to grow plants between the paving slabs, leave a very slight gap – 6 mm (¼ in) is enough – between one slab and the next. To keep your paving true, cut short pieces of wood of about that thickness, and use them as spacer pegs. When you've finished paving, brush seed compost into the cracks, and then mix some seeds with a little sharp sand, and brush it across the paving. They'll fall into the gaps, and germinate without difficulty. If you find you've got too many, just pull them up. Many alpines are perennial, and will come up every year, while annuals like *Alyssum maritima* seed themselves so freely that once you've sown it, you're never without it. (For a list of suitable alpines, see p. 65.)

Cutting slabs

You would have to have the luck of the devil when you lay your paving slabs to find that they all fit exactly, and you don't have to cut a single one. Chances are you'll have to cut at least one or two. If it's a straight cut, then it's easy enough to do with a brick bolster and club hammer. Measure where you need to cut and score down the surface of the slab with the edge of the bolster, leaving a groove. Turn the slab on its edge and nick the top edge front and back. Turn it through 180 degrees and do the same on what was the bottom edge. Then, with the slab face down, score down the back between the two nicks.

Now, lean the slab against your leg, put the edge of the bolster in the groove on the front, and tap gently with the club hammer. Turn the slab round and do the same on the back. Keep on until the slab cracks in two. If you have any complicated shapes to cut, to fit round a drainpipe, for instance, you could hire an angle grinder from the local hire shop, along with eye protection and some stout gloves. You will also need to buy at least one special stone-cutting disc. If you're going to be cutting a lot of slabs – to fit a curved shape, for instance – then you'll need more than one. The hire shop should stock them.

Mark the shape to be cut on the surface of the slab, although since the discs don't last long and are very expensive, it's best to cut a quarter of the way through from each side, and then tap along the line of the cut, on the bit that you don't need just in case, with the club hammer. If the cut is going to be on display, if you're cutting treads for steps, for example, then hang

Mediterranean plants like thyme are happiest growing in thin, poor, gravelly soil.

the expense, and use the angle grinder to cut right the way through. If you are not very experienced at DIY it's probably best to pay someone to do the cutting for you. Angle grinders can be dangerous in inexperienced hands.

Planting in paving

When you're laying slabs, it couldn't be simpler to create planting pockets by missing out a slab or two. Although there are a few plants that will stand up to being constantly trodden on, most won't, so it's best to plant away from the main walkway and the area where you're going to put your patio furniture. As for plants, you can choose anything that's happy with your soil conditions (see p. 40) and the amount of sun and shade it will get. Since you'll be spending a lot of time there, scented plants would be a good idea as would herbs, particularly if the patio is right by the back door, so you can just pop out and pick a handful for the kitchen.

You can also grow plants in the cracks between the paving slabs. Annuals like alyssum (which comes in pink, red and purple as well as white) are ideal, as are alpines like aubrietia, dianthus, and herbs like thyme.

Laying a brick path

If you have an old strip of concrete that you really want to be rid of, or indeed no path at all, then bricks or blocks laid on sand make a very attractive replacement. Once you've broken up the concrete and carted it away the method is the same in both cases.

First of all, choose the material for your path. If you're sensible, its width will be an exact number of bricks or blocks. No point in cutting bricks unless you absolutely have to! Before you start, lay them out in the pattern of your choice, with about 6 mm (¼ in) between them. Measure the width and add twice the width of the edging you'll need to stop your blocks moving sideways.

Measure and mark out the path with pegs and string. The depth to which you'll need to dig out the soil is determined by the depth of the blocks – usually about 6 cm (2¼ in) plus 5 cm (2 in) of sand. Again, if your soil is well compacted, you won't need to bother with a proper foundation. If it isn't, you'll need to dig another 5 cm deeper and put in 5 cm of dry ballast and cement in the ratio 10 parts ballast:1 part cement.

If the path is higher than its surroundings, the next step is to put in an edging to stop the sand and the blocks moving sideways. The easiest way is to use lengths of 8 × 2.5 cm (3 × 1 in) treated timber, fixed on the outside to pegs driven into the ground about 1 m (3 ft 3 in) apart. Once you have checked with a spirit level that the edges are level, you can keep them in place permanently with a thin fillet of concrete or soil around the outside. If your path curves, then help the wood to bend easily by making a series of sawcuts about 5 cm (2 in) apart and halfway through its depth.

Wet the sand just enough to make it uniformly moist – it should just hold together when you press a handful between your palms. Put it into the trench and level it roughly with a rake. For the final levelling you'll need a notched board, which you make yourself. Start with a piece of wood 10 cm (4 in) wider than the path and at least 5 cm (2 in) more than the depth of a block. Cut notches either side at exactly path width and 2 cm (¾ in) less than the depth of the block. That means when you lay the blocks initially they will be 2 cm higher than the finished level you want, but as you tamp them down they will settle to the right height.

Rest your notched board on the wooden edging and as you slide it along it will scrape off any excess sand and give you a perfectly level surface. Either get rid of the excess as you go, or if you come across any low patches use it to fill them in, and then level again. You don't have to worry about a 'fall' when you're laying this kind of path since any excess water will drain between the bricks and into the ground.

Once the final levelling is done, you can start to lay the blocks, leaving a 3 to 5 mm (⅛ to ¼ in) gap between each one. When you need to stand or kneel on the blocks you have just laid, put another board across the whole width and stand on that. Never stand on the blocks themselves, otherwise you could dislodge one that you've already laid, which would mean taking all the blocks out, back to that point, and starting again.

When all the blocks are laid, spread a thin layer of sharp sand over the surface and brush it into the gaps. Now tamp it down hard with a board and a heavy baulk of timber.

If it is a very long path, or you're using this method to make a patio, you'd be better off hiring a flat-bed vibrator from the hire shop, which tamps the blocks down very firmly indeed. If the area is to take any kind of weight – a driveway for example – then you must lay proper foundations first, and the blocks are best laid in a herringbone pattern, which forms a stronger bond.

Gravel

As well as being one of the cheapest surfaces you can have, gravel is also very adaptable. It can look very formal, with low clipped box hedges, or very informal, with colourful plants growing through it and seeding themselves everywhere.

Before you lay gravel, you must first surround the area with some kind of edging, to prevent it spreading everywhere. You could use treated timber, or a pre-cast concrete kerb. If you're lucky, you might even have uncovered some Victorian barley sugar twist edging tiles underneath the debris, which would be perfect. Alternatively, you could buy the reproduction ones which are available now, but they are very pricey. If you are planning to build raised beds for your plants, then the walls will retain the gravel and you don't need a special edging.

If your soil is chalky or gravelly already, you can simply spread 2.5 cm (1 in) of gravel on to the soil, and roll it in. If you've got a clay, or a sandy soil, then you'll need to spread a 7.5-cm (3-in) layer of hoggin which is a mixture of gravel and sand, available from builders' merchants, first, and compact it well with your feet, or better still a roller. On top of that, you spread 2 to 2.5 cm (about an inch) of gravel, and roll it in. You certainly don't want the gravel any deeper, or it becomes difficult to walk through.

If you want some slabs as well as gravel, then either lay them with five blobs of mortar (p. 61) directly on to the soil if you're not using hoggin, or lay them loose on the hoggin if you are.

To plant through gravel, initially, you'll need to make planting holes through both layers, so that the roots of the plants can reach the soil below. After a few years, you'll find that soil works its way into the hoggin and the gravel, and you'll be able to plant directly into it.

Plants for gravel

Many plants, particularly alpines, thrive in the good drainage that gravel provides. Among the best are:

Gravel is the best medium for showing off attractive alpines like gentians, the grey-leaved Oxalis adenophylla *and the white-flowered* Nierembergia rivularis *(above and below right).*

Yarrow (*Achillea*) Make sure you go for an alpine variety, like 'King Edward' which has delicate ferny grey-green foliage and primrose-yellow, daisy-like flowers from June to September. *Height*: 15 cm (6 in).

Alyssum saxatile This is a perennial, not to be confused with its white, annual relative. *A. s.* 'Compactum' has primrose-yellow flowers from April to June. *Height:* 15 cm (6 in).

Columbine (*Aquilegia*) Again, make sure you buy an alpine variety. *A. flabellata* (or *akitensis*) has attractive blue-green foliage and large blue and white flowers in late spring. *Height*: 15 cm (6 in).

***Arabis ferdinandi-coburgii* 'Variegata'** Its name is almost larger than it is! This plant forms low mounds of very attractive green and white variegated foliage and has white flowers in summer. *Height*: 10 cm (4 in).

Thrift (*Armeria*) Good, very low-growing varieties of this evergreen cushion plant include *A. caespitosa* 'Bevan's Variety' which has bright pink flowers and deep green foliage and *A. c.* 'Alba' with white flowers. Both flower in May. *Height*: 6 cm (2 to 3 in).

Aubrietia One of the most widely grown alpines, usually in its purple form, and often paired with the acid-yellow variety of *Alyssum saxatile*. There are other varieties in shades of pink, red and lavender for a softer, more subtle effect. Prevent them from sprawling everywhere by cutting them back hard after flowering. They are easily grown from seed. *Height*: 10 cm (4 in).

Bellflower (*Campanula*) Again, make sure you buy an alpine variety, like any of the *C. carpatica* or *C. cochleariifolia* hybrids. The former has blue or white flowers and you can grow it easily from seed, while the latter has blue flowers. Avoid *C. poscharskyana* and *C. portenschlagiana*, both of which spread like crazy.

Corsican thyme (*Mentha requienii*) It's not a thyme at all, but a member of the mint family, with tiny, very fragrant leaves and minuscule lavender-blue flowers in spring. *Height*: 2 cm (less than 1 in).

Dianthus alpinus These mat-forming plants have attractive flowers in shades of pink, red and white. Look out for *D.* 'Oakington' (warm, rose-pink), *D. deltoides* 'Brighteyes' (white flowers with a red 'eye') and *D. d.* 'Flashing Light' with brilliant scarlet flowers. You can also grow it from seed. *Height*: 5 to 15 cm (2 to 6 in).

Cranesbill (*Geranium*) Among the best alpine varieties are *G. cinereum* 'Ballerina', with lilac-pink flowers veined with red from May to July, *G.* 'Laurence Flatman' with soft, mauve-pink flowers mottled with magenta from May to September, and *G. subcaulescens*, with crimson flowers with a darker eye from May to July. *Height*: 10 to 15 cm (4 to 6 in).

***Lithospermum diffusum* 'Heavenly Blue' (or better still 'Grace Ward')** If you have an acid soil, do try this. It has the most intense Gauloise-blue flowers from May to August, carried above a mat of dark green foliage. *Height*: 15 cm (6 in).

White Cup (*Nierembergia rivularis*) A succession of white, inverted bell-shaped flowers are carried above a mat of bright green foliage from June to September. *Height*: 5 cm (2 in).

Saxifrage (*Saxifraga*) There are lots of excellent varieties with flowers in shades of red, pink, yellow and white to choose from. Buy them in flower from the garden centre. *Height*: 10 to 15 cm (4 to 6 in).

Sedum Again, there's a wide choice on offer, but do avoid the native *Sedum acre* with bright yellow flowers. You sometimes see it advertised in magazines, as some kind of miracle, ground-covering plant. Strictly speaking, that's an accurate description, but it doesn't know when to stop, and once you've got it, it's impossible to get rid of it. *Height*: 10 cm (4 in).

Houseleeks (*Sempervivums*) People become addicted to these and build up huge collections. Their rosettes of fleshy leaves in a range of colours are very striking, as are their spikes of flowers in June and July. *Height*: 10 to 15 cm (4 to 6 in).

Thyme (*Thymus*) There are lots of low-growing varieties to choose from – *T.* 'Doone Valley' with dark green and gold variegated foliage and mauve flowers, *T. serpyllum* 'Annie Hall' with shell-pink flowers, *T. s.* 'Coccineus' with rich reddish flowers, and *T. s.* 'Albus' with white flowers. *Height*: 5 to 8 cm (2 to 3 in).

CHAPTER 3

Borders

One of the relatively few early rewards from taking over a neglected garden is stumbling across what was clearly once a border, albeit a long time ago, and, once you've hacked the wilderness back a bit, finding a few horticultural gems alive and well beneath the waist-high grass and weeds. Even if you are a total beginner, you'll have no difficulty in recognising a rose, with or without its leaves, and you may recognise one or two other shrubs as well. But the chances are that you won't be able to identify most of the plants you've got, particularly if you take over the garden in winter when one cluster of bare brown twigs looks very much like any other to all but the most experienced eye, so you won't know whether you want to keep it or not.

So how do you find out what you've got in your garden? Obviously, you could ask the person who sold you the house, and if you're buying in the winter months ask them to show you any photographs they may have of the garden in spring and summer. At least that should give you some idea of what you might have and where. Although evergreen plants can be identified at any time of the year, it's obviously much easier to wait until any deciduous ones are at least in leaf, if not in flower, before you seek help in identifying what you've got. If you know any keen gardeners you could do it the easy way and ask them to make a tour of the garden with you. Take a notebook and pencil or, even better, some waterproof tie-on labels, so that as you're told the name of each shrub, you can write it down and attach the label firmly to its owner. Alternatively, you could snip off a sprig of the foliage with, if possible, a flower or two, and take it along to your local garden centre. Chances are there'll be someone there who can help. Don't cut your specimen twigs until just before you set off, though. Even the most expert expert would find it hard to identify a shrub from a few crisp shrivelled leaves which have been in your pocket for a couple of weeks.

Another pleasurable method of getting to know plants is to visit gardens open to the public, not just the grand stately ones but small private gardens which open once or twice a year for charity and which are listed in either of the 'Yellow Books'. There you will probably recognise many of the plants you have found in your garden, and what's more most of them will be labelled.

You could always look the plants up in a reference book, but you'll need a 'flora' type, in which plants' characteristics – their size, shape, shape of leaf, flower colour, flowering season and so on – lead to their identification. You could also try something like the *RHS Gardeners' Encyclopaedia of Plants and Flowers*, which groups plants according to size, flowering season and flower

Trees, shrubs, roses, conifers, perennials and alpines all play a part in this beautiful mixed border.

colour, but with a general alphabetical plant encyclopaedia, it would be like looking for the proverbial needle in a haystack.

You could also join the Royal Horticultural Society, which costs less than £30 a year. Once you're a member, their experts at Wisley in Surrey will identify a plant for you, if you send them a cutting from it. Put it in a polythene bag, inside a small padded envelope, and send it, along with a stamped addressed envelope, by first-class post.

Once you know what the trees, shrubs and perennials in your borders are, you then have to decide whether or not you want to keep them. There are a whole range of factors to be borne in mind, some less obvious than others. Legally speaking, where trees are concerned, you may have no choice. If you live in a conservation area, you will not be able even to prune a tree without permission in writing, let alone chop it down. And the same is true if you have an individual tree in your garden that is covered by a Tree Preservation Order (see p. 158). Most local authorities are not totally unreasonable, and will grant permission for the removal of dead or dangerous branches and a limited amount of pruning, although most will want you to use a qualified tree surgeon to do the work.

If your trees aren't covered by any kind of protection order, before you start chopping them down, you should try and imagine what your garden would look like without them. Maybe one of them actually screens an ugly tower block or deadens the noise from an elevated section of motorway half a mile away, or is the only thing that prevents your neighbours from looking straight into your garden and provides you with any privacy. Maybe, however, the tree itself is so unattractive, or casts so much shade that you still want to get rid of it, even though it serves a useful purpose. In that case, it's worth thinking about leaving it where it is in the short term, while you take alternative steps – plant a different sort of tree, more attractive or much smaller, to screen out the ugly view, or erect trellis and plant climbers to restore your privacy.

If you find you have inherited a collection of pretty dull, though mature shrubs, the temptation is to rip the whole lot out and start again with a blank canvas. But then you are throwing away the one thing that all new gardens or borders lack – size and maturity. Much better to keep a skeleton framework of mature shrubs for a year or two while your newly planted ones get established, and then remove the old faithfuls when they've served their purpose.

Once you've answered those questions, you need to look at the plants themselves. Are they basically good, sound specimens that have been neglected a bit and have become rather overgrown? Or are they spindly, bare at the base, riddled with disease and a very peculiar shape? Of course, you may not know what a good example of that particular shrub should look like, but you can get some idea from looking at books and catalogues and, besides, a really poor specimen will look just that, even to a non-expert eye.

Diseases

There are a whole range of diseases that are likely to flourish in a neglected garden. Many of them, like blackspot on roses for example, are relatively easily treated, but some are serious and need immediate action.

HONEY FUNGUS (*Armillaria mellea*) lives in the stumps and roots of dead trees and sends out tough black 'bootlaces' through the soil which then attack the healthy roots of shrubs and trees causing them to wilt and, usually, to die soon after. It is often the cause of sudden and unexplained deaths of trees

The fruiting body of honey fungus on a tree stump – one excellent reason for removing tree stumps whenever possible.

and shrubs. Honey fungus can spread a long way from its original host so have a good look round the garden and you may well find a dead tree or tree stump with a cluster of yellowy-brown mushrooms growing round its base – the 'fruiting body' of the fungus. If you peel away some bark, you'll find lacy sheets of white threads beneath it. It can affect a number of trees and shrubs (and some bulbs and rhubarb, too), but apples, lavender, lilac, cherries and plums (both fruiting and ornamental), privet, conifers like cypress and pine, viburnums and rhododendrons seem to be particularly vulnerable. The only solution is to dig up the infected plants, and the tree stump, and burn them. (Although bonfires are not eco-friendly, as we have said, this is the one case where you really have no alternative. Diseased wood must be burnt.) You should then treat the soil, bearing in mind how widely the disease can spread, with Armillatox, bleach, or with Jeyes Fluid. Remember, also, to disinfect any tools you have used with Jeyes Fluid, methylated spirits or a 3 per cent lysol solution. Don't replant the area with woody plants like trees or shrubs for a year or two. Grow herbaceous perennials or annuals instead. Your best bet for avoiding problems in future is to plant trees and shrubs that seem resistant to honey fungus – box (*Buxus*), elaeagnus, elder (*Sambucus*), robinia, holly, ivy, clematis, honeysuckle, mahonia, smoke tree (*Cotinus*) and conifers like yew and Douglas fir.

CORAL SPOT is another fungus which lives on dead wood. It is easily identified by a rash of tiny coral-red pustules, and although it is usually found on dead wood, its airborne spores can spread into live wood nearby and kill that too. It will attack a wide range of trees and shrubs, but fruit trees and bushes like apples, plums, red- and blackcurrants, are particularly susceptible, as are magnolias and maples.

If the plant isn't too badly infected, prune out all the infected wood, cutting at least 10 cm (4 in) below the infected area, and burn it. If you have to remove any large branches, you could paint the wound with a wound sealant that contains a fungicide to kill off any spores that remain. There is another school of thought, though, which maintains that by painting the wound with any sealant, there is always a chance that you will seal disease in and so you're better off leaving any wounds alone.

Once you've got rid of coral spot, make sure it doesn't return in the future by removing and burning all dead wood as soon as you see it. Make sure you clean and disinfect your secateurs or saw with methylated spirits.

PHYTOPHTHORA ROOT DEATH is another fungus disease which attacks the roots of a wide range of shrubs and trees, causing them, and soon after, the plant, to die. It is often quite hard to diagnose, especially if the plant has been dead for some time, because honey fungus may have developed on the dead wood. It attacks a wide range of plants but apple, beech, lime, ornamental plums and cherries are particularly vulnerable, as are yew and Lawson cypresses. The only treatment is to dig out infected plants and burn them. Since the fungus can linger in the soil, you must kill it by sterilising the affected area, and avoid planting susceptible species there again. Phytophthora thrives in heavy, moist, warm soil, so improve the drainage before you plant trees and shrubs and avoid mulching with too much farmyard manure or garden compost. Clean and disinfect any tools you have used.

FIREBLIGHT is a virulent bacterial disease which leaves the trees and shrubs it attacks looking as if they've been burnt, hence its common name. The first symptoms are often the withering and blackening of the flowers when they first appear, followed by the death of the leaves and twigs. It attacks pears and apples, and among ornamental trees and shrubs cotoneaster, firethorn (*Pyracantha*), japonica (*Chaenomeles*), hawthorn (*Crataegus*) and mountain ash (*Sorbus*), are particularly vulnerable. To confirm whether a tree or shrub is infected, peel back the bark. If the wood is reddish-brown underneath, it is.

In some parts of the country – north of a line between Hull and Preston – fireblight is still a notifiable disease, which means, if you suspect it is present in your garden, you must contact the nearest office of the Ministry of Agriculture immediately. If a plant is heavily infected, the only answer is to dig it up and burn it. If it doesn't seem too badly infected, cut back the diseased wood, until the remaining wood looks white, with no trace of any brown stain. Burn all the prunings and disinfect all the pruning tools you have used.

Pruning

With luck, though, most of the shrubs in your garden won't be suffering from a serious disease. They may be horribly overgrown, or very spindly, and whether or not they are worth trying to save will depend on how they respond to pruning and feeding.

Some shrubs will respond astonishingly well to a good, hard prune – an overgrown butterfly bush (*Buddleia*), for example, will stand being hacked right back to within a few inches of the ground in spring and will reward you later that summer with a mass of scented flowers. It's possible to give an old rose bush a new lease of life with the same treatment, provided you also give it a generous feed of rose fertiliser after you've cut it back.

Remember, though, that roses, like all plants, have only a limited life of, say, twenty-five to thirty years' maximum, and after that they are really not worth saving. And it's worth bearing in mind that, in many cases, there are new varieties of roses and shrubs that are more vigorous, more free-flowering, more disease-resistant, and have a better range of colours and so you really are much better off starting from scratch.

Other shrubs, like lavender, for example, and most conifers, with the notable exception of yew, resent being cut back hard into the old wood (wood that is at least one season old) and will either not produce any new growth from it at all or will do so only very slowly, and look so awful in the meantime that it's best to dig them out and start again.

Coral spot (above) and an apple tree afflicted with fireblight (right).

Tools

You will need a decent pair of secateurs, the best you can afford. If you have branches to deal with that are more than about 2 cm (¾ in) in diameter, you will also need a pruning saw and it's worth investing in a really stout pair of gardening gloves to protect your hands from thorns.

You should look after *all* your garden tools, of course, but make sure you clean all your cutting tools thoroughly each time you use them and wipe the blade with a lightly oiled rag. Sharpening is best left to the professionals, although good-quality secateurs should not need sharpening for some years.

When?

As a general rule, shrubs that flower *before* the end of June are flowering on last season's growth and are pruned immediately flowering is over. Those that flower from July onwards are flowering on growth made this season and are pruned in early spring.

What?

When you prune any shrub or tree, always cut out wood that is dead, diseased or damaged. Cut out any thin, weak stems, and stems that rub or cross other stems, in which case you cut the weaker of the two. Always cut just above a bud.

Assume that all shrubs that have been pruned hard will benefit from a feed of blood, fish and bonemeal or pelleted chicken manure (for the organic gardeners) or rose fertiliser or Growmore (for the rest) after pruning, unless stated otherwise.

How to prune neglected shrubs – a guide to the most common species

(M/E denotes those shrubs that can be moved easily. M/D denotes those that are more difficult)

Barberry (*Berberis*) For deciduous varieties, like *B. thunbergii* 'Aurea', 'Helmond Pillar' or 'Rose Glow', thin overgrown bushes by cutting back the oldest, roughest-looking woody shoots to ground level after flowering in June/July. If they are in a real tangle, then cut all the stems right back to the ground. Once it's back in shape, it doesn't need pruning annually.

For evergreen varieties like *B. darwinii* and *B. stenophylla*, prune regularly after flowering in April/May. If you want berries in the autumn, wait until the following spring and remove only the shoots which have carried berries, *not* the new ones which will be carrying the buds for the next crop of flowers. M/D

Butterfly bush (*Buddleia davidii*) Cut back hard in spring to the lowest pair of leaf buds on each of the main stems in late February/March. Don't feed it, or it will produce too many leaves at the expense of flowers.

With *Buddleia alternifolia*, remove the shoots that have borne flowers once flowering is finished in June. M/D

Camellia Shorten any straggly twigs by cutting them back to sturdy-looking side shoots in spring. Once camellias are back in shape, they do not need regular pruning. M/E

Blue Spiraea (*Caryopteris*) Thin overgrown bushes in late February/March by cutting up to a third of the main shoots right down to ground level and thinning the rest by cutting back the previous year's growth to within 2.5 cm (1 in) of the old wood, which is thicker and darker in colour. To keep it in shape, cut the previous season's growth back to 2.5 cm of the old wood each spring. M/D

Ceanothus Deciduous kinds, like 'Gloire de Versailles' and 'Topaz', which flower from July onwards, should be pruned in spring. Cut back last season's growth to two or three pairs of buds from the main stems.

Evergreen kinds, like 'Thyrsiflorus repens' or 'Burkwoodii' which flower in April/May, should be pruned after flowering, by cutting back any straggly shoots by half their length, and by removing any frost-damaged shoots (the leaves will be brown and shrivelled), cutting them back to the old wood. Don't cut into the old wood unless you have to, as it is very slow to produce new growth. M/D

Ceratostigma willmottianum The frost will usually cut this back to ground level in the winter, but any growth surviving should be cut down to just above ground level in spring. M/E

Japonica (*Chaenomeles*) With overgrown, free-standing specimens cut back up to a third of the main stems to ground level in spring, after flowering has finished, to keep the centre of the bush open. With wall-trained specimens, pinch back the young shoots to four or five leaves in June/July, and reduce the resulting side shoots to two leaves in the autumn. This creates spurs on which the flowers will be produced year after year. M/D

Mexican orange blossom (*Choisya ternata*) Cut out any frost-damaged and straggly shoots after the first flush of flowers in April/May. M/E

Dogwood (*Cornus alba*) Many dogwoods are grown for their brightly coloured stems in winter, and, as it is the new growth that produces the best colour, you should prune them back almost to the ground each spring. To get the longest possible display from the stems, wait until just before the leaves break. M/E

Smoke tree (*Cotinus coggygria*) The purple-leaved varieties (*C. c.* 'Royal Purple' or 'Notcutt's Variety'), which are grown primarily for their foliage, can be pruned in spring. Cut back the previous season's growth to three or four leaf buds from the main stems. That way, you lose the flowers, which are produced on the previous season's growth, so if it's the flowers you want, only prune any straggly growth back to a strong-looking shoot in spring. M/D

Cotoneaster Prune overgrown deciduous bushy varieties in late winter/ early spring by cutting the oldest wood down to ground level, leaving only the previous season's growth. With ground-covering, or wall-trained varieties, like *C. horizontalis*, remove any shoots that are growing upright or outwards and if they have outgrown their allotted space, prune the shoots that need shortening.

Prune evergreen varieties in April. M/D

Broom (*Cytisus*) Broom does not produce growth from old wood, so where plants have become very straggly and bare at the base, you're better off digging them up and starting again. To prevent new plants becoming straggly, prune them after flowering each May, cutting back the wood that has produced the flowers to where strong new shoots are growing. M/E

Heather (*Erica*) Summer- and autumn-flowering heathers (*E. cinerea* and *vagans*) which have become very straggly with age can be cut hard back, virtually to ground level after flowering. In following years, keep them in shape by clipping them with shears to remove the dead flower spikes, and most of the previous year's growth in late winter.

Clip winter- and spring-flowering heathers (*E. carnea* and *E. × darleyensis*) with shears after they have finished flowering to remove the dead flower heads and most of the previous season's growth. M/E

Elaeagnus Deciduous kinds, like *E. angustifolia*, should have their side shoots pruned back hard in March.

Prune very overgrown evergreen kinds, like *E. pungens* 'Maculata', right back to ground level in spring. Otherwise, prune them back to keep them within bounds and in shape in spring. If there are any shoots with plain green leaves on a variegated shrub, cut them out at their point of origin. If you leave them, the whole plant may eventually revert to plain green. M/E

Forsythia You should prune a really overgrown or very large specimen over three years, cutting out a third of the old wood right down to ground level each year in April when flowering is over. If you're lucky, *F. suspensa*, which is usually grown against a wall, will have been trained in a fan-shaped framework, from which its long, weeping stems then grow. Prune these hard back to the framework when flowering is over. M/E

Fuchsia The frost usually prunes hardy fuchsias for you, cutting them down to the ground each winter. If it doesn't, then cut the surviving stems almost down to ground level in March/April. M/E

Hebe Cut out the oldest branches of overgrown specimens. With others, after flowering, remove the shoots that have carried flowers and any straggly ones. Since most hebes are not hardy, remove any frost-damaged shoots in spring. The plant may recover and produce new growth, but if it's been too badly frosted it won't. M/E

Hydrangea With the mophead and lace cap types (*H. macrophylla*), cut some of the oldest stems (the roughest, and darkest in colour) and some of the weaker new growth in March leaving a low framework of old wood, with some strong new stems growing from it.

With a badly neglected *H. paniculata*, either prune the old wood hard back to ground level, or if there seems to be one, to a low framework 15 to 20 cm (6 to 8 in) high. It's best done in March though you will lose that summer's flowers. M/E

St John's wort (*Hypericum calycinum*) Clip it hard back with shears in early spring. It will quickly produce new growth to cover the cut stems. If it has spread too far, as it usually does, chop it out with a spade. Don't worry about being brutal; it is virtually indestructible.

Winter-flowering jasmine (*Jasminum nudiflorum*) This can soon become a tangled mass if it's been neglected for long, in which case the answer is to cut it right down to the ground in spring. Otherwise cut out most of the stems that have borne flowers when flowering finishes in April. M/D

Kerria On neglected plants, cut all canes that have borne flowers in April/May back to ground level. On other plants, cut back all the canes either to ground level or to low down where strong new shoots are already growing. M/E

Oregon grape (*Mahonia*) Straggly specimens of the smaller-growing mahonias like *M. aquifolium* can be cut back to within 15 cm (6 in) of the ground, to encourage new stems, and can be kept bushy by being cut back as hard every three or four years. Taller varieties, like *M.* × 'Charity' and *M. japonica*, can be cut back by a half, after flowering. Do it over two seasons, pruning half the old stems one year, and half the next. M/D

Mock orange (*Philadelphus*) Really overgrown, tangled bushes should be cut right back to the ground in spring. Obviously there will be no flowers that summer, since they flower on old wood. With less overgrown shrubs, prune out the older stems which have borne flowers, once flowering has finished in June/July. M/E

Cinquefoil (*Potentilla*) In spring, cut out some of the old woody stems from the centre of tangled bushes and reduce the previous year's growth by about half or trim them lightly with shears. M/E

Cherry laurel (*Prunus laurocerasus*) Overgrown bushes that have become bare at the base can be pruned right back to just above ground level in spring. Prune ornamental almonds (*Prunus triloba*) after flowering by cutting back the growth that has borne flowers to two or three buds from its junction with the old wood. M/E

Rhododendron, including azalea If they grow too large, or straggly, or become bare at the base, they can be cut back hard to about 1 m above the ground. New shoots will grow again from the stumps, but it will be four or five years before they will flower again. Can you wait that long for them to start justifying their existence? M/E

Flowering currant (*Ribes*) Bushes that are too large can be pruned hard after flowering in April by cutting the old stems back to a point low down where you can see live buds growing from the bark. Otherwise cut back shoots that have borne flowers to a new young replacement shoot lower down. M/D

Rosemary Rejuvenate old straggly plants by cutting back woody stems by half their length in April. Give them another trim after they have finished flowering. M/E

Roses (see below)

Golden cut-leaved elder (*Sambucus racemosa* 'Plumosa Aurea') To get the most attractive-coloured foliage, cut the stems back to within a few inches of ground level in late winter. You will lose the flowers and berries by doing so, but this variety is grown mainly for its foliage. M/E

Cotton lavender (*Santolina*) Prune straggly growth hard back in April to just above a point close to the base where new shoots can be seen. If you're growing the plant primarily for its foliage, then give it a light prune again in summer to remove the flower buds which are forming. If you want the flowers, wait until after flowering, then remove the flower heads and trim the new growth. M/E

Bridal wreath (*Spiraea arguta*) Rejuvenate an overgrown plant by cutting the old stems hard back to where young shoots are growing after flowering has finished in May. Remove the end section of each shoot which has actually borne flowers. M/E

Spiraea japonica Cut back all stems to within a few inches of the ground in February or March. M/E

Lilac (*Syringa*) Lanky, overgrown bushes can be cut back hard to about 80 cm (2 ft 7 in) of the ground in April. They won't flower again for two or three years. If they have become just a bit overcrowded, cut out a few shoots in autumn and remove any weak growth. M/D

Weigela Really old, neglected plants can be cut right down almost to ground level in spring, although they won't flower that summer. With plants in slightly better shape, prune back the shoots which have borne flowers to two or three leaf buds from the point where they join the main stem. On the variegated varieties, cut out completely any shoots with plain green leaves. M/D

Roses

There are whole books written about pruning roses, which makes the whole business seem very daunting to most beginners. In fact, it isn't that complicated *provided* you stick to a few basic rules.

First of all, you always prune to just above an outward-facing bud, so that the shoot that will grow from it grows outwards, leaving the centre of the bush open to allow air to circulate and help prevent diseases like mildew. The cut should start about 1 centimetre above the bud and slope downwards, at about 45 degrees, away from it. The reason for this is to ensure that rainwater doesn't trickle on to the bud and encourage it to rot. If you cut too close to the bud, you could damage it. If you cut too far above it, the wood could die back and you'd have to prune again, losing that bud. The best time to prune is early spring, although if you have any really tall, overgrown bushes, you can cut them back by about a quarter in the autumn. This will prevent them being buffeted too badly by winter gales which can otherwise loosen or even snap their roots.

It's worth saying again that roses, like all plants, have a limited life, and if those that you've inherited look very weak and spindly they're probably not worth saving. But if they're just overgrown and untidy, it's worth having a go.

Different types of bush roses need pruning in slightly different ways, but you may not know, especially if you've taken over the garden in winter, which type yours are. That isn't a major problem because, if the roses have been neglected for some time, it will take a couple of years to get them back into shape, and, until then, both hybrid tea (large-flowered) roses, and floribunda (cluster-flowered) roses should be treated in the same way.

First of all, in late winter, remove all the dead, diseased and damaged wood, any weak, spindly growth, and any branches that cross or rub. Then cut the youngest stems back to two or three buds from their junction with the older wood. Feed the bushes well with blood, fish and bonemeal, rose fertiliser or Growmore, mulch them with a good few inches of well-rotted organic matter (composted straw is ideal) and make sure they don't go short of water throughout the summer. They should produce new growth from low down and even a few flowers that summer.

The next winter, prune one of the oldest stems right back to ground level, and where strong new shoots have been produced low down on old wood, cut out the old stem just above the new shoot. Cut back all the new shoots to two or three buds from the point where they join the old wood. Again, feed, mulch and water them well.

Do the same the following winter. By the third summer, the bush should be producing lots of young growth and bigger flowers. If the bush isn't responding after a couple of years, then dig it up and replace it.

Once your roses are back in shape, the rule of thumb for pruning is that weak growth should be pruned harder than strong growth. Floribundas are more vigorous than hybrid teas, generally speaking, and so should be pruned more lightly – back to four or five buds. (By now, since your roses will have flowered, you will know which is which – hybrid teas have large, individual flowers, floribundas carry their flowers in clusters.) The same is true within an individual rose bush, too. Prune strong growth back to four or five buds, and weaker growth back to two or three.

Neglected shrub roses and 'old-fashioned' roses need slightly different treatment. They don't flower well on new wood, like hybrid teas and floribundas. They flower best on side shoots that develop from it the following year, and on the shoots (sub-laterals) that develop from those. So once you have cut out any dead, diseased or damaged wood, any weak growth and any that rubs or crosses, cut back any side shoots that have borne flowers to two buds from the point where they join the main stem, and 'tip' the rest – remove the top few inches of growth – to encourage more side shoots to form. Feed, mulch and water well.

With the exception of miniature varieties, roses are difficult to move.

Climbing and rambling roses

Climbing roses have stiffer stems than ramblers, and usually flower throughout the summer, while ramblers only flower once, and require slightly different treatment. If you have a neglected climbing rose growing against a wall or fence, it may well have been trained into a fan shape in its youth. If so, then in late winter cut out one of the oldest stems (the most woody and gnarled-looking ones) completely, to encourage the rose to produce new growth low down, and prune back all the side shoots to two or three buds from the point where they join the main stem. Feed, mulch and keep well watered. As strong new shoots appear low down, train them as near horizontally as you can and remove another of the oldest stems the following winter.

Rambling roses produce long, flexible 'canes' from the base of the plant each year, and in an ideal world, pruning consists of cutting out completely all the old canes which have borne flowers in the autumn, and tying in new ones to replace them. With an overgrown rambler, cut out as many of the oldest canes as you can and feed, mulch and water freely. The following year, provided the plant has produced enough new canes, cut all the old ones which have borne flowers, right down to ground level. If it hasn't produced enough new growth from the base, cut out the weakest of the old canes and cut the side shoots on the stronger ones back to buds from the point where they join the main stem.

If possible, untie the rambler from the pillar or fence up which it's growing, lay it on the ground, prune it there and then tie the new canes back up again.

Other climbers

Clematis The pruning of clematis is another subject that can be made to seem dauntingly complicated but it isn't really. You can divide them into two basic types – those that flower in spring and early summer on the previous year's growth, which can be pruned if necessary *after* flowering, and those which flower in late summer on the current year's growth, which should be pruned hard in the spring, otherwise you get lots of bare stem lower down and flowers 3 or 4 metres above the ground.

The first group includes the small-flowered, rampant *Clematis montana* which blooms in April/May as well as large-flowered hybrids like 'Nelly Moser', 'The President' and 'Lasurstern' which flower in May/June. The second includes large-flowered hybrids like 'Ville de Lyon', 'Jackmanii' and 'Perle d'Azur', and the small-flowered *texensis* and *viticellas*, like 'Duchess of Albany' and 'Etoile Violette'.

Of course, in winter, you won't know what you've got. While it's relatively easy to identify *Clematis montana* because it's likely to be a tangled mass of thick, dead-looking stems covering 10 metres (some 30 ft) or more, the thin, dead growth of one large-flowered hybrid looks pretty much like any other. If you can leave it unpruned, it will produce flowers either in early summer if it turns out to be one of the first group, or high up above the ground in mid to late summer if it's one of the second. Then at least you'll know which group it belongs to! If you can't leave it, because it's growing through a rose that you must prune, say, or because the wall or fence up which it's growing needs attention, cut the stems back to pairs of fat leaf buds between 15 (6 in) and 60 cm (2 ft) above the ground. If it's one of the first type, you'll lose almost all the flowers that summer, but if it's the second, you've ensured a good spread of flowers up the wall or fence from July onwards.

Clematis of all types are very greedy feeders and should never be allowed to go short of water. Their roots must also be kept cool, so plant them in shade if possible – on the shady side of a shrub at the back of a sunny border, for example, or apply an extra thick mulch after pruning.

Climbing hydrangea (*Hydrangea petiolaris*) Cut back this self-clinging climber if it has outgrown its allotted space. Remove the shoots that have borne flowers in April, since the dead flower heads are rather attractive and provide interest in the winter months.

Summer-flowering jasmine (*Jasminum officinale*) Neglected plants can become extremely untidy, so thin them out at the base, and cut back excessive growths after flowering.

Honeysuckle (*Lonicera*) Most varieties of the common honeysuckle (*L. periclymenum*) flower on the previous season's growth, so overgrown plants are best pruned after flowering by removing some of the oldest, most woody stems, and cutting back the rest to within their allotted space. Some varieties, though, like the 'Late Dutch' honeysuckle (*L. p.* 'Serotina'), flower on the current season's growth and, if necessary, should be pruned hard back in winter. If you're not sure, you can either prune it back in winter and risk losing the following summer's flowers if it turns out to be an early-flowering kind, or you can leave it and, if it's a late-flowering kind, you'll have to put up with it being overgrown until next winter.

Virginia creeper (*Parthenocissus*) Cut it back in winter to prevent it from taking over the world, or at least, from getting into gutters, or under slates.

Russian vine (*Polygonum baldschuanicum*) If you have inherited one of these, probably the most vigorous of all climbers, you'll be lucky to find your garden at all! If you want to keep it, clip it back with shears in April, and again after flowering in September, and thin it by cutting out some shoots at the base.

Chilean potato tree (*Solanum crispum*) In April, cut out any shoots damaged by frost and, if the plant has outgrown its allotted space, cut last year's growth back to about 15 cm (6 in) from the point where it joins the main stem.

Wisteria Wisteria is at its most magnificent when it is rampant, but if it has outgrown its allotted space then you can prune hard in August by cutting back the main stems to within the allotted space, and the side shoots of the side shoots ('sub-laterals') to two leaves from the base. (Many gardening books advise you to prune wisteria by pinching back the sub-laterals to five leaves in August and again to two buds in winter, but if you've got a huge wisteria all over the back of the house, you're doing well if you manage to prune all those shoots once a year, let alone twice.) Once it is more or less within bounds, then keep it that way by cutting it back each August where it's grown too far, either with shears or secateurs.

Suckers

You might find woody shoots growing in the middle of the lawn or in borders which could well be suckers. Trees like cherry, plum, willow, and the lovely stag's horn sumach are particularly prone to producing these woody shoots along the length of their roots. There is no point in cutting them off, either with a rotary lawn mower or with secateurs, because you will simply encourage more suckers to grow. Nor can you treat them with a weedkiller because you risk killing the parent tree. The only answer is to trace them back to their source, and tear them off. Sadly there is no guarantee that they won't send up more suckers somewhere else.

Some shrubs, like magnolia, camellia, rhododendron, lilac, and most roses, are sometimes grafted on to a different, more vigorous rootstock (you can tell if a plant is grafted by a knobbly kink in the main stem, the 'union', just at or below soil level) and you will often find strong suckers growing from below ground level from these rootstocks.

It is essential to remove any suckers because they are more vigorous than the grafted plant, and if left to their own devices would soon swamp it. Again, the only answer is to trace them back to their source and tear them off. With roses, it's usually quite easy to tell the suckers from the rest of the plant because the leaves and thorns look quite different. With other shrubs it's slightly more difficult. Lilac, for example, is usually grafted onto a privet or wild lilac rootstock, so while you can easily recognise any suckers from the former as different, it's not so easy with the latter. In that case, treat *any* shoot growing from below the soil as a sucker.

Many rhododendrons are grafted on to a rootstock of *R. ponticum*, which is so vigorous that it is considered virtually a weed in some parts of Wales. Since it *is* so vigorous, it's vital to remove any suckers as soon as they appear, otherwise it will soon take over. If you find a rhododendron that was meant to have pink or white or red flowers suddenly starts producing pale pinky-purple ones, that is the explanation.

Moving shrubs

You might find that you have some splendid shrubs, or even small trees, in your garden, which are healthy and which haven't been neglected, but which are simply in the wrong place. Most shrubs can be successfully transplanted, either to another part of the garden or into a container. Those that move most easily are ones with fibrous roots – masses of thin roots that don't push very deep into the soil. It's relatively easy to dig right underneath the root system, and if a few get broken in the process there are so many others that the plant won't have any problems in re-establishing itself in its new home.

More problematic to move are those with tap roots – much thicker roots and fewer of them – which grow very deep. Obviously, it's much more difficult to dig out this group of shrubs without breaking the roots and, since they have comparatively few of them, it's also more difficult for them to get established in a new position. But it can be done.

The best time to transplant both types of shrubs is while they are dormant, between late autumn and early spring. Choose a day when the ground isn't frozen or waterlogged. (Conifers should be transplanted a bit later, in April or even May when the sap has begun to rise.)

Before you start, decide where you want the shrub to go. Take the opportunity to dig over the ground where you're going to plant, remove any perennial weeds and incorporate lots of bulky organic matter. If you're not completely sure where you want the shrub to go, then put it in a container while you make up your mind.

Shrubs that are easy to move (see p. 75)

You will need a spade, and a large piece of sacking (or tough polythene sheeting). Start by digging a circular trench around the shrub with a radius of between 30 and 45 cm (12 and 18 in) depending on the size of the shrub and keep digging down until no more roots are visible. Then push the spade under the shrub, and lever it gently upwards to free the remaining roots. You may have to do the same thing on the other side as well.

Roll up half of the sacking, rock the shrub and its rootball (the ball of soil containing the roots) away from you, then push the rolled-up bit of sacking underneath it. Rock the shrub back in the opposite direction on to the flat piece of sacking, then unroll the rolled-up bit and, with a bit of luck, you've got the shrub positioned neatly in the centre. Tie the sacking tightly round the rootball and lift the whole thing out. If it's a very large shrub, like the camellia in our over-mature garden, you may have to lash it to a pole and even call in a neighbour to help you lift it. Water it well.

While you can leave a shrub like this for a week or two, provided you keep it well watered, it's best to replant it as soon as possible in its new home or in a pot.

Dig a hole, slightly larger than the ball of soil. Put the shrub in it, and make sure that when the hole is refilled, the shrub will be at exactly the same level in the soil as it was before. There will be a distinct soil mark on the shrub, so it's very easy to gauge. If it's too low, replace some soil in the bottom of the hole. If it's too high, make the hole a little deeper. When it's just right, put the shrub into the hole, and slide the sacking out or cut away as much as you can reach. If you can't remove it all, don't worry – sacking will soon rot down in the soil. Polythene won't rot, so if that's what you've used, you must get it all out.

Mix a handful of blood, fish and bonemeal (or rose fertiliser or Growmore) in with some of the soil you've dug out, and use it to fill in the hole. Firm it in gently with the ball of your foot to get rid of any air pockets, and then give it a good soaking. Large shrubs may need bracing for a year or so with four stakes around the base and ropes.

If you are moving conifers and other evergreens, it's worth spraying them with an anti-desiccant spray before and after you move them. It helps to stop them from losing too much water through their leaves and either developing brown patches or even dying.

Shrubs that are difficult to move

If you have a particularly choice shrub which has a tap root, the way to move it is to dig a wide trench around it which you then fill with organic matter, like composted straw, and leave it for a year. In that time, it will produce lots of new roots which will grow out into the organic matter, so that it will have formed a good rootball before you lift it and snap the tap root. The new roots it has formed in the previous year will compensate for the loss of the tap root, and help it get established in its new home.

Moving a camellia

Getting a sheet of strong polythene under the camellia's rootball is relatively simple if there are two of you . . .

. . . but actually lifting a big mature shrub like this one, plus large rootball, may require additional muscle . . .

. . . as will replanting it some months later in a different part of the garden.

Herbaceous plants

As a rule, herbaceous plants (plants which aren't woody like shrubs and which, in most cases, die down in the winter and re-emerge in the spring) don't live as long as shrubs, but there may well be some treasures in your borders which, although a bit neglected, can certainly be rescued.

Again, you need to look at the state of the plants. Even a beginner can see that a spindly clump of Michaelmas daisies (*Aster amellus*) with their leaves covered in powdery mildew isn't worth saving. Besides, the newer, dwarf varieties like *Aster novi-belgii* 'Little Pink Beauty', 'Lady in Blue' or the white 'Kristina' are more suitable for small gardens, and are disease-resistant, too.

If there is no sign of disease, though, and the clump has just got too large, or is maybe looking a bit tired or bare in the centre, then it's certainly worth digging it up and dividing it to give you several new plants. This is a job that should be done either in the autumn after flowering is finished but while the soil is still warm, or better still, in the spring when the plants are just beginning to shoot, when the soil isn't frozen or waterlogged and when frost isn't forecast. Which time is best varies according to the plants in question, but, if in doubt, leave it until the spring.

You'll need a fork (in fact you'll probably need two – borrow one from a neighbour in exchange for some of the new plants you are about to create by division), a sharp knife, secateurs and possibly a bucket of water to wash soil off the roots, so that you can see what you're doing. Cut down any remaining stems to ground level and carefully dig up the clump by pushing the fork into the soil and levering it upwards. Move the fork round 90 degrees, and do the same. Repeat twice more, then lift the clump out.

In most cases, the object of dividing is to remove small, vigorous young pieces of the plant, complete with roots and growth buds, from the outside of the clump, and then to discard the old, tired, worn-out centre.

Some plants, like polyanthus, can be easily pulled apart with your fingers. Others, like phlox, or Michaelmas daisies which form tough, matted clumps, need to be prised apart using two garden forks. Stick the forks into the centre of the clump, back to back, and move them backwards and forwards until the clump breaks in two. Then divide each half again. If you can, prise pieces, each with about six shoots or growth buds, away from the edge with your fingers. If not, then cut away the old woody part with a sharp garden knife or an old bread saw. Be sure to trim off any dead or rotting roots before you replant them or pot them up.

The best way to divide plants with fleshy roots, like hostas or lupins, is to cut them into pieces with a sharp knife, or an old bread saw. This must be done in spring, just as they are starting into growth so you can be sure that each piece has some growth buds and roots. Hostas dislike being disturbed, so don't expect them to look too wonderful the first summer. If you replant three or five new divisions in the area where you had one clump, you'll be covering the same amount of ground, but your plants will be young and vigorous, and good, probably, for another five years before they'll need dividing again.

Plants like elephant's ears (*Bergenias*) grow from a fleshy underground stem called a rhizome. To divide them, dig up the rhizome, which grows just below the surface of the soil, and shake off the soil. Choose a few young growths, each with at least two or three strong growth buds or healthy-looking shoots, as well as clusters of roots, and cut them off with a sharp knife flush with the old rhizome. Trim each piece to just below a cluster of strong, healthy roots, and at the same time cut off any dead leaves or bits of rotting stem. Discard the old stem, which can be put through the shredder. Plant the young pieces right away, with their roots downwards, and their growth buds, or new shoots, above the soil.

Some plants, particularly those which grow from a crown like Oriental poppies and columbines (*Aquilegias*) can't be divided easily. The answer there is to take cuttings or to collect seed after flowering and sow them in late winter or early spring. The best way to increase your stocks of poppies is to take root cuttings in spring. Dig up the plant as before in autumn, cut off one or two thick roots, and put the parent plant back in the soil. Cut the roots into pieces 5 to 7 cm (2 to 3 in) long, and make a slanting cut on the bottom of each cutting so you can't forget which way up they should be. Put them vertically in a 15-cm (6-in) pot filled with sandy compost, slanting end downwards, about 5 cm (2 in) apart. Cover them with 1 cm (½ in) of sand and stand the pot in a closed cold frame (a home-made wooden box covered with a sheet of clear, rigid plastic will do). In spring they should have rooted and developed three or four pairs of leaves. Put them into individual small pots in a good cutting compost, leave them outside throughout the summer and plant them out in the autumn.

They also seed themselves pretty freely, so have a careful hunt through the surrounding undergrowth for seedlings, which you can either dig up and transplant right away, or pot up until you've decided where to put them.

Bulbs

Bulbs that have been growing undisturbed for four or five years benefit from being lifted and divided, because once they become overcrowded, they don't flower as well as they used to.

Once they have finished flowering, push a fork (a handfork for small bulbs like crocuses, a garden fork for larger ones such as daffodils and tulips) into the soil well away from the clump and deep enough to avoid damaging the bulbs, and then lever the clump upwards. Carefully remove the soil from the clump and separate the bulbs with your fingers. You will find that many of the larger bulbs have little bulbs attached to them at the base. Remove them, and if you have the room and the patience, you can plant them in narrow trenches about 10 cm (4 in) deep, on a bed of sharp sand, at a distance from each other of twice their own width. Leave them for two years or until they reach a decent flowering size, and then plant them in their permanent position.

In the meantime, you can replant the larger bulbs right away at the right depth and distance from their fellows for that particular species. As a rule of thumb, most bulbs need twice their own depth of soil above them and twice their own breadth of soil between them, so a daffodil bulb 5 cm high, for instance, needs to be planted in a hole 15 cm deep, 15 cm from its neighbour. Leave the foliage on and don't be tempted to tidy it up by tying it in knots. The leaves manufacture the food for next year's flowers, and knotting them interferes with that process.

You can leave bulbs like daffodils and crocuses to dry and replant them in the autumn if you want to get the existing borders dug over, or you're creating new ones. It's probably best to leave tulips until November anyway (if you plant them much earlier, they could start into growth and the young shoots would get clobbered by winter frost) but bulbs like snowdrops and winter aconites must be replanted right away – 'in the green', as the experts say.

Brightening up your borders

It may be that in the garden you've inherited there are some groupings of shrubs that are reasonably healthy, and worth saving, but they are all much of a muchness when it comes to size, shape and colour, and so look rather dull. What you can do then is to leave the existing, mature planting and, by adding just a few new shrubs or perennials, brighten up the whole area. Obviously flowers can do a great deal, but so can foliage, and shrubs that have variegated or coloured leaves – silver and gold especially – are particularly valuable here. Alternatively, you can actually use existing shrubs as a host for flowering climbers, like the less vigorous varieties of clematis (the rampant ones like *C. montana*, *C. orientalis* or *C. tangutica* would very rapidly smother their host), the Scotch flame flower (*Tropaeolum speciosum*), and annual climbers like sweet peas, and Canary creeper (*Tropaeolum peregrinum*).

What you plant will depend largely on how much sun, and shade, the plants in that particular spot get.

For south- or southwest-facing borders, which get sun for most of the day

Against a background of tall shrubs, you could plant the variegated weigela, *W. florida* 'Variegata', which has green and yellow leaves and mid-pink foxglove-like flowers in June. It will eventually reach about 1.5 m (5 ft) in height and 1.2 m (4 ft) across. For small gardens, try *W. f.* 'Nana Variegata' which has creamy white and green leaves and the same colour flowers but won't reach much more than 1 m (3 ft 3 in) in height and spread. There is another lovely, even smaller variegated form, *W. praecox* 'Variegata', which has larger pale pink flowers with a honey scent, and cream and green variegated leaves, and only reaches about 75 cm (2 ft 6 in) in height. But it's more difficult to find.

In front of smaller shrubs, you could plant one of the variegated hebes like *H.* ×*franciscana* (or *elliptica*) 'Variegata' which has long, green and pale creamy yellow leaves with long pale violet flowers from midsummer on, or *H.* × *andersonii* 'Variegata' which has pale lavender blue flowers in early to mid summer and oval silver-margined grey-green leaves. For something more dramatic, you could plant a phormium, with its long sword-like leaves. *P. tenax* 'Yellow Wave' has golden leaves with green edges, while *P. cookianum* 'Cream Delight' has olive-green leaves with a central cream stripe. Both these hebes and the phormiums are slightly tender, which means that a hard frost can damage them, or even kill them off, so in winter cover them with straw, or even temporarily with a plastic bag slid over four bamboo canes pushed into the soil around the plants to make a frame.

Most silver or grey-leaved plants thrive in a sunny spot, so to lighten shrubs with rather dark dull foliage, like the winter-flowering viburnums, for example, you could try the butterfly bush, *Buddleia fallowiana* 'Alba'. Its leaves are silvery-white when they're young, and fade to a very pale grey, and from July onwards it has sweetly-scented white flowers with an orange eye. It can reach up to 1.5 m (5 ft) in height, and benefits from being cut hard back, almost to ground level in spring. The best silver foliage plants are the artemisias. *A. arborescens* 'Faith Raven' which grows to about 1.2 m (4 ft), has delicate feathery silver foliage and, unlike the ordinary *A. arborescens*, is not killed off by frost. *A. absinthium* 'Lambrook Silver', which grows to about 90 cm (3 ft), has lovely silver filigree foliage and insignificant grey bobbly flowers, while the slightly smaller *A.* 'Powys Castle' has the same foliage but no flowers at all. They are, in fact, evergreen, but they usually look pretty scruffy in early spring, so you should prune them hard back to a few inches above the ground, to just above a point where you can see new shoots emerging from the stem.

Most plants with golden foliage (see below) prefer a little shade, particularly at midday, as too much sun can scorch their leaves, so it's better not to plant them in a south-facing border unless they will get a little protection from overhanging trees.

The late-summer-flowering Clematis viticella *growing through a conifer hedge certainly adds welcome colour to its rather dull host.*

Annuals

In the first season, of course, annuals are a marvellous way of brightening up any dull border. For a sunny spot, the choice is enormous, as is the range of colours, although, given that the object of the exercise is to brighten up rather dull planting, go for colours like white, pink, clear yellow and light red, rather than purples, blues or deep reds.

For something tall, mallow (*Lavatera trimestris*) is hard to beat, either in its white form 'Mont Blanc' or one of the pinks like 'Silver Cup' or 'Pink Beauty'. The mixed pink, blue and white form of love-in-a-mist (*Nigella damascena* 'Persian Jewels') is well worth growing, as is *Bartonia*, which has large clear yellow daisies all summer long. These are all hardy annuals, so you simply sow the seeds where you want the plants to flower, from March to June to give you a succession of flowers. Alternatively, you could buy some tall half-hardy annuals (which need to be sown indoors) from the garden centre. *Cosmos* is a good choice, with its large open daisy-like flowers in shades of red, pink and white, and its light green feathery foliage. So are asters, but for this purpose make sure you buy the taller varieties. The dwarf ones, like the 'Bedder' range, only grow to about 15 cm (6 in), but would be a good choice for the front of a border. Other good half-hardies for this purpose include fibrous-rooted begonias (*Begonia semperflorens*), busy Lizzies (*Impatiens*) and petunias (look for 'Resisto', bred to stand up to the vagaries of the British summer). Among the low-growing hardy annuals which you can sow directly into the soil, alyssum, which comes in pink, red and purple as well as the best-known white, is a good choice, as is candytuft, and the very pretty *Nemophila maculata* 'Five spot', which has a purple spot on each of its five white petals. Be warned, though, that the slugs love its young foliage so it will need a bit of protection (sawn-off sections of plastic bottles, for example) until it has toughened up.

Climbers to grow through shrubs

Some of the smaller-flowered types of clematis – the spring-flowering *C. alpina* and *C. macropetala* and the mid- to late-summer-flowering *C. viticella* and *C. texensis* – are ideal for growing through and over shrubs, since they are not too vigorous. Like all clematis, they like their heads in the sun but their feet in the shade, so make sure you plant them on the shady side of the shrub. Good varieties to look out for are *C. alpina* 'Frances Rivis' with large cornflower-blue and white flowers, *C. a.* 'Columbine White', and *C. macropetala* 'Markham's Pink'. Among the *viticellas*, the wine-red 'Madame Julia Correvon', and the double-flowered 'Purpurea Plena Elegans' are both good, while the creamy-white-flowered 'Alba Luxurians' would sparkle against any dark green foliage. As for *Clematis texensis*, the two most widely available varieties, the 'Duchess of Albany' which has deep pink flowers with a cherry red bar down the centre of each petal, and the ruby red 'Gravetye Beauty' are both well worth having.

Clematis viticella and *texensis* are particularly good companions for winter- or early spring-flowering shrubs like *Viburnum tinus*, camellias, and japonica, because their spent growth can be cut hard back in late autumn when they've finished flowering and their leaves have died, leaving their hosts free to flower unencumbered.

As for climbing annuals, sweet peas are an excellent choice. You can buy trays of young plants from your local garden centre, but do make sure they are tall varieties, not dwarf ones. Even simpler, you could plant some nasturtium seeds in the soil around the shrub from March to June, and, when the stems are long enough, train them into the shrub. Look for a tall variety, like 'Tall Mixed Climbing'.

A couple of less well-known relatives of the nasturtium are both worth a try. Canary creeper (*Tropaeolum peregrinum*) has lovely fringed yellow flowers and very attractive pale green leaves. Again, you simply sow the seeds directly into the soil around the shrub from March to May, or you could start them off in pots on the kitchen window sill in February.

The Scotch flame flower (*Tropaeolum speciosum*), so-called because of its stunning bright red flowers from summer well into the autumn, can transform a dull green shrub or an evergreen hedge into a thing of beauty. It seems easier to grow in the north than the south, but even then it is notoriously temperamental. If it's happy, it will grow like a weed; if it's not, it won't grow at all. It grows from tubers, and it's so spectacular that it's worth a try, but don't pin your hopes on it!

For east- or west-facing borders which only get sun for half the day

Although most shrubs with variegated foliage would grow well in this situation, it's here that golden-leaved shrubs and herbaceous plants really come into their own because they get enough sun to bring out the gold in their leaves, but are not exposed to the full heat of the midday sun which can scorch them.

One of the best is the golden cut-leaved elder, *Sambucus racemosa* 'Plumosa Aurea', or the newer form *S.r.* 'Sutherland Gold', which has deeply cut bright gold leaves throughout the summer. Since you get the best colour if you cut it back hard each spring, it will never grow to much more than 1.5 m (about 5 ft). The new *Spiraea japonica* 'Golden Princess' not only has bright gold foliage all through the summer, but also flat heads of bright pink flowers from mid-summer on. The new growths of the older variety, *Spiraea × bumalda* 'Goldflame' are startling pinky-orange-gold when they first emerge, fading to a softer yellow by the time the dark pink-red flowers open in July and August.

For gold foliage all year round, the new golden Mexican orange blossom (*Choisya ternata* 'Sundance') is a good bet. It really does create a pool of sunlight amongst dark or mid-green shrubs. It is slightly tender, so it's better planted in a west-facing border, sheltered from icy cold easterly winds, although it should be all right in a very sheltered east-facing border as well.

There are many dwarf conifers which would fulfil this function perfectly, too. Among the best are *Thuja occidentalis* 'Rheingold', which slowly grows into a broad pyramid of golden foliage (about 1 m (3 ft 3 in) high after ten years), turning a rich coppery colour in winter, and the even smaller *Thuja orientalis* 'Aurea Nana' which makes a small oval bush, golden-yellow in early summer, then turning golden green. There are two excellent golden forms of yew – the narrow column of *Taxus baccata* 'Standishii', which will only grow to about 1 m in ten years, and the low-spreading 'Summergold' which could create a little pool of sunshine at the base of existing shrubs.

Among herbaceous plants, you could try golden marjoram (which you can also use in the kitchen), Bowles' golden grass (*Milium effusum* 'Aureum'), the ornamental grass with foliage stems and flowers all of which are golden yellow, and the ground-covering golden creeping Jenny (*Lysimachia nummularia* 'Aurea') which produces long trailing stems of round golden leaves and buttercup yellow flowers in June and July.

Annuals

Most of the annuals recommended for sunny borders should do well enough in these situations as well.

*The golden foliage of the Golden cut-leaved elder (*Sambucus racemosa *'Plumosa Aurea') would brighten up any dark border.*

Climbers

The varieties of clematis recommended for south-facing borders should be happy enough there. You could try sweet peas and nasturtiums, but they won't flower as freely if they're not in full sun.

North-facing borders which are in shade for most of the day

One of the best ways to liven up a dull, shady border is to give it a bright background, and for this purpose one of the golden-variegated ivies like *Hedera helix* 'Goldheart' or the much larger-leaved *H. colchica* 'Paddy's Pride' would be ideal. If you wanted flowers, too, you could try the semi-evergreen, gold-netted Japanese honeysuckle, *Lonicera japonica* 'Aureo-reticulata', which has fragrant cream and yellow flowers from June to September, although it doesn't flower as freely as it would in a sunnier spot.

As for brightening up the existing planting, variegated shrubs are ideal. Among the evergreens, *Elaeagnus pungens* 'Maculata' is a good choice, with its large, bright green and gold leaves. It's very slow-growing, not reaching more than 2 m (6ft 6in) in ten years. Some of the variegated hollies are worth considering too – *Ilex* 'Golden Queen' for instance, or *I.* 'Silver Queen' although unless you keep them pruned back, they will reach 5 or 6 m (16 to 20 feet) in twenty years. A better bet might be the white and green-variegated hedgehog holly, *Ilex aquifolium* 'Ferox Argentea', which forms a rounded shrub and doesn't reach more than 2 m (6 ft 6 in) in twenty years.

In really deep shade the only variegated evergreen shrub which will give a good account of itself is the spotted laurel (*Aucuba japonica* 'Variegata' or 'Crotonifolia' which has larger leaves). It has been out of fashion for years, since the Victorians filled their shrubberies with it, but if you want a splash of brightness in a really shady place, it's that or nothing.

In medium shade the variegated deciduous dogwoods like *Cornus alba* 'Elegantissima' with its truly elegant pale green and silver leaves, and *C.* 'Spaethii' with green and gold leaves, are good bets. They also have bright red stems in winter, if they are pruned hard back each spring (see p. 76).

To liven up the front of a dull shady border try Bowles' golden grass, the golden creeping Jenny (*Lysimachia nummularia* 'Aurea') and the Golden Dead Nettle (*Lamium maculatum* 'Aureum' which has purple flowers.

Annuals

There are comparatively few annuals that thrive in shade, but this is a case of quality rather than quantity, for those that will grow are all excellent. Perhaps the best is busy Lizzie – a clump of pale pink, pale salmon, or white ones, especially from the new 'Mother of Pearl' ranges, really does gleam in a shady spot. Fibrous-rooted begonias (*Begonia semperflorens*) and the monkey flower (*Mimulus*) are also good choices here, although again, go for the paler colours if you can because the deeper colours tend to get a bit lost in shade.

Climbers

Most of the small-flowered species of clematis listed on page 92 will grow in a shady spot but won't flower as freely as they would in a sunnier position.

Containers

For the owners of a small city backyard, where borders are not a practical proposition, container gardening is the answer. In some ways, it's better than growing plants in borders because you can suit the conditions to individual plants.

The basic rules of successful container gardening are that you can grow almost anything you like – trees (as long as you stick to very small species, of course), shrubs, herbaceous plants, alpines, bulbs, annuals, even food crops (runner beans, salads, or even a small apple or plum tree) – provided you give your plants enough space for their roots (in other words, a large enough container for the plants you choose), enough food and water, and, at the same time, make sure the drainage is good enough to prevent the compost becoming waterlogged.

The choice of containers is vast, and depends largely on taste and your bank balance. Terracotta pots are lovely and, even unplanted, add a real touch of class, but they are expensive. If you do buy them, make sure you buy those which are guaranteed frost-proof. Real stoneware containers are hugely expensive, if you can find them, but there are some very good reconstituted stone pots and troughs around now. Even concrete can look okay, especially if you paint the containers on the outside with yoghurt or liquid manure as soon as you buy them. This encourages lichens and mosses to grow very quickly, and in the case of the liquid manure the deep brown colour adds to the desired ageing effect, too. They are very heavy, so choose their permanent position with care, before you fill them with compost and plant them up. Afterwards, they'll be so heavy that moving them will be a major operation. (If you have lots of heavy containers, it might be worth investing in a sack barrow or one of those wheeled devices that DIY car mechanics use to slide under cars. They're very low, so you don't have far to lift the container, and strong enough to take the weight of a large person.)

Good wooden tubs and troughs are quite expensive, too, but also look very attractive. Try to buy containers made from hard woods which should last a lifetime. Those made from soft woods are cheaper, but make sure they have been pressure-treated with wood preservative, otherwise they'll rot. Make sure that the bottom of the container isn't in contact with the ground. Even standing it on a couple of battens 1.3 cm (½ in) thick will help. Half barrels are ideal for small trees or large shrubs, if you can find them.

Plastic used to be sneered at, but there are some very good plastic containers around these days, either pretending to be something else like stone or terracotta, or just being themselves with good lines and colours. Don't forget that once a container is filled with trailing plants, much of the container is hidden anyway.

Good drainage is absolutely essential for successful container gardening, so, first of all, make sure your chosen containers have plenty of drainage holes in the bottom. With terracotta pots, there isn't much you can do to increase the number, but with wooden tubs you can drill a few more, and with plastic you can make holes in the bottom with a heated skewer. The object of the exercise is to allow excess water to drain freely, but not to wash the compost out of the drainage holes, which not only makes a mess on your paving in the short term, but also, in the long term, can block the drainage holes. In the bottom of the container, you will need something to cover the drainage holes without blocking them. Pieces of broken slate, or, for larger containers, bits of brick are ideal, and in a garden like our city backyard in plentiful supply! If all else fails, broken up bits of polystyrene packing will do.

As for the compost, the best choice for most containers is a soil-based kind, like John Innes No. 2. Peat-based composts are lighter, which makes them more suitable for roof gardens, and for hanging baskets, where weight is an important factor, but they have several disadvantages. Because they are light, containers filled with them are more likely to blow over in a gale. They also dry out more quickly than the soil-based kinds, which means they need watering much more often. And if they do dry out, it is very difficult to get them to absorb water again.

Some plants need special composts. Acid-lovers, like rhododendrons, camellias and pieris, need a lime-free compost, sold as 'ericaceous compost', and alpines need a really gritty mixture – equal amounts of soil, or soil-based compost, and grit.

With hanging baskets, the principle is the same but the technique slightly different. The best baskets to choose are the plastic-covered wire mesh ones because it's much easier to plant around the sides than it is with the solid plastic kinds. For the same reason, it's easier to line the baskets with sphagnum moss (available in bags from good garden centres) than use the pre-formed basket liners. When you've lined the inside of the basket with a good, thick layer of sphagnum moss, making sure that it comes right up to and over the top, forming a collar, cut a circle of polythene – an old supermarket carrier bag will do – to fit into the bottom of the basket. Make a few inch-long cuts in it before you put it in. That way the polythene will prevent the water draining away too quickly but, at the same time, the cuts will let enough drain away to stop the compost from becoming waterlogged. Then add the compost. As we've already said, soil-less composts are lighter than the soil-based ones – an important factor with hanging baskets – but they do dry out more quickly. One answer to this problem is to choose a special compost which contains a water-retaining gel.

Watering

Once your containers are planted, they will need regular watering and feeding. In hot weather containers will need watering every day, even twice in really hot dry weather and, unless it's poured for weeks, you can more or less discount rain. The surface area of your container is very small anyway, and as it's likely to be covered in plants, the amount of rainwater that actually gets through is nowhere near enough for the plant's needs. Give the container a thorough soaking each time you water it. Carry on until the water runs out of the bottom of the pot. And make sure that you water the compost, not the plants themselves. If you do, the water will just run off the leaves and won't get down to where it is needed.

An apple growing on the smallest dwarfing rootstock, M27, is clearly happy and productive in a pot (right).

One plant – the purple-leaved Heuchera *'Palace Purple' – in a beautiful pot can be all you need to make a stunning container (left). A single-colour window box can be very attractive as this one, planted with a range of yellow flowers, demonstrates (below).*

Feeding

Feeding is slightly more difficult, as it depends on the plants. Trees and shrubs need feeding infrequently; after all, the aim is to keep them healthy, not encourage them to make huge amounts of growth. In spring, sprinkle a handful of a slow-release fertiliser, like blood, fish and bonemeal, on to the surface of the compost, and water it in. Alternatively, give them a weak liquid feed of something like Phostrogen or Farmina once a month throughout the summer. Every couple of years, carefully scrape away the top few inches of compost, taking care not to damage the roots, and replace it with fresh. Composts like John Innes contain fertiliser anyway, so you won't need to add any more that year.

Herbaceous plants are more shallow-rooted and need feeding more often, once every two weeks from May to September with liquid seaweed or some other soluble general fertiliser.

Annuals are the greediest of all, and should be fed once a week with liquid seaweed or tomato fertiliser which encourages flowering.

Planting your containers

The choice of what to grow in your containers is limited only by the size of the plant, and the conditions you're offering – a sunny spot or a shady corner.

Trees

Obviously Californian redwoods or even oaks are out of the question, but you could certainly grow a small tree, and bear in mind that because it's in a container, which restricts its root growth, it will be even smaller than it would be growing in a border.

In a sheltered spot, in part-shade, one of the lovely Japanese maples would be ideal. Among the best is *Acer palmatum dissectum* 'Garnettii' which has delicate feathery wine-red foliage, and eventually forms a small mushroom-shaped tree.

For full sun or part-shade, one of the smaller crab apples, like the weeping *Malus* 'Red Jade', would be a good choice, with blush-white flowers in spring, followed by bright red fruits, and bright green leaves that turn gold in autumn. Even planted in the garden it would only grow to 3 m (about 10 ft) high × 5 m (16 ft) across in twenty years, and with its roots restricted in a container it certainly won't reach that size.

One of the smaller flowering cherries would also be a good choice especially if it's grafted onto the dwarf rootstock 'Colt'. The Lombardy cherry

(*Prunus serrulata* 'Amanogawa') makes a tall, narrow column of pale, candy-pink flowers in spring, and won't grow to much more than about 3 m × 1 m (about 10 ft × 3 ft 3 in). You could think about the small Cheal's weeping cherry (*Prunus subhirtella* 'Pendula Rosea'), with rose-pink flowers, which is easy to find in garden centres. More difficult to find, but even better is *Prunus × yedoensis* 'Shidare Yoshino' with pale pink flowers fading to white. Neither of them will grow to much more than about 3 m × 3 m (10 ft × 10 ft).

Dwarf conifers are also a good choice for a container but make sure that what you buy really is a dwarf variety! There are many first rate varieties to choose from, but among the best are the upright juniper, *J. communis* 'Sentinel', which forms a narrow green column, not much more than 1 m (3 ft 3 in) high after ten years, the intense silver-blue *Picea pungens* 'Globosa' which forms a flat little pyramid no more than 60 cm (2 ft) high, and the oval *Thuja orientalis* 'Aurea Nana' which doesn't even reach a metre in height after ten years.

The slender blue-grey Lawson's cypress, *Chamaecyparis* 'Ellwood's Pillar' is another excellent choice – a pair of them in matching wooden tubs, underplanted with dwarf red tulips and white hyacinths, looked stunning either side of the steps up to Gay's front door. Clearly the burglars who stole them one night thought so, too!

Fruit trees

Thanks to the miracles of modern plant breeding, it's now perfectly possible to grow apple or plum trees in pots, and figs, particularly the variety 'Brown Turkey', are more productive when their roots are contained in a pot than they are in open ground. With apples, you can either grow the new 'Ballerina' types, which make a narrow column, no more than 3 m (10 ft) in height, or choose a variety grown on the smallest dwarfing rootstock, M 27. You need to grow at least two of different varieties, to ensure good pollination. For plums, look out for familiar varieties, like 'Victoria' grafted on to a 'Pixy' rootstock.

Shrubs

The choice is vast but perhaps the most important point to bear in mind is that shrubs in containers are centre stage, and must really earn their keep. So choose something that gives you the longest possible season of interest. You don't really want something that flowers for a couple of weeks in June and then just sits there with its unremarkable plain green foliage for the rest of the season.

Most rhododendrons come into this category, but one very notable exception is *R. yakushimanum*. In late spring it has deep pink buds which open into pale pink flowers which gradually fade to white. What makes it much more attractive than any of its hybrids is its long narrow leaves, which have a silvery sheen when young, fading to a deep leathery green, and brown furry undersides.

Pieris forrestii 'Forest Flame' is an excellent choice because it has such a long season of interest. In spring it carries clusters of bell-shaped, creamy-white flowers, rather like those of lily-of-the-valley, at the same time as the new foliage. The crowns of shiny, slender, spear-shaped leaves are a vivid shade of scarlet when they emerge, slowly fading to pink, cream and pale green before settling, in midsummer, for mid-green. In the autumn, clusters of small red buds form for next spring's flowers, and add colour through the winter months. *Pieris formosa* 'Wakehurst' has shorter, broader leaves, but is otherwise very similar. Both rhododendrons and pieris need ericaceous compost and enjoy some shade.

For a sunny spot patio roses are hard to beat, for they will go on flowering from June to November or even into December in a mild winter. There are more and more new varieties coming on to the market all the time, so it is worth visiting a specialist rose grower and having a look at what's on offer. Of the existing varieties, 'The Fairy' is an excellent choice, with sprays of rose-pink flowers for months and dark glossy foliage. The Rose of the Year in 1988, 'Sweet Dream', has clusters of apricot flowers while 'Cécile Brunner' produces masses of pale pink flowers, like miniature hybrid tea roses. For something really bright, the orange-red 'Anna Ford' is hard to beat. It also has lovely, deep green, glossy foliage.

Herbaceous plants

Again, the plants you choose must really earn their keep, either with a very long flowering season or with very attractive foliage. Some of the cranesbills, the hardy geraniums, flower for months. 'Wargrave Pink' which almost all garden centres stock just keeps on producing shiny bright pink flowers in sun or part shade. A new variety, 'Ann Folkard', flowers from July to October, although its combination of magenta flowers and golden foliage is a bit overpowering for some tastes. In a sunny spot, some of the dwarf campanulas flower all summer long – look out for 'Birch Hybrid' or *muralis* 'Resholdt's Variety', both with lavender blue flowers. Two to avoid are the very invasive *C. portenschlagiana* and *C. poscharskyana*.

The purple-leaved heuchera, *H.* 'Palace Purple', has sprays of tiny white flowers in early summer, but is grown primarily for its wonderful purple leaves that often take on a bronzy sheen. It would look marvellous with a silver-leaved plant like *Artemisia* 'Powys Castle', whose delicate feathery foliage would contrast very well with the shape and colour of the heuchera's leaves.

For a shady spot, hellebores and hostas are both excellent. The stinking hellebore, *H. foetidus*, has thin, spiky, glossy leaves, pale green when they're young, fading to dark green, with pale, creamy green flowers in winter, lasting for months. Even better, though not as easy to find, is *H. foetidus* 'Wester Flisk' with rich red stems. *H. corsicus* has paler green, broader leaves with clusters of apple-green flowers in early spring. There are any number of hostas to choose from, with leaves in every size, shape and colour imaginable. A simple large terracotta flowerpot planted with the huge, blue-grey-leaved *Hosta sieboldiana* 'Elegans' which has broad ribbed leaves up to 30 cm (12 in) long, looks stunning all summer, and, as a bonus, has tall sprays of white flowers in June and July. Smaller-leaved varieties, particularly the variegated kinds, are also very attractive. 'Francee' makes a mound of heart-shaped green leaves edged with cream, and 'Thomas Hogg', also cream and white, is widely available. Slugs and snails love hostas, and in borders can destroy large plants with ease, so growing them in containers gives them a better chance of remaining unscathed.

The cool colour scheme of the planting – white verbena, marguerites, petunias and silvery Helichrysum microphyllum *– complements the classic, grey lead urn perfectly.*

Bulbs

Bulbs make excellent companions to shrubs and perennials, and of course are excellent in their own right for pots, tubs and window boxes. Go for small bulbs like crocuses and the dwarf kinds of daffodils and tulips which are more in proportion to the rest of the planting than the larger, classic garden varieties would be and also are less liable to get flattened by the March gales. There are some real stunners available now – dwarf narcissi like 'Tête à Tête', 'February Gold', 'Hawera' and the white 'Jenny', and tulips like *T.*

kaufmanniana 'Show-winner' which is a vivid crimson-scarlet red and the yellow and white *Tulipa tarda*.

You can plant them in layers, larger, tall-growing bulbs like tulips and narcissi deeper than the smaller, shorter-growing ones like crocuses, grape hyacinths and irises like *Iris reticulata*.

Colour schemes are entirely a matter of personal taste, but it's worth considering the surroundings when you make your choice. Bright red doesn't look too good against a red brick wall, for example, but marvellous against grey brick or stone, or against white walls.

Bedding plants

Annuals and some half-hardy perennials, like geraniums and fuchsias, are the ideal plants for containers. Without spending a great deal of time or money, you can create wonderfully colourful containers with just bedding plants alone. Again, when it comes to choosing colour schemes, it's very much a matter of personal choice. If you want your window boxes and baskets to be every colour of the rainbow, that's fine. But sometimes, just two or three colours together – blue, gold and white, for example, or pink, pale blue and silver can look stunning as can a container in shades of just one colour – an all-white basket, for example, or a window box in different shades of yellow, from near-orange to almost cream.

Even in a shady spot, you can create a colourful display with fuchsias, busy Lizzies (*Impatiens*), fibrous-rooted begonias, lobelia, and don't forget trailing foliage plants like ivies or the variegated ground ivy, *Glechoma hederacea* 'Variegata'.

Trailing plants of all kinds – lobelia, trailing fuchsias, ivy-leaved geraniums – are perfect for containers, spilling over the sides of tubs and urns, as well as hanging baskets.

The secret of success with hanging baskets, incidentally, is to use far more plants than you think you can possibly get in and plant them everywhere – through the sides, up through the bottom, as well as on the top. One magnificent hanging basket – a ball of flowers and foliage almost a metre in diameter – was the result of over eighty plants crammed into a 36 cm (14 in) basket! Obviously, where every plant has very little compost to itself and is fighting with its neighbours for food, regular weekly feeding is absolutely vital.

CHAPTER 4

Features . . . and eyesores

Many old gardens which have become overgrown and neglected were once well laid out, and you may discover you've inherited a number of features – an old pool, for example, or a pergola which has seen better days – some of which may well be worth saving.

Of course, the first question to ask is whether or not you want to keep the feature. Maybe you quite like the idea of a rockery, but not where it is, since that's the perfect site for a patio. In that case, you could think about saving the plants, demolishing the existing rockery, and either creating another one somewhere else, or even making a scree garden instead. If it's a pool, and you have very small children, then it might be worth filling it in for now, and maybe restoring it later when it's no longer a source of potential danger.

The second question to ask is whether the feature can be saved. With a shed that has a leaking roof, rotten boards and a distinct list to starboard after the last gales, for example, you might find it costs you more in terms of time and money to repair than it would to consign it to the local dump and start again. If it is basically sound but just very unattractive, it's astonishing what you can do with a few tins of wood stain, a bit of trellis, a few climbers and some imagination.

Rock gardens

If you've discovered a rockery, smothered in weeds, with a few alpines bravely struggling on, the first thing you need to do is take a good, hard, critical look at the rocks themselves. Are they large slabs of rock well positioned so that they look like a natural outcrop in the wild? Or are they bits of rock, or, worse still although by no means uncommon, lumps of old hardcore, dotted around on a bank of soil, like so many warts on a toad?

If it's the former, then it is well worth having a go at tidying it up and replanting where necessary. If it's the latter, to be honest, you're better off demolishing the whole thing and, if you really want a rock garden, starting again. Even if you spend a great deal of time and effort cleaning it up, getting rid of the weeds, replacing the plants, it will never look right.

Assuming the fates have been kind and the structure of your rock garden is basically okay, than you need to look at the weeds which have infested it. In a rock garden that's been neglected for some time, perennial weeds like bindweed and ground elder will have had the chance to get their roots well and truly entwined with the plants' roots, and of course well and truly established under the rocks. Simply chopping off the top growth or even pulling out as much of the root as you can will not solve the problem, since many of these weeds can regrow from even the smallest piece of root left in the soil.

If your rockery is covered in couch grass you can use a special weedkiller called *Weed Out*, which kills only grass, and doesn't harm broad-leaved plants at all so you can use it safely all over the rock garden. The best time to use it is between March and September when the couch grass is growing strongly. Remember, it will kill all grass, so if you find ornamental grasses in the rockery, as we did in one that we restored, then protect them with a large plastic flowerpot with the holes in the bottom covered over with sticky tape before you spray. If your rock garden is near the lawn, choose a very still day to spray for the same reason.

If other perennial weeds, apart from ground elder, have infested your rock garden, you need to decide first of all whether the plants outnumber the weeds sufficiently to make it realistic to leave the former in place while you tackle the latter individually, or whether the weeds have the upper hand, in which case it's a question of deciding which plants are worth saving, and then killing off everything else.

The first rockery we tackled at first glance looked very colourful and full of plants, but when you looked closer you could see couch grass, creeping buttercup, thistles and nettles growing in among the plants and in fact much of the colour came from euphorbias which had self-seeded so freely that they were virtually weeds. In this case, it was worth tackling the weeds individually – spraying the couch grass with *Weed Out*, digging out the thistles and nettles, painting the creeping buttercup with glyphosate, and pulling out the shallow-rooted euphorbias by the handful!

The second rockery fell clearly into the second category! It was a bank with a few shrubs – *Rhus typhina*, *Hypericum*, *Ribes* – showing above the tangle of weeds. When we first saw it, though, it was full of bluebells, so we decided to leave the spraying until they had died right down and so wouldn't be harmed by the weedkiller.

If you inherit a weed-infested rockery that really does need spraying, the first thing to decide is which plants are worth keeping. You may have a few choice dwarf shrubs or conifers, though of course this is also an opportunity to get rid of those that really are in the wrong place. In our first rock garden we found a *Juniperus* 'Pfitzeriana Aurea', which you can still see sometimes in the 'Dwarf conifer' section of garden centres, even though it can reach up to 3 m (10 ft) high and 6 m (20 ft) across! This one had been pruned back to try and keep it in check with the result that it was a real mess. We took it out and replaced it with the very slow-growing, narrow *Juniperus communis* 'Compressa' which will never grow to more than about 1 m (3 ft) tall. We

Although at first sight this rockery looks very colourful, most of the colour comes from self-seeded annual spurge and snow-in-summer, which are crowding out the more attractive plants.

also took out a couple of azaleas, which were also too big for the rock garden, and were not doing very well in the thin sandy soil or in full sun. We replanted them in another shadier part of the garden where the soil is less free-draining.

If you've got any plants like *Alyssum saxatile*, that have become straggly and bare at the centre but have healthy-looking new growths on the outside of the clump, it might be worth taking a few cuttings before you get rid of them.

In June, cut the new growth off as close to the parent plant as you can. Trim each one back to 5–8 cm (2–3 in), leaving two or three leaves at the top, and make a clean cut just below the lowest leaf joint, or node. Put them in a 50/50 mixture of coconut fibre compost and sharp sand, in either pots or seed trays, and, if you have inherited one, put them in a cold frame. If you haven't, then a wooden orange box, with a sheet of clear plastic over the top, will do. With plants like rock cress (*Arabis*) and some saxifrages which form rosettes of leaves, remove new rosettes which haven't borne flowers, and pot them up in the same way.

Once you can see the new growth at the tip (it should take three to six weeks) pot them up individually. You can stand them in the open in the summer, but they're best put back in the cold frame during the winter. That way they are protected from alpines' worst enemy, the wet. Plant them in the rock garden the following spring.

A large clump of aubrietia which hasn't been trimmed back each year after flowering and has become straggly and sprawling is probably not worth saving. New plants are cheap enough and, indeed, there are new varieties and new colours which can be even better than the old. And don't forget you can raise plants very easily from seed.

Once you've chosen the plants you're going to keep, cover each one with a large plastic flower pot as before. Then spray the whole area with glyphosate to kill off the weeds. Wait until the weedkiller has dried before you remove the flower pot. In three to six weeks, the weeds should have died. Remove the dead growth, and then you can replant, making sure you give each new plant some fresh compost or garden soil mixed with plenty of gravel. You may well find that the odd weed will regrow. If it does, simply paint its leaves carefully with glyphosate diluted according to the instructions, and with a squirt of washing-up liquid added (much cheaper than buying the gel and just as effective), each time new shoots appear. Eventually it will give up the ghost.

Ground elder and bindweed are in a class by themselves. Since they grow in among the plants, it's impossible to spray with the liquid, without running a real risk of splashing the plants themselves. You could paint each weed leaf individually with gel, but you would have to be extremely careful. Really, you have no option but to dig it all out. Carefully dig up any plants you want to save, and untangle the plants from the weeds, making sure you remove any traces of weed roots you find growing through the roots of the plants themselves. Pot the plants up in a gravelly compost. Wait a couple of weeks until the weeds are growing strongly and then spray with glyphosate. When all the weeds have died and no more have appeared for a few weeks, then you can assume it's safe to replant.

If you want to garden organically and don't want to use weedkillers even once, then there are only two options open to you. First, you could dig up the plants you want to save, as before, carefully removing all trace of weed roots from the plants' own roots, then cover the whole area with black polythene and leave it for two years. Or, you can remove the plants, dismantle the rock garden and either cart away all the old soil and import fresh, or you can sieve it all, and make sure you get out every piece of root. Nobody ever claimed that gardening organically was an easy option!

You may find that what has actually smothered all the alpines in the rock garden is not, technically speaking, a weed at all, but a fellow alpine. Snow-in-summer (*Cerastium tomentosum*) is often the culprit, as it was in our first rock garden, because although it is very attractive with its silver foliage and masses of white flowers in spring, it can easily spread 1.25 m (4 ft) or more, smothering everything in its path. If you must have it in your garden, give it space where it can rampage at will, tumbling over a sunny wall, for example, or be prepared to hack it back with a spade each summer when it has outgrown its allotted space. A more radical solution is to dig it all out and replace it in your rock garden with its much more restrained cousin, *C.t. columnae*. Other thugs you may find smothering your choicer rock plants are the blue-flowered *Campanula poscharskyana*, and biting stonecrop (*Sedum acre*) with its fleshy pale green leaves and tiny bright yellow flowers. Again, be prepared to keep on hacking them back or remove them from the rock garden and replace them with a more refined, non-invasive relation like *Campanula* 'Stella' or *Sedum floriferum* 'Weihenstephaner Gold' with bright yellow flowers, or *S. spathulifolium* 'Capablanca' which has pale yellow flowers and lovely rosettes of creamy-grey leaves.

If you're unlucky enough to have it in your rock garden, you'll understand why Bouncing Bette (*Saponaria ocymoides*) got its name. It is very pretty with its bright pink flowers, but much better as a ground-cover plant in a sunny spot than dominating the rock garden, like an over-energetic relative at a family gathering.

When it comes to choosing new alpines for your rock garden, it is well worth making the effort to visit a specialist grower rather than relying on the local garden centre, unless, of course, it happens to have a huge selection of rock plants. And the choice of alpines is vast. When you visit a large rock garden or a specialist nursery, it's easy to see how people become hooked on them.

Obviously you need to bear in mind your soil type when you're making your choice – some alpines, for example lithospermum and gentians, are lime-haters and must have an acid soil – and whether the site is in full sun or part shade. While it's true that most alpines like an open sunny position, there are some, like ajuga, lewisia, pratia, some saxifrages, and violas that will do well in shade, although you should never plant them under trees. What alpines hate more than anything except waterlogged roots is waterlogged foliage, both of which cause them to rot and die. Planted under trees, where they can be dripped on all year and in autumn, smothered with soggy leaves, they are most unlikely to survive the winter.

When you're choosing alpines, think, too, about their different shapes and habits and make sure you choose some of each type. You'll want a few upright ones, like the tiny juniper, *J. communis* 'Compressa', which is like an Italian cypress in miniature, or something bushier like the lovely silver-leaved *Convolvulus cneorum*. You must have some mat-forming ones, like *Arenaria balearica*, aubrietia, and thyme, growing on top of the rocks and spilling over the sides, as well as some rounded, clump-forming ones like thrift (*Armeria*), the yellow-flowered *Hypericum polyphyllum* and bellflower (*Campanula*). Make sure, though, that you buy non-invasive varieties, or else you will simply be recreating the problem you have just solved!

Finally, the rosette-forming types, like houseleeks (*Sempervivums*) and many types of saxifrage, are ideal for growing in the vertical crevices of rock. So are lewisias – in fact they have to be grown in this way in the open, because if they get water in their rosette of leaves it will rot and they will die. Push the rootball of the plant into the crevice, then fill in underneath and above with gravelly compost.

Other ways of growing alpines

If the rockery you inherited was beyond the pale, and you really can't face the thought of ordering several tons of rock to build a new one (a ton of limestone equals about 13 cubic feet or, roughly, 3 ft × 2 ft × 2 ft) but you would love to grow alpines, there are a number of alternatives open to you. If you have decided to use gravel in your garden, in place of lawn, perhaps (see p. 65), or combined with paving slabs to form a path, then you can grow alpines in that. Or if you have laid a patio, you could grow alpines in the gaps between slabs.

For something more elaborate, you could make a small scree garden. (Scree in the wild is the loose stone chippings at the bottom of a mountain.) If you've got a slight natural incline in the garden, facing south or west, you could use that and go for a natural look. Or you could make it on the flat, and go for a more formal look – a brick-edged circle, perhaps.

Drainage is the key to success with alpines, so having marked out the site, you need to dig it out to a depth of about 60 cm (2 ft). Put a 20-cm (6–8 in) layer of hardcore in the bottom, and then cover that with either a layer of coarse grit about 5–8 cm (2–3 in) thick, or, if you have any spare, a layer of turves, grass side down. Then fill up the hole with a mixture of good garden soil, coarse gravel and, instead of peat which always used to be recommended for the purpose, either well-rotted garden compost if you've got any or, failing that, composted straw from the garden centre. Measure it in shovelfuls – two of soil, one of gravel and one of compost.

Once the hole is filled, leave it to settle for a couple of weeks, and top it up with the same mixture if it sinks. Then you can plant your scree garden. When all the plants are in, spread a thin layer of gravel over the soil, making sure you get it right up to the base of each plant, under the leaves. It not only looks very good, it also serves as a mulch, suppressing weeds and conserving moisture in the soil. Most important, it also keeps the plants' leaves from direct contact with the soil, which could encourage them to rot. (For a selection of alpines, see p. 65.)

Pools and ponds

You may find it hard to believe when you look at a half-empty, stained concrete pool, choked with weed, but water in the garden is probably the most attractive feature you can have. Still water is very calming, and so is the sound of gently moving water – a trickling wall fountain, for instance, or a small waterfall, or even water bubbling up through an old millstone, real or fibreglass.

Water also provides you with the chance to grow some of the many stunning aquatic plants – exquisite waterlilies in ice-cream colours, beautiful

A shadow of its former glory. This formal lily pond contained just a few inches of slime, a couple of goldfish, the odd straggly plant and thousands of tadpoles (left).

Although it's teeming with wildlife, this pond has become so overgrown with aquatic plants and grass from the lawn that it's impossible to tell where grass ends and water begins (right).

variegated irises, marsh marigolds and so on – and any kind of water in the garden is a magnet for wild life. You'll soon find you have frogs, newts, toads, dragonflies, birds, including duck and herons, which may or may not be good news depending on whether you want to have ornamental fish in your pool.

If you have decided that you want to keep the pool, and that it's in the right place, then you need to find out what's wrong with it. In the case of the first pool we tackled, once a beautiful formal lily pool, set in a sunken gravel garden, the problem was glaringly obvious. It was made of concrete, rectangular in shape, with half-circles cut out on each side, and edged with lichen-encrusted stone, but like so many concrete ponds, it had sprung several leaks and now contained about two inches of water, an equal depth of thick foul-smelling silt, four water plants in various states of terminal decline, three rather sad-looking goldfish, half a million tadpoles, and, as we discovered when we got right down to the slime, about fifteen frogs!

Our second pool could hardly have been more of a contrast. It was a wild-life pool, dug out of the ground and lined with a butyl liner, but it had become so clogged and overgrown with giant reedmace (*Typha latifolia*), duckweed and coarse grasses growing in from the surrounding lawn that it didn't simply look a mess, it was also potentially dangerous, too, since around the margins it was impossible to tell where grass ended and water began. It was hugely successful in its aim of attracting wildlife, though. It was absolutely pulsating with frogs and tadpoles as well as newts, water beetles and the odd, large goldfish.

Repairing a concrete pool

The first thing to do is to find somewhere to put the living contents while you work on the pool. A folding children's paddling pool is ideal, although a series of tubs and buckets will also do the trick. Putting the animal and vegetable contents of the pool into tap water would cause yet another shock to their systems, so it's best to keep them in the water they've been living in. Scoop some out with a bucket and put it into your temporary container before you start the removal operation.

If you're lucky, the plants will be in plastic baskets, so its just a question of lifting them out. If they're growing in mud at the bottom of the pool, lift them carefully out keeping as much mud around the roots as you can. Catching the wildlife will no doubt take you back to childhood beach holidays with your fishing net. Two points worth remembering – first, don't underestimate the ability of something as gaudy as a goldfish to hide itself in muddy water and water weed, and don't underestimate how far and how fast a frog can jump!

If the water is still reasonably deep, then scoop it out with a bucket. If it's very shallow, as it was in our first pool, then the best implement for the job is a plastic dustpan. You can pour relatively clear water down the drain, or on to the surrounding garden but the thick sludge, which could clog the drains, is best put on the compost heap.

Incidentally, once we got down to the last really smelly centimetre or so of silt, we discovered a drain hole in one corner of the formal pool, but of course there was no way of knowing, until we'd got down that far, that it was there! If you're in the same situation, it might save you a lot of time and mess to prod carefully over the bottom of the pool with a bamboo cane to see if you can locate a drain hole that way.

Once the pool is empty, scrub it thoroughly with clean water and a stiff brush, removing any stubborn green algae still clinging to the cement with a bit of household bleach, and then leave it to dry out.

The cracks in your pool will probably be immediately obvious, as they were in ours. One ran along the junction of the bottom with one of the long sides, and the other ran from the top of one of the curves and right down over the shelves for marginal plants.

To repair the cracks you need special pool repair compound, reinforced with fibres, to help prevent it cracking again, which you can get from water garden specialists.

Before you start, brush over the area around each crack with a wire brush to remove any bits of dry debris. Then soak the whole area around the crack with water (the easiest way is to use a large paint brush), mix up the compound, and apply it with an old trowel, smoothing as you go. If you're dealing with a particularly deep hole or crack, it's worth filling it in a little at a time, allowing it to dry completely between each application.

Once the compound is dry, apply a primer, followed by two coats of a special liquid plastic, which forms a lasting plastic membrane sealing the concrete permanently. It's available from specialist water garden specialists, and comes in three colours – swimming pool blue, stone and black. To make sure you get an absolutely watertight finish, apply the first coat horizontally, and then two or three days later when it's completely dry, apply the second coat vertically. Or vice versa.

Once the plastic sealant is dry, refill the pool with water and leave it to settle for at least ten days to allow any harmful chemicals in it to disperse. If your plants were already growing in baskets, and are in good shape, then you can simply put them back. If they look pretty ropey, take them out of the old basket, cut off any dead roots and dead or old foliage, and repot them. Line a new plastic basket with a piece of sacking (or, failing that, a loose-woven dishcloth) to prevent the compost washing away, half-fill them with ordinary garden soil or special aquatic compost (*not* potting compost, since the fertilisers it contains will help turn your water green by encouraging the algae responsible to thrive), put in the plant and then top up with more soil. Put a layer of gravel on top of the soil. This will not only stop the soil washing away, but if you're planning to have fish in the pool it will stop them rooting around in the soil and possibly dislodging the plants. If the plants were originally growing in the mud on the bottom, you're better off, for future ease of maintenance, planting them in the special baskets in the same way. Don't forget to add oxygenating plants, like Canadian pool weed (*Elodea canadensis*) or curled pondweed (*Potamogeton crispus*) to keep your pool healthy and prevent the water turning green. You'll need two bunches for every square metre of the pond's surface area. In the first season, you'll need to plant them in pots, like other water plants, but the following year there will probably be enough sediment on the bottom of the pool for you to drop weighted cuttings into the water, and let them root. Wait a couple of weeks before returning the fish, not forgetting, of course, to feed them in the meantime.

Using a liner

Another good way of dealing with some leaking cement pools is to put a sheet liner in. This certainly solves the problem of lots of very fine hairline cracks that are impossible to find, and it also means that even if more cracks appear in the concrete the pool won't leak. It wasn't an option with our first pool because of the shape and the fact that the stone coping could not be lifted to hide the edges of the liner, but for a pool surrounded by paving slabs or bricks, it would be an ideal solution. Butyl is the best liner and should last a lifetime, provided it's installed carefully. If it does spring a leak – water voles have been known to nibble through it, even in inner city Paddington! – there are repair kits available. It is also the most expensive. Thick polyethylene or PVC sheeting is almost as good and is cheaper, while polythene is the cheapest of all, but you'll be lucky to get more than three years out of it before it needs replacing.

To estimate the size of liner you need to buy, measure the maximum length, maximum breadth and maximum depth of the pool. Add twice the greatest depth to the length and also to the breadth and add an allowance to be tucked under whatever edging you choose. Liners come in lots of different standard sizes, so buy the one closest to your actual measurements. Unless a liner is literally only a fraction shorter or narrower than the size you need, you'll have to buy the next size up.

To stop the rough surface of the concrete damaging the liner, you could either put a 2-cm (½-in plus) layer of sand, a sheet of polythene or even old newspapers over the surface of the pool before you fit the liner. To make sure you get it even, stretch it over the pool, and, making sure you've got an equal amount of overlap all round, weight down the edges with bricks or stones. Put the hosepipe on to the liner, and turn it on. As the water flows in, it will weight the liner down, pushing it flat against the contours of the pool. Keep smoothing the liner to avoid masses of creases, and neatly tuck the surplus in at the corners. When the pool is full to the brim, turn off the hose. Remove the bricks or stones and trim the liner to about 15 cm (6 in) all round. Edge the pool with slabs or bricks to fit in with the rest of the garden. Make sure the edging overlaps the pool by at least 5 cm (2 in) so that, unless you kneel down at the water's edge, you can't see any of the liner.

Restoring an overgrown wildlife pool

Before you empty the pool, you need to preserve what's worth keeping in the way of wildlife and plants, in exactly the same way as you would with a concrete pool. Ours was large and deep, and scooping out the water with buckets would have taken hours, if not days, so we took advantage of the fact that it was on a slight slope, and had a field owned by a friendly farmer at the bottom, to siphon it out. It's quite easy to do. Fill a length of hose with clean water and when the pipe is completely full, kink the end furthest from the pool to prevent any water escaping. Make sure that end is lower than the end you are about to put in the pool, then put one end in the pool and immediately unkink the other. With a bit of luck, and the laws of gravity on your side, you should find the pool water will start running through. If you have a really big pool, and it's not possible to siphon it out, then hire a pump for half a day and pump the water away into a nearby drain.

Once you are down to the primeval slime at the bottom, then you have to scoop it out, although be prepared to find large numbers of frogs, beetles and so on living in it. Remove any plants growing in the mud that you want to keep and pull out the rest along with the blanket weed and duckweed which, it must be said, can be a tough and very messy job.

Once the pool is clear, you can see the state of the liner. In the case of our wildlife pond, we actually found couch grass growing through the butyl liner because it had been laid directly onto the soil, with no under-lining at all. In a situation like that, you have two choices. Either you can start again

This is how the renovated pond looks six months later, complete with lilies.

– rip out the old liner, then, ideally, line the hole with heavy duty polythene, through which couch grass can't penetrate, then put in an underlining – newspapers, sand or even a special fibre lining – before you put in the new butyl liner. Or you can do as we did, and use a polyethylene liner, which couch grass can't penetrate, either, and leave the old butyl one in place to act as an underliner.

Measure it and fit it as you would the liner for a cement pool (see p. 112). When the liner is in place you can either finish it with crazy paving slabs or, for a really natural effect, cut under the turf around the edge of the pool for about 30cm (1 ft), then peel it back, tuck the edge of the liner underneath, and roll the turf back over it. Do be sure to keep the edges of the grass trimmed, though, or else you'll have the same problem we had – grass growing into the pool.

The next step is to put an 8-cm (3-in) layer of heavy soil in the bottom of the pool, covering the liner completely. Once you refill the pool with water, of course, it will look like a vat of chocolate for a day or so, but it will soon settle down, and you're less likely to have problems with the water turning green. Then replant the pool, using baskets for waterlilies, and planting all the marginal plants and oxygenators directly into the layer of mud on the bottom. As the owners of our pool wanted it to be a real wildlife pool, we were going to find the goldfish a new home, since they eat a lot of the insect life which rather defeats the object. If you do want to put fish into your pool, then wait a couple of weeks until the water is really clear before you put them in.

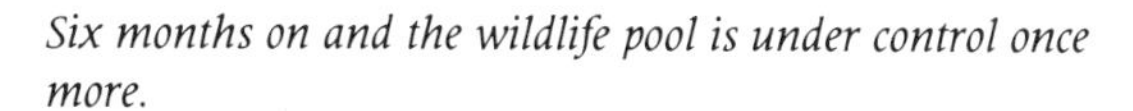

Six months on and the wildlife pool is under control once more.

Clogged pools

You may find your neglected pool is simply clogged with blanket weed or pool weed, in which case pull it out by the handful, and keep on doing it as it grows. Other pool plants may have been choked to death, in which case you'll need to restock.

The pool you inherit may well be one of those rigid plastic affairs that look like a large, vivid turquoise Jerusalem artichoke – all knobbly and misshapen. The problem with them, apart from the purely aesthetic one, is that they are usually too shallow to sustain a balanced ecosystem, and the water in them is usually green. The best bet is to remove any surviving fish and plants (see p. 111), then dig it out, cart it off to the tip and start again.The shape of hole you'll be left with will be as knobbly and as unnatural as the turquoise monstrosity itself, so you're better off starting again. To be fair, you can now get preformed pools in black and some are quite deep, but most of the shapes still leave a lot to be desired, so you really are better off digging out the shape you want and using a sheet liner. If you don't want a formal shape, then go for one with clean sweeping curves, not lots of little fiddly ones, and give it sloping sides, not straight ones. Not only does it look better, but it makes it easier for frogs and newts to climb out.

Use the hosepipe to get the shape you want, and when you're happy with it, dig it out, removing the topsoil first and piling it separately. You can use that elsewhere in the garden. You can cart the subsoil away. From then on, it's just the same as lining an old concrete pool (see p. 112).

Fountains and waterfalls

You might find a submersible pump with a fountain jet in your pool. If it works, and you want to keep it, fine. If it doesn't, then you're better off getting a qualified electrician in to look at it. The same is true if you want to put a submersible pump into a pool. Laying on an electricity supply in the garden, whether it's for a pump or for lights, is a job for a professional. Do remember, though, that some plants, like waterlilies, don't like moving water very much, nor does much wildlife, although goldfish don't mind.

Pergolas

There's no doubt that a pergola can make a very attractive feature in a garden, and if you have inherited one that is past its best it could be worth saving. First of all, you need a good look at the basic structure, and that could well mean removing all the climbing plants that cover it. If they're rambling roses, with fairly lax, whippy stems, then you can untie them from the pergola's uprights and lay them on the ground. If the stems are just too tangled, then you can cut them hard back in spring although you'll lose this summer's flowers. If it's covered with the tangled, thick brown stems of *Clematis montana*, and you can't tease any of them free from the posts, cut it back either after flowering in May, or, if you can't wait until then, to a pair of fat leaf buds at a convenient height in early spring, although of course you will lose this season's flowers.

If you find that one post has rotted at ground level, drive in a short post (no more than 1 m (3 ft) in all) as close to it as you can. Bolt it to the old post, well clear of the rotten part. If you can, cut away the rotten section and treat the cut with wood preservative. If you can fix the new post (they're called 'godfathers' incidentally) on the inside of the pergola then it won't be as noticeable as it would be on the outside. Either way, once the plants are growing up again, you won't really notice it.

When the repairs are finished, prune the climbers if necessary (see p. 81) and tie them back around the posts. The neatest way to fix climbers like clematis (if they're not growing through roses), summer-flowering jasmine and honeysuckle, is to fix a wire on opposite sides of the post. Knock a nail almost all the way in at the top, wrap the wire round it three or four times, then knock it the rest of the way in. Pull it tight and do the same at the bottom. Then force a small piece of wood 2.5 cm (1 in) thick under the wire to hold it clear of the post and nail it in place. This allows you to tuck the plants behind the wire without damaging them.

You could do a 'godfather' repair on two of the posts in a pergola, but after that it's probably not worth saving. If half the posts have rotted, then it's likely that the others will soon, so you're better off taking it down and starting again. If you're unlucky, the pergola's builder will have concreted the posts straight into the ground, in which case you really have no option but to get the concrete out. Even if you don't want to put another pergola there, you'll find that very little will grow in an inch or two of soil on top of concrete.

If you're going to replace the pergola or put one somewhere else in the garden, then do your heirs a favour and use Met-posts or Erecta posts – metal sockets to hold the uprights, with a long, metal spike underneath which is driven directly into the soil. That way, if ever a post rots in future (and it shouldn't for many years since the metal socket holds it clear of the soil) it's very easy to remove it and replace it with a new one. It also means that if anyone wants to get rid of the pergola altogether in future, they just have to pull a few metal spikes out of the ground, and don't have to worry about smashing up concrete. Incidentally, if you have opted for a hard surface in your tiny backyard, or want to put a pergola on an existing patio, you can buy special fittings to hold the uprights which can be bolted on to a hard surface. Then you can grow your climbers in pots.

The ready-cut, ready-drilled pergola kits you can buy at garden centres or big DIY superstores are probably the best bet, though make sure you choose one made by a reputable manufacturer. They cost from about £70.

Remember, though, to put it up section by section, as you go. Don't put up all the posts first and trust to luck the the cross-struts will all drop neatly into place. Chances are they won't!

Dry stone walls

You may find a few low, dry stone walls in the garden, either as decorative edgings to borders, or as retaining walls, holding back the soil where the garden changes level. Well-made from natural stone, and filled with colourful alpine plants, they can look wonderful. Falling down and full of dead vegetation and weeds, they look a mess.

If yours is only a very low wall, no more than 60cm (2 ft) high, and it's only crumbling away a bit at the top, then it's worth having a go at restoring it. Carefully remove the stones, layer by layer, to a level where the wall is no longer crumbling, getting out as many weeds and their roots as you can. If there are any alpines surviving, remove them too as carefully as you can and pot them up for the time being. If some of the stones have actually crumbled or were missing, then buy some to match from the local garden centre or builders' merchants, making sure you choose chunky, roughly rectangular pieces, at least 5 cm (2 in) thick. The key to success is to make sure that the stones slope slightly from front to back, and the face of the wall slopes backwards at about 20 degrees from the vertical. Replant as you go, allowing slightly wider gaps between some stones, putting in some gritty compost and planting into that. The soil acts as mortar and, as they grow, the plant's roots will help bind the wall together. Good alpines for dry stone walls include yellow alyssum, pink, blue and purple aubrietia, blue and white campanula, pink cranesbills (*Geranium lancastriense* or *dalmaticum*), evergreen white candytuft, and fleabane (*Erigeron mucronatus*) with its daisy flowers that change from white to pink and then purple.

If the wall is so far gone that it needs to be taken down and rebuilt from scratch, it's not really a job for a beginner. Either get a professional to do it for you, assuming that the stone is worth saving or, if it's not, cheat. There's now a range of 'dry stone' blocks available called Ryedale Walling, made by Marshalls, which are simply stuck together with an outdoor brick and tile adhesive like Tetrafix or Febtile – you don't even have to mix up sand and cement! It looks very effective, especially with a coat of yogurt or liquid manure painted on to get the algae and lichens growing, and it is very strong. You could plant into it, by leaving gaps between each block, although since each one is 14 cm (5.5 in) high, it would look a bit odd until the plant had spread enough to cover the gap. You'd need to leave a gap the same width in each course of blocks, although obviously not in the same plane, so that the overall length was the same.

Broken or uneven paving

You may find that you have inherited a patio which is basically sound, except for one or two cracked or shattered paving slabs or bricks. If you're lucky, you'll find they are bedded on sand, so you should be able to lift them out without too much difficulty. In the case of large slabs, you might need a couple of old screwdrivers or something similar to help lever them up. If they've been set on mounds of mortar, it's a bit more tricky. You might need to smash up the slab a bit more, until you can remove a few pieces and get a cold chisel underneath to chip away at the mortar.

Finding a replacement that matches could be a bit of a problem. Your best bet is to start at an architectural salvage yard, which specialises in second-hand, and therefore weathered, bricks and slabs. Failing that, you could try the local garden centre or builders' merchants and match it as closely as you can. It won't ever be perfect, but you'll soon learn to live with it. In one sense, it might help to sow some seeds, or plant a few alpines in the gaps to cover the newcomer, but then, that might just draw attention to it. To replace the slabs or bricks, bed them down as you would on a new patio.

Rocky paving is another problem that's quite common in old gardens, either on the patio or in a path. If you can, put a crowbar or the blade of an old spade in between the rocky slab and its stable neighbour, and lever it up. Rather than risk injury by lifting it up, get a piece of strong metal tubing, or even an old broomstick, that's wider than the slab to be lifted, and slip it underneath the raised end. You can then roll the slab clear. If the slab was bedded on sand, level it out and add a bit more. If it was laid on mounds of mortar, chip them out with the crowbar or a cold chisel, and mix up fresh.

Replace the slab and tamp it down well, checking that it is level all round, by using the spirit level on the slab and each of its neighbours in turn.

If it's just impossible to lever the slab out, then you could try knocking small wooden wedges in between the rocky slab and its neighbours at either end. The wedges will eventually rot away, but you might well find that by the time they do the slab has stabilised anyway. If not, then knock in some more wooden wedges.

Having been laid carefully on the lawn while we replaced the wobbly old pergola with a new, stable one, the honeysuckle can now be tied back in place (left).

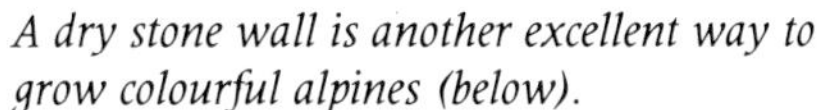

A dry stone wall is another excellent way to grow colourful alpines (below).

Dirty or stained patios

A patio that has mellowed with the years, its slabs encrusted with lichen, is one thing. A patio that's just plain dirty, or worse, stained in patches by engine oil, is something else. There are a whole range of patio cleaners on the market now, but when *Gardening from Which?* tested a number of them in 1989, they found that in most cases ordinary washing powder, a scrubbing brush and a powerful hose were just as effective and infinitely cheaper. None of the cleaning materials got rid of lichen stains, and, while you could bleach them with ordinary household bleach or hydrogen peroxide, they may actually look worse afterwards than they did before. If the patio drains on to a lawn or flowerbeds, make sure that you don't splash any of the concentrated solutions on to the grass or plants. Once you've hosed them off with water, they should be too dilute to do any damage. If the problem on the patio slabs is moss or algae, incidentally, you can only use products approved by the Government under the Pesticide Regulations for this purpose so, in this instance, household bleach is out. You can use washing powder though . . .

If you're not happy about using chemicals, even biodegradable ones, the alternative is either to buy or to hire a high-pressure water sprayer for a day, and blast the dirt off with that. Do wear eye protection, though, and be aware that this powerful jet of water can remove loose bits of mortar from between bricks and paving slabs.

Oil or creosote stains are more of a headache. There are a number of products on the market, and while most are quite effective on comparatively fresh oil stains, they are not particularly effective on oil which has really soaked in or on creosote.

Statues and ornaments

If you're lucky, you might find an old birdbath or sundial, or even a statue in among the debris. They can all make marvellous focal points in a garden but, again, whether or not you keep them depends on the state they are in and your personal taste. A Roman emperor with his nose chipped off still has great appeal, and certainly having no arms hasn't done the Venus de Milo any harm! A headless gnome with all his paint rubbed away, on the other hand, is probably best consigned to the great wishing well in the sky.

If you find any ornaments – urns, birdbaths, even statues – that are broken but could be stuck back together, as opposed to those with bits missing that need patching or remodelling, you could try a new product from the USA called JB Weld, available from DIY superstores, and shops. It's a cold welding compound that will stick metal as well as stone or cement and can stand extremes of temperature. It needs between six and twelve hours to 'cure', so you'll need to tie or wire or otherwise hold the pieces together while the compound sets.

If you find a rather nice sundial, say, with a large hole in its base, you could repair it with special repair compound. Once it's quite dry, paint it with either plain yogurt, or liquid manure to encourage lichen and algae to grow and give it the same weathered look as the rest. If the base is too badly damaged to repair, buy a new one from the garden centre as close in colour as you can find to the part you're going to keep, and, again, paint it with yogurt or liquid manure

Inspection covers

One of life's mysteries is why the people who put in drains always choose to put inspection covers right in the middle of the best place for a patio or lawn. It's also a mystery why they always put them at a slight angle so that you can't pave easily around them with standard paving slabs, without lots of fiddly and irritating cutting.

While you can't do anything about the former, you can do something about the latter. You'll find the inspection cover fits into a metal frame, which has been cemented into place on top of a brick 'chimney' leading down to the drain. Chisel the cement away, and remove the frame. Lay the paving slabs first, and when you're close to the opening, adjust the metal frame so that it lines up neatly with them. You'll find you've got just about the width of a brick to play with. When it's right, cement it back in place. The fact that it's no longer square to the hidden brickwork doesn't matter. If you find the inspection cover is a bit too high, remove the metal frame, and the top layer of bricks, and, using a cold chisel, knock off the 'frog' – the indented bit of the brick. Cement the half bricks back in place and, using more cement to get the level just right, put the metal frame back, too.

A lot of books advise you to stand a planted container on top of the inspection cover to disguise it, but in our opinion that only draws attention to it. A better bet is to group a collection of containers carefully on and around it. It looks more natural and on the odd occasion you do need access to the drain it's really no hardship to move them.

You can buy special drain planters which hold enough soil in which to grow plants. These work best if the inspection cover isn't bang in the centre of your patio. If it is, not only will the planter look rather odd, but you're likely to walk on it. While it's strong enough to bear the weight of several sumo wrestlers, so you would come to no harm, the plants wouldn't like it.

The best solution in that situation is to buy a special inspection cover with a tray deep enough to hold paving slabs or blocks, so that once they're filled with the same material as your patio, all you see of the cover is a narrow metal rim.

Inspection covers in the middle of lawns are another favourite trick of

A drain planter designed to take paving slabs or bricks is probably the best way to cope with inspection covers right in the middle of the patio.

house builders. One option is to buy another special inspection cover, which you can then fill with turf, or soil and grass seed. Again, all you see is a narrow metal rim.

One solution that's often suggested is to plant a low-growing conifer like a juniper next to the cover, so that it spreads across to hide it, but can be lifted whenever access is needed. The problem is, it's become such a cliché that if you see a juniper growing in a lawn you can be pretty certain there's an inspection cover underneath! The other problem is that many prostrate junipers grow much too large for the purpose, and although you can cut them back, they never look as good as they do if they're allowed to sprawl. Perhaps the most attractive solution we've seen to this problem is a small, formal circular scree garden built around the inspection cover. The alpines grow in the soil round the edge, and the cover itself is hidden by the same gravel that's used to mulch the soil, and by a sundial. On the rare occasions the owner needs access to the drain, the sundial is lifted off, and the gravel swept to one side. When the job is finished, the gravel is simply swept back over the cover again and the sundial replaced. In this case, the inspection cover was pretty well in the middle of the lawn, and so a formal circular shape worked well. If it was off-centre, then you'd need to adapt the shape a bit – a kidney shape, maybe, with the inspection cover close to one edge covered with gravel, and surrounded by mat-forming plants.

Inspection covers in borders aren't such a problem since you can disguise them with shrubs and herbaceous perennials much more easily. If you find they stick up too much, then remove the frame as before and remove the top course of bricks. Make sure you don't make it too low, though. If it's below soil level, soil will spill on to it, and roots may grow into that, and it won't be possible to remove it, if you have to, without damaging plants. If you've moved to the country, you might have a septic tank or cess pit, instead of main drainage, with a stink pipe sticking up in your border, as well as an inspection cover. One easy, attractive solution to that problem is to plant a group of conifers, a tall one, like *Chamaecyparis lawsoniana* 'Ellwoodii' or *Thuja occidentalis* 'Smaragd' to hide the pipe, a low-growing one – something like *Juniperus virginiana* 'Grey Owl' is spectacular where it has room to spread its wings – to hide the inspection cover, and maybe a rounded shape, like *Thuja occidentalis* 'Rheingold' or *T. orientalis* 'Aurea Nana' just to complete the group. Conifers are ideal because they are shallow-rooted and they will be growing in only a foot or so of soil on top of a concrete tank. Avoid anything that is deeper-rooting. Not only will the roots soon hit concrete, which will be harmful to the plant, but they could also do the tank some damage, which would be expensive, and messy, to put right.

The ivy-filled trellis pillar on the left has been strategically placed so that, when you're sitting on the patio, you don't see the neighbours' windows, which look directly into the garden (above).

This is what the ivy-filled trellis pillar conceals (right).

Telegraph poles and the like

If you move into the country, you might find a telegraph pole in your garden (though they're tele*phone* poles these days) or, more likely, a pole carrying the electricity cables. The telephone company or the area electricity board concerned will probably pay you a very small sum for having the pole on your land, but it remains their pole and what they say goes. You are not allowed to grow anything up it, for instance. For one thing, it would be dangerous if a rampant climber got tangled up with the cables, and, for another, it would make it very difficult if ever one of their employees needed to climb up it. You can always ask if they will move the pole, but they may want a great deal of money to do so.

If it really is right in your line of vision, the best thing to do is create a focal point somewhere else, to draw your eye away from it. You could plant an attractive small tree (see pp. 169–80) in the foreground between it and the place you usually sit, so that when you look in that direction, the tree catches your gaze first.

Screening eyesores

If you have a view of an electricity pylon or an ugly tower block in the distance, then obviously you'll want to hide it as quickly and effectively as you can. The way *not* to do it is to plant a row of huge conifers right on your boundary. While it is true that they will eventually blot out the view, they will also blot out most of your light as well, and starve any other plants close to them. Much better to use the rules of perspective to your advantage and to use a carefully sited small tree (or even a couple of them) or a pergola covered with climbing plants either to block out the ugly view completely, or, if that's not possible, then to block it partially and distract your eye so you don't notice it quite as much.

It may be, of course, that to screen the eyesore effectively the tree ought to be planted in your neighbour's garden. If you're prepared to choose something that will suit both your purposes, to pay for it and to plant it, you may find your neighbour is more than happy to oblige.

If the view really is so awful that you really can't wait long enough for a tree to reach that height, you could plant a large shrub as well, much closer to the house, and take it out once the tree has reached the desired height. Alternatively, you could build a pergola close to the house, cover it with climbing plants and screen it that way.

Sheds, oil tanks, compost heaps

Sheds can actually be made to look very attractive with a bit of imagination. They can be painted, or covered in climbers. A shed that's covered, literally, in ivy, neatly trimmed clear of the windows and door, can look terrific.

Oil tanks, dustbins and compost heaps are all necessary but none of them adds to the beauty of the garden, so the best thing to do is to screen them. The last thing you should do, though, is put a fence straight across in front of any eyesore. It will just draw attention to it, and make your garden look shorter. Setting fencing panels, trellis or even hedges at an angle, from opposite sides of the garden is a different story altogether. They can make the garden look larger, suggesting that it continues well beyond the barrier, and hide the eyesore just as effectively. With a smaller eyesore, like an oil tank, you can screen it with a hedge or a trellis with climbers growing up it, allowing access to it with the sort of overlap arrangement you often find around public conveniences in the park. Don't try and grow climbers over the tank itself, though. It will simply look like a tank with climbers growing over it, and besides, in the case of one tank covered with Russian vine, the poor delivery man needed a machete to get to the inlet pipe every time he came!

Dustbins are a particularly tricky problem, especially in a front garden. You can build a special housing for them in the same material as the house or your boundary wall or fence. Or, a simpler solution is to make a paved bay for them, with a couple of loose-laid paving slabs, in a shrub border, or even a hedge. That way, the bin men have easy access to them, but from at least some angles they remain hidden from view.

CHAPTER 5

Boundaries

There are lots of reasons for having some form of barrier around your garden – all of them valid. For a start, it will keep unwelcome visitors out, be they dogs, deer, sheep, cattle or humans (the person who devises a 100 per cent effective means of keeping cats out of gardens deserves a Nobel prize in our book!), and afford you some privacy. It can offer some protection from the wind, and wind-blown litter, and possibly screen an unattractive view. It can also be an attractive backdrop to show off your garden to best advantage.

So the first question you must ask when you inspect the walls, fences, or hedges you have inherited is, are they doing their job? Clearly a straggly, neglected privet hedge with gaping holes in the bottom will not keep out next door's dog, nor will it add to the beauty of the border you are renovating. A broken-down fence does little for your privacy and perhaps reveals an ugly view. A brick wall may be structurally sound, although in need of re-pointing and, since one of the previous owners seems to have used it for cleaning his paint brushes, it's no longer a pretty sight.

The second question you should ask is, whose walls, fences or hedges are they, anyway? Unless you live in the first or last house in the street, or in splendid isolation in open countryside, you are very unlikely to be responsible for all the barriers around your garden. You will certainly be responsible for one of those running lengthways down your garden and possibly jointly responsible for the one at the bottom of the garden. As a rule of thumb, the person on whose side the posts or brick piers are is responsible for the fence or the wall. With hedges it's more difficult. The only way to be certain is to look at the deeds to the house. If they don't tell you, you'll just have to ask the neighbours on both sides and at the bottom of the garden whose is which, and trust to their memories and good will. There's an old saying 'Good fences make good neighbours' and that's certainly true. If the most dilapidated fence surrounding your garden is your neighbour's responsibility and he seems reluctant to do anything about it, then you have two choices. You either live with a constant eyesore which means that your garden will never be the little paradise you dream of, or you replace it yourself. That way, you might even shame him into bearing some of the cost.

If your boundaries need work – either renovating or even replacing – you should tackle it sooner rather than later. You don't want to be grubbing out an old hedge or putting in a new fence post after you've cleaned up and replanted the border in front of it.

Hedges

Whether or not the hedge is worth saving depends, as usual, on what it is, what state it's in, and whether you like it. Unlike shrubs, you can't really leave a hedge you're not sure about for a couple of years, until the rest of the planting has matured a bit because you're likely to do a lot of damage to the new planting if you do decide to take it out later.

If you've got a privet hedge that is just a bit overgrown and a bit bare at the base, then prune it hard back in the spring. Cut back the side branches to within a couple of inches of the main stem, and either cut the main stem to about 30 cm (1 ft) below the height you want it to be, or, if it's really scrawny, cut it down to a few inches above the ground.

Clear the base of the hedge of all weeds, dead growth and rubbish. Carefully fork over the surface of the soil, and give the plants a feed – about 120 g (4 oz) of blood, fish and bonemeal to every square metre if you're an organic gardener, or something like Growmore if you're not. Finally, mulch it with a good few inches of well-rotted garden compost, farmyard manure, or composted straw and make sure it never goes short of water throughout the summer. You should find new foliage soon starting to shoot from the base of each plant, although don't expect it to grow much more than about 30 to 45 cm (12 to 18 in) in the first year, and less if you cut back almost to ground level.

Badly overgrown privet hedges like this one, which have become gappy and bare at the base, need pruning back hard (above left). Just five months later, it's a pretty decent privet hedge once more (above right).

You can treat box (*Buxus sempervirens*), shrubby honeysuckle (*Lonicera nitida*), and informal flowering hedging plants like barberry (*Berberis* × *stenophylla*) in the same way. An evergreen cherry laurel (*Prunus laurocerasus*) or holly hedge can be pruned hard back, too, but it's better to use secateurs to do the job than shears since the large, glossy leaves turn brown and look awful if they're chopped in half.

Opinions vary about overgrown beech hedges. They can be cut hard back, both in height and width, but they are very slow to regrow and, to be frank, look a mess in the meantime. One compromise, if you are keen to keep the beech hedge, is to cut it hard back one side in late winter/early spring this year, and give the other side the same treatment next year. When it's the turn of the side you look at most often, you can at least walk round to the other side to remind yourself why you're doing it!

If you live in the country, you may have inherited a hawthorn hedge, which can make a fine, prickly, animal-proof barrier. If it's become bare at the base, you can either cut it down by half, or even to ground level, or you could have it laid. This is an old country craft, which involves partly cutting through young saplings, bending them over at the height you want the hedge to be and weaving them into each other. If you are really keen, the British Trust for Conservation Volunteers* run courses for amateurs. Alternatively, you could ask local farmers for the name of a professional in the area or even look in the yellow pages.

Conifer hedges are extremely popular, but the only type that can really be cut hard back is yew (*Taxus baccata*). Unlike all the rest, it will produce new growth when you cut back into the old wood, and in fact the trunk produces more new growth than the branches. The only snag is that it regrows rather slowly – about 22 cm (9 in) a year. If you do cut an old hedge back, cut it so that it's broader at the bottom than at the top. This means that it's less vulnerable to snow damage (a heavy snowfall on a top-heavy hedge is likely to break it open) but, more important, that the growth at the bottom of the hedge gets as much light as the growth at the top, so it's not likely to become bare again in the future.

If you have inherited a garden surrounded by a leylandii hedge (× *Cupressocyparis leylandii*) which is now taller than the house, you have our sympathy. If it's too wide all you can do is trim the sides back a bit, but you must always leave at least 10 cm (4 in) of live foliage on each shoot, since it won't regrow from the old wood. If you want to reduce the height, you must do so very gradually. When fully grown, they are very impressive tall trees, and lopping too much off them just makes them look hideous. Basically, the truth is that if your leylandii hedge is more than twice the height you would like it to be, the best solution is to take it out and start again.

---

* 36 St Mary's Street, Wallingford, Oxfordshire OX10 0EU. Tel: 0491 39766

If you've got a conifer hedge that's not too large, but has just become bare at the base, one solution would be to grow other plants in front of it to cover up the gaps. (If the neighbour's dog is getting into your garden through the gaps, then some fine meshed plastic netting fixed across the larger holes should solve that problem.)

Hedges are greedy feeders, so the soil around them is usually poor and dry but, that said, there are a number of plants for both sun and shade which will tolerate such conditions.

For shade, one of the variegated spindles (*Euonymus fortunei*) like the gold and green 'Emerald 'n' Gold' or the cream and green 'Emerald Gaiety' would be ideal as would *Spiraea* × *bumalda* 'Goldflame', brightening up the plain green foliage of the hedge. Among the herbaceous plants, the tough spurge *Euphorbia robbiae*, with its yellow-green bracts (like flowers, but technically speaking not) all summer long, lady's mantle (*Alchemilla mollis*) with its pale green fan-like leaves and tiny lime-green flowers, cranesbill (*Geranium endressii* or *G. macrorrhizum*) and, as ground cover, the silvery leaves of dead nettle (*Lamium maculatum* 'Beacon Silver' or 'White Nancy') would all do an excellent job. Although a variegated ivy would brighten up the shady side of a hedge, it's best avoided here since it could eventually get out of control and throttle its host.

For the sunny side of a hedge, there's a wide range of shrubs and herbaceous plants to choose from. Among the best are the pink, wine red and cream variegated barberry (*Berberis thunbergii* 'Rose Glow'), rock rose (*Cistus* × *corbariensis* or *C.* 'Silver Pink'), lavender and cotton lavender (*Santolina chamaecyparissus*), and herbs like rosemary and sage. Rose campion (*Lychnis coronaria*) with either white or bright magenta-pink flowers would be a good choice, as would silvery catmint (*Nepeta mussinii* or × *faassenii*).

If your hedge is infested with weeds, like bindweed and brambles, then pull as much as you can out of the hedge taking care not to damage it and then paint or if there's too much of it, carefully spray the remaining weed growth with glyphosate. Pull it clear of the hedge and lay it on the ground. Then lean a piece of old hardboard or even strong cardboard up against the hedge as a temporary screen while you spray. If you want to garden organically, then pull the weed growth clear of the hedge and cover it with black polythene, weighted down at the edges with bricks or stones. Leave it for a few months, then remove it and pull out the dead or spindly growth you find underneath. Mulching will help keep annual weeds down, but be prepared to use the hoe regularly.

Thin hedges

Your hedge may look rather thin and straggly, and even have gaps where individual plants have died. If more than one or two have died in the case of a privet hedge, the cause may well be honey fungus (see p. 71). If so, you must dig out the remaining plants and burn them.

If there's no sign of honey fungus, it could just be that the hedge has been slowly starved over the years. Try pruning it back just as it's starting into growth in early spring to the point where new growth is appearing and give it a feed of either blood, fish and bonemeal or Growmore (120 g or 4 oz to the square metre or yard).

If there are distinct gaps, then you could try filling them with new plants. That should be successful with something like laurel, and with some conifers, although you'll need to buy larger, more mature, and therefore more expensive plants than you'd buy if you were planting a hedge from scratch. The newcomers also have to compete for food, moisture and light with the bigger, established plants, and for standard-sized hedging plants it's an unequal contest. That's why the failure rate with in-filling is so high. Sometimes books and magazines advise you to fill the gaps in your hedge with other plants – berberis, forsythia, even rugosa roses. While they would certainly fill any gaps, unless you were very careful in what you chose and the gaps were evenly spaced, the result would look a bit of a dog's dinner.

The modern equivalent of Sleeping Beauty's castle – a modern house, hidden by a leylandii hedge which was never pruned. It's too late now to cut it back, so the only answer is to take it out.

Brightening up a dull hedge

While a well-grown hedge is an asset to any garden, you may be one of those people who find a large expanse of rather patchy, although generally healthy mid-green hedge less than exciting, in which case you could brighten it up with climbers. If you're going to clip the hedge every year, then you should choose either an annual climber, one that also needs pruning every year as well, or one that dies down in the autumn. See p. 92 for suitable varieties.

Canary creeper (*Tropaeolum peregrinum*) is a good choice for a plain green hedge with its bright green leaves and fluffy bright yellow flowers all summer long. And its much more temperamental cousin, the Scotch flame flower (*Tropaeolum speciosum*) with its flame-red flowers, looks very striking against a dark hedge, like yew. The Chilean glory flower (*Eccremocarpus scaber*) would also be a good choice here, and much easier to grow, given a sunny spot and a well-drained soil. It dies back to ground level in all but the mildest winters, but will usually shoot again in spring, and, if it doesn't, it's easily raised from seed.

For something a bit more subtle in terms of colour, the everlasting pea (*Lathyrus latifolius*) is worth growing. It has pinky-mauve or white flowers (like sweet pea flowers, only smaller, not frilly and without any perfume) all through the summer and into the autumn.

Although clematis needs plenty of moisture, and would not thrive in the poor, dry soil close to a hedge, you can still use it in this situation if you're careful. The trick is to plant it a good metre (3 ft) away from the hedge, and train it along the ground before training it up into the hedge itself. The best varieties to use are those that can be cut hard back in autumn or early spring. Among the large-flowered kinds, the pink 'Hagley Hybrid', the red 'Ville de Lyon', the blue 'Ascotiensis' or 'Perle d'Azur' (either of them would look marvellous on any golden hedge) or the purple 'Jackmanii' are all first class. Among the smaller-flowered kinds, look out for varieties of *C. viticella*, like the wine-red 'Madame Julia Correvon', the double purple-flowered *C.v.* 'Purpurea Plena Elegans', the creamy-white and pale mauve 'Little Nell' and *C. texensis*, either 'Duchess of Albany' with mauve-pink urn-shaped flowers, each petal of which has a darker central bar, or the deep red 'Gravetye Beauty' whose blossoms look more like small lily-flowered tulips than anything else.

Removing a hedge

If the hedge is really too far gone to be worth saving, then the answer is to take it out. How you do it will depend on a number of factors. If you have a hawthorn hedge, for instance, which is very difficult to get out, the best way is to find a local contractor or farmer with a tractor and get him to pull it out. But of course, that depends on whether or not you have access for a tractor.

If you've got an ordinary garden hedge of, say, privet, or shrubby honeysuckle (*Lonicera nitida*), then it shouldn't be too difficult to dig it out yourself. If the hedge is badly overgrown, cut it down to about 1.2 m (4 ft), then dig a trench around the roots, chopping through them as you find them with an axe or, better still, a mattock. Tie a rope or some thick twine round the top of the plant, and get someone to pull on it, first in one direction, then in another while you carry on chopping through the roots as they're exposed. Eventually, the remaining roots will snap, and the plant will pull free. Pull out as much of the roots remaining in the soil as you can. With more difficult hedges, like beech and some conifers like yew and Leyland cypress, the answer might be to winch them out. It should be said, though, that doing it yourself is only worth thinking about if you are very fit and strong (and can call on one, if not two, equally fit and strong helpers) and if you have a suitably robust tree nearby to which you can anchor the winch. Obviously, if you anchor the winch to a tree that isn't strong, you're likely to pull it out of the ground rather than the one that has to go! Otherwise, call in a contractor.

You can hire a winch at the local hire shop, although do make sure that you check it very carefully before you take it home. Make sure that the cable isn't kinked or frayed at all, or, if it has a chain, that none of the links are rusted. Check, too, that all the fittings are in good condition.

Before you attach the winch to the anchor tree you need to protect the trunk from damage with something thick like a couple of layers of old carpet. Attach the winch's strap to the tree as low down as you possibly can, and attach the other end of the cable or chain to the plant you're going to pull out, as high up as is feasible. When it is securely fastened, begin to winch. Once the cable or chain is tight, it might take two of you to increase the strain, unless of course one of you is Arnold Schwarzenegger. As the shrub begins to move, get the third person to hack away at the roots with an axe or a mattock, and eventually you'll pull it clear. It usually works like a charm, but just very occasionally, it doesn't. You might find that although you've got the cable as tight as you can possibly get it, and the shrub is bending like crazy, it's just not coming out. In that case, you will need a third pair of hands, just to help you pull the ratchet back the one notch necessary to finish the job.

Hedge or fence?

Once you've pulled the old hedge out, you'll have to decide whether to plant another hedge, or to put up a fence. If the reason for pulling out an old privet hedge was that it was infected with honey fungus, you'll either have to choose something resistant to it, like yew, or put up a fence.

If there is nothing to restrict your choice, both methods have their advantages and disadvantages. On the plus side, fences are virtually instant – it shouldn't take you more than a couple of weekends at most to put up a fence round an average-sized garden. They also take up very little growing space, even if you cover them with climbers, which is an important consideration in a small garden. On the minus side, fences are relatively expensive, they don't look very attractive (although the rather garish bright ginger colour of most new fencing can be disguised by painting it with a darker wood stain), they don't last for ever and they are no use as a windbreak. When wind meets a solid barrier like a fence, it tends to go up over it and down the other side, with, if anything, increased speed. Hedges, on the other hand, make much better windbreaks because they filter the wind rather than trying to stop it. They also look more attractive than fences, either in their own right or as a living background to borders, and while a fence gradually deteriorates over the years, a hedge looks better and while it doesn't have to grow taller or wider than you want it to be, it will get denser and more effective as a screen.

The down side with hedges is that they are slow to establish – even the fastest-growing plants will take three or four years to look anything very much. They take up a lot of room and suck much of the nutrient and moisture out of the soil on either side of them. They also need looking after. Young plants need to be kept well-fed, well-watered and free of weeds, and when they are established they will need clipping to keep their dimensions in check, and feeding to prevent the kind of problems that caused you to get rid of the old hedge!

Choosing a new hedge

If you've decided to plant a new hedge, then the first decision is what kind of hedge do you want. Do you want a formal hedge, one that is clipped regularly to form a green wall, or do you want an informal one, consisting of flowering shrubs, which are left to grow more or less as nature intended? Again it's swings and roundabouts. Formal hedges need more looking after, but informal ones take up much more space. Formal hedges look good all year round. Some informal ones, like forsythia, look spectacular when they're in flower, but less interesting when they're not. In the end, it's down to personal taste and which fits in better with the kind of garden that you want.

Formal hedges

Conifers

The Lawson cypress (*Chamaecyparis lawsoniana*) has many different varieties, some of which are excellent for hedging. *C.l.* 'Green Hedger' is a good rich green colour, while *C.l.* 'Pottenii' is a lovely subtle sea green. *C.l.* 'Allumii' has blue-grey foliage, and while 'Pembury Blue' is an even more striking colour, it doesn't form as dense a hedge as 'Allumii'. If you want a golden hedge, *C.l.* 'Lanei' is the best Lawson cypress, though if it's going to form a background for other plants, like any golden foliage, it's probably a bit too bright. Plant 90 cm (3 ft) apart.

Leyland cypress (× *Cupressocyparis leylandii*) is the fastest-growing conifer of all, which is why so many people planted it as a hedge from the sixties onwards. The problem with it is that, unchecked, it can reach 15 m (50 ft) in fifteen years. While a leylandii hedge that has been regularly trimmed can look very good, as a general rule in a small garden it's best avoided. It's also less attractive than most of the other hedging conifers, although it has to be said it's a good bit cheaper. There is a gold variety, × *C.l.* 'Castlewellan Gold', which is less vigorous – marginally! If you really must have a leylandii hedge, then be prepared to prune the top and the sides regularly to keep it within bounds. Plant 90 cm (3 ft) apart.

Yew (*Taxus baccata*) is probably the best conifer for hedging you can have. Its reputation – for belonging in stately homes or churchyards, for being sombre, or for being very slow – has led to it being less widely planted than it might otherwise be. It's not that much slower than other evergreens, it is quite happy growing in shade, and if for some reason you do neglect its pruning in later life, you can always get it back into shape by cutting back hard into old wood. It's true it is a bit dark, but you can brighten it up with colourful planting in front of it. Plant 60 cm (2 ft) apart.

A well-trimmed conifer hedge is an asset to any garden. This is Thuja plicata.

Western red cedar (*Thuja plicata*), particularly the variety 'Atrovirens' is an excellent hedging plant with its bright green, shiny foliage which catches the light as it moves. *T.p.* 'Fastigiata' is a very slender, upright variety which needs very little clipping, although the foliage isn't quite as bright. There's another excellent thuja for hedging, *T. occidentalis* 'Smaragd' which means 'emerald' and which describes the colour of its foliage. Thujas have an advantage over almost all other conifers in that, if the outer leaves are scorched by the frost or cold winds, and turn brown, they will produce new growth from the inside. Plant 90 cm (3 ft) apart.

Although you sometimes see conifers offered very cheaply by mail order in the papers, it is all too often a false economy. They're almost always bare-rooted plants, often of very poor quality. A *Gardening from Which?* survey a couple of years ago found the failure rate for these plants was between 43 and 77 per cent. Container-grown plants cost more, but they're much more reliable.

Other formal hedges

Box (*Buxus sempervirens*), with its small, leathery evergreen leaves, makes a good formal hedge, especially if you're ambitious enough to have a bit of topiary in mind. There are variegated forms, like the gold and green

B.s. 'Aurea Maculata' (or 'Aureovariegata') or the cream and green 'Elegantissima'. Plant 30 cm (1 ft) apart.

If you want to plant low edging hedges within the garden, in a herb garden, say, then you want the dwarf variety *B.s.* 'Suffruticosa'. Plant 15 cm (6 in) apart.

Beech (Fagus sylvatica) isn't evergreen, but it keeps its dead leaves all through the winter, giving you a very attractive bright russet-brown screen until the new growth pushes its way through in spring. If you buy bare-rooted plants in the autumn it will be a lot cheaper than most good conifers – certainly a factor if you've got a lot of hedging to plant. There is a purple variety of beech, and you sometimes see the two colours planted alternately. It's an idea if the hedge is to stand in splendid isolation, but if it's to be a background for other plants, the overall effect is messy.

The one snag with beech is that it needs a light, well-drained soil if it is to thrive. If you've got a heavy clay soil, you could plant hornbeam (*Carpinus betulus*) instead. It's very similar in many ways. It, too, keeps its dead leaves throughout the winter, although it has to be said they're not quite as bright or attractive as those of the beech. Plant 60 cm (2 ft) apart.

Privet (*Ligustrum ovalifolium*) is one of the most common hedging plants there is, and yet for the kind of small garden in which you usually see it, it's really not suitable. For one thing, it is incredibly greedy, and sucks all the nutrients and moisture out of the soil for a good metre either side of it. For another, it is very susceptible to honey fungus. and for a relatively short run of hedge, there are other much more attractive alternatives. Plant 30 cm (1 ft) apart.

This yellow-flowered Potentilla fruticosa *makes a pretty, informal hedge, while the clipped conifer balls on each side of the gate make a very attractive formal contrast.*

Shrubby honeysuckle (*Lonicera nitida*) has tiny, oval evergreen leaves and it responds well to clipping. Look for a form sometimes sold as 'Yunnan', 'Yunnanensis' or even 'Fertilis' which is stronger growing and more upright than the one most commonly sold. The golden form, 'Baggesen's Gold', is more attractive than the plain green. Plant 30 cm (1 ft) apart.

Cherry laurel (*Prunus laurocerasus* 'Rotundifolia') has large, wonderfully glossy evergreen leaves and makes a very handsome hedge. The only two snags with it are that, like all large-leafed hedges, it needs pruning with secateurs rather than with shears, since the cut edges of the leaves turn brown and look very ugly, and the other is that it's quite expensive. Plant 90 cm (3 ft) apart.

Informal hedges

Barberry (*Berberis*), in some of its evergreen forms, like *B. darwinii* and *B.* × *stenophylla*, makes excellent barriers. The former has prickly, shiny dark green leaves and orange flowers in April and May, while the latter has graceful arching branches producing yellow-orange flowers at the same time. Look out for a new variety, *B.* × *s.* 'Cream Showers', which has, as the name suggests, masses of creamy-white flowers. There is another new one, too, called 'Claret Cascade', but the combination of wine-red foliage and orange flowers is not for the faint-hearted! For a hedge that will keep anything on two legs, four legs or even tank tracks at bay, try *B. julianae*. It forms an impenetrable thorny thicket but, of course, it's also the very devil to prune. Plant 60 to 90 cm (2 to 3 ft) apart.

Escallonia makes an excellent informal semi-evergreen or even evergreen hedge in a seaside garden. It flowers from May to July, with a second crop of red, pink, or white flowers sometimes in late summer. Any variety with 'Donard' in its name is worth growing. The Slieve Donard nursery in Northern Ireland, where they were raised, is the country's leading escallonia specialist. Plant 75 cm (2.5 ft) apart.

Forsythia with its bright yellow flowers certainly makes for one of the most startling hedges you could wish to see for a few weeks in early spring, but after it's finished flowering its leaves are nothing to write home about and of course it loses them in winter. For those reasons, it's not a particularly good choice. You sometimes see it grown as a mixed informal hedge, along with the bright pink flowering currant (*Ribes sanguineum*) – a combination that can either be described as 'cheerful' or 'toe-curling', depending on your taste – or lack of it! Plant 60 cm (2 ft) apart.

Firethorn (*Pyracantha*) makes an excellent informal hedge because it has evergreen leaves, white flowers in late spring and early summer and red, orange or yellow berries in the autumn. Its long thorns also make it a pretty effective barrier. *P. rogersiana*, with red berries, is a good choice, as is 'Orange Glow' and the yellow-berried 'Soleil d'Or'. Plant 60 cm (2 ft) apart.

Roses (*Rosa rugosa*) are often advertised in the papers as providing the miracle hedge, and the pictures of it suggest it forms a neat barrier, smothered in flowers for months on end. The reality is that its flowers are rather sparse, it's an untidy grower, it loses its leaves in winter and you're left with ugly, spiny brown stems from October to March. Plant 45 to 60 cm (18 in to 2 ft) apart.

Laurustinus (*Viburnum tinus*) makes an excellent evergreen hedge in shade with its large heads of pink buds which open into white flowers from November to March. The variety 'Eve Price' is particularly attractive. A viburnum hedge can look a little dull in summer, but can soon be brightened up either with a clematis grown over it (see p. 92) or by colourful planting in front of it. Plant 90 cm (3 ft) apart.

Planting a new hedge

Since you want your new hedge to get away to a good start and you hope that it will last several lifetimes, you must prepare the soil really well. Clear away as much of the old hedge's remaining roots as you can, and, of course, all traces of weeds.

Fix a garden line as a guide, and dig out a trench, one spade's depth deep and 90 cm (3 ft) wide, throwing the soil to one side. With a fork, break up the subsoil in the bottom of the trench and then put in a good deep layer of organic matter – garden compost if you've got it, composted straw if you haven't. Put back half the soil into the trench and sprinkle it with an organic fertiliser like pelleted chicken manure (if you use bonemeal, do make sure that you always wear gloves when handling it) or Growmore if you're not gardening organically – a handful for every 90 cm (3 ft) of trench. Don't forget, the soil in which the old hedge grew will be virtually exhausted so it needs all the help it can get. Then spread another layer of organic matter along the trench, replace the rest of the soil, and finally spread some more organic matter on top. Obviously, the trench will now be higher than the surrounding soil, so you'll need to leave it to settle for a few weeks.

You can plant container-grown hedging plants at any time of year, assuming the ground isn't waterlogged or frozen, but autumn is best. For one thing, the soil will still be warm which will help the young plants to get established, ready to take off in spring and, for another, although you'll still need to make sure they never go short of water, you'll get more help from the elements than you would in summer. Planting a beech or hornbeam, quickthorn or, if you must, a privet hedge in autumn also means you can buy either bare-rooted or root-wrapped plants which are quite a bit cheaper than the container-grown ones. We don't recommend buying bare-rooted conifers for the reasons we gave earlier (see p. 134). There is really no merit in buying large, more expensive plants for hedging. They're slow to get established, and they'll probably need staking. Small, young cheaper ones will get established more quickly, and will soon catch up and even overtake the larger ones. They will make lots of bushy growth low down, which is exactly what you need from a hedge and they won't need staking.

Once you're ready to plant your hedge, sprinkle some bonemeal on to the surface of the soil – a couple of handfuls for each metre – and fix a garden line straight down the middle of the trench. If you're planting container-grown plants, give them all a thorough watering and then place them at the right distance apart along the line, so that you can make any minor adjustments to the spacing before you start planting.

Dig a hole just larger than the container, and check before you plant that the soil will be at the same level on the plant's stems as was the compost in the pot.

When you take the plants – conifers particularly – out of their pots, you may well find that the roots have started to grow in a circle. If you just plant them as they are, the roots will carry on growing that way, and you may find, in a few years' time, that a gale will topple them like ninepins because they have no real anchorage in the soil. So, before you plant, gently tease out the roots.

The Scotch flame flower (Tropaeolum speciosum) *looks stunning against a dark yew hedge. It's quite fussy about where it grows, but it is so spectacular that it's always worth a try.*

If you're planting bare-rooted plants, put the spade into the soft soil of the trench at right angles to you and twist it through 90°. That will make a big enough hole to take the root system. As you go to put each plant in the soil, give it a quick, downward flick with your wrist, to make sure the roots aren't all bunched up. Make sure the plant is at the same level at which it was growing in the nursery, remove the spade, and then firm the plant gently with your heel.

If you've planted privet or shrubby honeysuckle then you should cut it hard back right away – to within 5 cm (2 in) of the ground. It's very hard to see your already very small hedge plants decimated in this way, but such brutal treatment will give you a much bushier, denser hedge with leaves right down to the ground.

Windbreaks

If you've planted a hedge as a windbreak, particularly a conifer hedge, you'll need to give it some protection in its early years. Strong winds can dehydrate the foliage of young conifers, turning it brown, and although thujas will produce new growth from the inside if this happens, other conifers won't, so your hedge will look unsightly. A screen of special windbreak plastic nailed to stout posts on the windward side of the hedge will give it the best protection until it is well enough established to counteract the drying effects of the wind. Admittedly, these screens are not a pretty sight, but if you don't want to lose your new hedge, you really have no option and, besides, it will only be there for one winter.

Looking after your new hedge

It is absolutely vital that new hedges don't go short of water. Check the soil round them regularly and if we do have another hot, dry summer, then, while you can still use the hose, spray over the foliage whenever you water the plants. Keep the plants free of weeds, and give them a good feed each year in spring. If you've planted the hedge in autumn, you'll need to check in the spring that the frost hasn't loosened the plants. If it has, just firm them in again with your heel.

Pruning depends on which hedge you've planted. Beech and hornbeam are best left alone for a couple of seasons. Then you can trim the sides lightly, but don't trim the top until it's reached the height you want.

As for conifers, opinions vary. Some people say you should cut the main shoots back by up to a half the season after planting, otherwise you'll get an open hedge that's easily damaged by snow. Our view is that you should start trimming back the sides lightly in the second season, otherwise the inside of the plant will go bare and since most conifers won't produce new growth from old wood you'll be stuck with it. You shouldn't cut the main shoots back until they have reached the required height. If you do, the main shoots will fork and that will result in a gappy, open hedge. The one exception is yew. If you want to produce a superb, dense hedge for which your grandchildren will bless you, cut back a third of the previous year's growth each August. You'll still have a pretty marvellous hedge if you only give it a very light trim instead.

Laurel hedges are best given a light trim with secateurs the spring after planting, to encourage bushy growth.

Don't forget, the long-term aim in pruning any formal hedge is to form a wedge-shape – broader at the base than at the top.

Once it's reached the required height, your hedge should only need clipping once a year in August or, in the case of very fast-growing hedges like leylandii, in May as well.

You should prune informal flowering hedges with secateurs after they've flowered, cutting out the older shoots which have borne flowers. (For the treatment of particular shrubs, see the section on pruning on p. 75.)

Put all your prunings through a shredder, and compost them for a few months before you use them in the garden (see p. 36). If you don't have a shredder, or access to one, then either cart them away to the local dump, or sweet-talk the dustmen into taking them away for you. Don't burn them.

Front gardens

Although the most commonly grown front garden hedge is privet, it's really not suitable (see p. 135) and something like shrubby honeysuckle, box, lavender or an informal flowering hedge would be a much better bet. Apart from those already mentioned, you could try a mixture of shrubs – evergreens and deciduous kinds – making more a narrow border than an actual hedge.

Fences

Repairing a fence

You may have inherited a fence that is basically sound but has one or two posts that have rotted below ground level, so that the fence leans here and there. Provided the other posts are sound (scrape away the soil from around each one and stick a bradawl or small screwdriver blade into the wood – if it goes in easily, the post is beginning to rot), the easiest way to repair them is with concrete spurs, called 'godfathers', bolted to the sound, upper part of the post.

First of all, remove any gravel boards – the piece of wood tacked on to the bottom of the fence – and support the fencing panels either side of the post with bricks. Then saw through the post just above ground level and paint the cut surface and the lower part of the post with wood preservative (not creosote, which can harm plants).

Start digging a hole on the side where the spur is going to be fitted, and dig down to the bottom of the rotten post stump. If you're lucky, you'll find it was just held in place with hardcore and soil and so it's easy to remove. If you're not so lucky, you'll find it was concreted in place. It's important to remove all the rotten wood, so try and lever up the concrete and stump in one piece with a crowbar. If that proves impossible then break up the concrete with a sledge hammer or pick axe and remove all the pieces. Fill the hole with hardcore, rammed well down, to within about 15 cm (6 in) of the top. Prop the spur in place on top of it, close up to the post, and mark the holes for the bolts on the post through the pre-drilled holes in the spur. Take the spur away, then drill the holes right through the post. Put the spur back again, and bolt it to the post. You should use galvanised coach bolts, with the heads of the bolts on the post side, and the nuts and washers on the spur side.

Remove the supports you put under the fencing panels on either side and then check the level of the fence with a spirit level. Adjust the spur if necessary. Either put some more hardcore underneath it if it is too low, or take some away if it's too high. When the post is absolutely level, hold it steady with two braces (lengths of batten nailed to a short stake pushed into the ground at one end, and nailed temporarily to the fence post at the other), and fill the hole with concrete. Try to slope the surface of the concrete away from the post to encourage water to run off.

If you need to replace a whole post, then put supports under the fence panels on either side of it and brace them before you remove the screws or nails that are holding them to the post. Remove the rotten post, either by levering it out with another post or, if you have to, by digging it out. To avoid creating a similar problem for yourself, or your heirs in future, use a Metpost or Erectapost when you put the new post in. You can buy these posts with a long metal spike that you simply hammer into the ground using a special 'dolly', and so you don't have to bother with digging holes and mixing up concrete at all. But, as in this instance, if the hole is already there, you might as well use it. Besides, if you filled the hole with soil, and then drove the spike in, it wouldn't be as solid in the ground and as stable as it ought to be.

The new post you buy needn't be as long as the old one – 20 cm (8 in) longer than the finished height of the fence (the height of the panel, plus 5 cm (2 in) at the top and 15 cm (6 in) at the bottom) should be enough. Fill the hole in with hardcore to about 30 cm (1 ft) from the top. Fix the new post in the socket before you put it into the hole. Check that it's at the right level by laying a plank on top of the new post and its neighbour, and then using the spirit level. Do the same with the neighbouring post on the other side. It's easy to tell if it's upright by checking the alignment of the two fencing panels that will be fixed to it. If they run parallel with it all the way down, then it's upright. Fill the hole with cement, and brace the post in position. Leave the braces in place for 24 hours at least. When you re-attach the panels to the post, use special metal brackets that you screw in place. It'll make life much easier if you ever need to remove a panel again, and you won't run the risk of splitting the panels as you might with nails.

Broken arris rails

The arris rail is the piece of wood running horizontally along the back of vertically boarded fence panels. If you are responsible for the fence, then the arris rail should be on your side. If it is broken, and the panel is otherwise sound, then you can repair it with special metal brackets, available from DIY shops.

Broken fencing panels

If you've got one or two panels that have seen better days, while the rest of the fence looks pretty sound, it's worth taking them out and replacing them. If more than that look as though they're on their way out, or soon will be, then you're better off replacing the whole lot. Look for a panel in the same style, whether it's weave or closeboard or lapped. Of course, you won't be able to match the colour exactly. Your existing fence will be weathered and the new panels will be that aggressive bright orange so beloved of fence makers. It will eventually weather too, of course, but if you can't stand it sticking out like a sore thumb for a season or two, then you can paint all the panels with a wood preservative or wood stain in a darker colour. Incidentally, don't use creosote. It gives off fumes that can kill plants and many of the newer preservatives, which are plant-friendly, do the job just as well.

Remove the old panel from the posts at either end – not an easy task, admittedly, as you'll have to break, or cut, it out – and prop up the new one in its place, using bricks and slivers of timber to get it exactly the same height as the rest of the panels. Fix it to the posts with the special metal brackets that you screw on.

Replacing a fence

When it comes to choosing a replacement for the old fence, there are a whole range of options to choose from. Certainly, the simplest way to put up a new fence is to use ready-made panels which come in a variety of styles – weave, lap (both horizontal and vertical), close boarded, and so on. They vary in price, too, and you should always go for the best you can afford.

Cheap panels won't last as long and so end up being more expensive in the long run.

If a boundary fence is to provide you with some privacy, it needs to be about 2 m (6 ft 6 in) high. In fact you can't put up a wall or a fence higher than 2 m in your back garden without applying for planning permission, which is why you can't get standard fencing panels more than 1.8 m (6 ft) high. In a very small garden, though, that could feel rather claustrophobic, so it might be better to choose panels 1.5 m (5 ft) high and top them with 30 cm (1 ft) of trellis. That way you've still got privacy, particularly if you train climbers up the fence and through the trellis, but you haven't got a solid wooden barrier at eye level.

If you want to create barriers within the garden, then heavy-duty, ornamental trellis panels are well worth thinking about. They achieve the desired effect of dividing up the space, without being too heavy or oppressive and making the garden look small.

There are a number of specialist firms, making a whole range of designs, although they tend to be very expensive. In our city back yard we only needed a small amount of trellis so it was worth spending the money and buying more expensive, architectural panels. But many garden centres and DIY stores stock a range of basic styles – panels of square trellis with curved tops or domed tops, diagonal and herringbone trellis and so on – which can do the job very well as the screen we put up in our over-mature garden demonstrates clearly.

As well as providing support for climbers, they can look very attractive in their own right. In an informal garden, you could just leave the trellis the colour it is, or stain it another natural colour – a wood shade, or green as we did in our over-mature garden. In a more formal setting, you could make a real feature of it and paint it with a coloured wood stain – subtle colours like sage green for instance, or the fashionable duck-egg blue that Monet used in his garden at Giverny or something brasher like bright blue, or red.

The best way of putting up a fence is to use Metposts or Erectaposts, the metal brackets mentioned earlier (see p. 141), concreted into the ground.

It's highly likely that the old fence panels were the standard 6-foot width so all the holes for the posts will have already been dug. Even so, you should still abide by the cardinal rule for putting up fences – fit post, then panel, then post, then panel, and so on. If you put all the posts in first, you've only got to be slightly out with one of them and you're in serious trouble.

Bolt the metal fitting to the post, then fill the first hole with hardcore to within 30 cm (1 ft) of the top. Put the post into the hole and check that it is at the right height – 2 m (6 ft 6 in) above the ground which will allow for the height of the panel (or panel plus trellis), plus 5 cm (2 in) at the top to make it look neat when it's finished, and 15 cm (6 in) at the bottom to allow for a gravel board to be fitted. (This stops the bottom of the fence panel rotting from being in contact with the soil and if it eventually rots itself, then it's much easier and cheaper to replace than the panel.)

This post will dictate the height of the whole fence so it's important to get it right. Once it is, then use a spirit level to check that it's upright and then concrete it into place. Then fit the first panel to it with special metal brackets, supporting the free end of it with bricks and wedges of wood to make sure it's absolutely level. Then put the second post into its hole, and check the height. It's very simple to do if you cut a small piece of wood that is the same length as the distance between the top of the panel and the top of the first post and use that each time. When the second post is at the right height, fix the panel to it, and then concrete it in. Check all the levels again, and then brace the panel either with a timber batten each side or with a spare fence post with a nail hammered halfway into it at one end to hook over the top of the panel. Leave the support in place for 24 hours. Carry on like this until the end of the run. You might just find that the last panel and post fit the space exactly, but then pigs might also fly. It's actually not that difficult to cut a panel to fit.

First of all, measure the space to be filled carefully, and mark it exactly on the panel. Then lever off the two struts at one end of the panel – a claw hammer and a big screwdriver should do the trick. Place one strut on the panel, with its outside edge on the mark you made earlier, and nail it in place. Turn the panel over, mark the exact size on that side too, and do the same with the other strut. If you have to remove a large part of the panel, you'll need to move the centre strut too. Then saw off the excess, and fit the reduced-sized panel in place.

If you are putting trellis on top of your fence, fix it directly to the fence posts, making sure it just clears the top of the panels and that it is parallel with them. The last job is to nail the caps, or, if you want something fancier, caps and finials (wooden balls) on to the tops of the posts.

If you really are working on a tight budget, and it's not possible to replace the old fences with new wooden fences right away, you might think about a cheaper chain link fence as a temporary measure for a few years. But think again. They don't provide any privacy nor are they very attractive, although admittedly you can solve both problems by planting a screen of evergreen shrubs in front of them. You might think you could compromise by putting up permanent posts, fixing chain-link fencing to them for now, and then replacing them with wooden panels when you can afford to. But since fences should always be erected post–panel–post–panel and so on, if you did put all the posts in first, you would run the risk of finding the fencing panels won't fit exactly when you come to replace the wire, which will create major problems. And once the plants in your border are getting established, you're going to be very reluctant to risk damaging them, which you're almost bound to do when you're replacing the chain link with wooden fences. So have a look at the budget again, and see whether, by smiling nicely at the bank manager, you might just be able to afford to do the job properly first time round.

Brightening up the fence

Once you've repaired or replaced the fence, the best thing you can do is get climbers growing up it as quickly as possible. There are climbers and wall shrubs that will thrive in every situation – sunny, part shade, even deep shade – and in every type of soil. For all practical purposes, they fall into three main types – self-clingers, like ivy, which don't need any support, twiners, like clematis which need something around which to twine themselves or their leaf stalks, and wall shrubs, like climbing roses, which need supporting totally. In the list of plants that follows, they're marked C, T or W accordingly.

The self-clingers may need a bit of help to get started. Ivy, for instance, only produces roots that cling on new growth, so when you plant it, none of the growth it has already made will attach itself to the fence. The simplest thing to do is leave in place the cane up which the plant was growing in the pot, and point it at the fence. The ivy will do the rest.

Twiners seem some kind of framework up which to climb. You could nail thin plastic trellis on to the fence, but it doesn't look very good and it's expensive. Cheaper, and almost invisible, is a framework of wires, stretched horizontally at 30-cm (1-ft) intervals along the length of the fence, and held tightly in place by a staple nailed into each post, with thinner vertical wires woven through them also at 30-cm (1-ft) intervals. Once the plants are in, and you've woven the growths around the lower wires, they should be able to look after themselves, although if you do see any growths waving free, tuck them round a wire. Alternatively, you could use a large piece of chicken wire, nailed to the fence top and bottom.

You can use the same system for wall shrubs, except you'll always need to tie the stems to the wire framework as they grow.

Climbers and wall plants for shade

Clematis, which like their heads in the sun and their roots in the shade, can be suitable for shady walls or fences, although the majority do prefer a sunnier situation. They also do best in a limey soil, although they will grow well enough in a neutral or slightly acid soil.

Good large-flowered varieties to look for include the widely available 'Nelly Moser' whose pale pink-mauve petals are striped with a deeper pink, the mauve-pink, free-flowering 'Comtesse de Bouchaud' (which both actually prefer some shade since bright sun fades the colour of their flowers), the pure-white 'Marie Boisselot' and the lavender blue 'Mrs Cholmondeley'.

A plain fence is almost hidden by two late-summer flowering Clematis viticella – *'Royal Velours' and 'Etoile Violette'.*

The fiery autumn colour of Virginia creeper is spectacular – a real consolation for the onset of winter.

Small-flowered varieties also grow well in shade. Avoid the rampant *Clematis montana* unless you have masses of space, but varieties of *C. alpina*, for instance, which have nodding blue and white flowers in spring, are marvellous growing through evergreen shrubs, like firethorn (*Pyracantha*). The late-flowering *C. viticellas*, with small flowers in wine-red, purple or white are also good for growing through other shrubs. Most varieties are either pruned back hard in winter to encourage better flowering, or, in the case of *C. alpina*, are simply pruned to keep them within their allotted space.
Flowering: March to October (depending on the variety). *Height and spread*: 3 to 5 m (10 to 16 ft) T.

Climbing hydrangea (*Hydrangea petiolaris*) is a marvellous climber for all soils, and for shade. It has masses of bright, fresh green leaves in spring, and large flat heads of white flowers in early summer, which turn brown in autumn and look good on the bare stems in winter.
Approx. height and spread after 5 years: 1.5 × 2m (5 × 6 ft). *After 10 years*: 3 × 4 m+ (10 × 16 ft+) C.

Ivy (*Hedera*) Ivy is the best evergreen climber for shade and tolerates all kinds of soil. One of the variegated kinds, like the small-leaved, bright gold and green 'Goldheart', or the much larger-leaved *H. colchica* 'Paddy's Pride', really would brighten up a dark corner. If you want a plain green, as a background for variegated shrubs, perhaps, then the glossy dark green *H. helix* 'Hibernica' is ideal.
Approx. height/spread after 5 years: 4 m (13 ft). *After 10 years*: 5 m (16 ft) C.

Honeysuckle (*Lonicera*) Honeysuckles usually prefer sun (although, like clematis, they like their roots in moist shade), but a few varieties will thrive

in shade. *L. americana* has very sweetly scented flowers which open white and slowly fade to yellow, flushed with pink. The gold-netted Japanese honeysuckle, *L. japonica* 'Aureoreticulata', is not as vigorous as *L. americana*, but has attractive semi-evergreen foliage, as well as sweetly scented small yellow flowers in summer.
Flowering: June to September. *Height and spread*: 3.5 × 8m (14 × 32ft) T.

Roses Roses prefer a sunny situation to do well, but there are several ramblers and climbers that will do well on shady walls, provided the soil is moist enough. Look for 'Morning Jewel' with bright pink flowers, the pearly, blush-white 'New Dawn', 'Pink Perpetue' with carmine-pink flowers, the yellow-flowered 'Golden Showers' and the red 'Danse du Feu', all of which go on flowering throughout the summer.
Flowering: June to October. *Height and spread*: 2.4 × 1.8 m (8 × 6ft) W.

Virginia creeper (*Parthenocissus*) All varieties have superb autumn colour, but look for *P. henryana*, the leaves of which are a beautiful dark, velvety green, deeply veined with silver and pink in summer. It's not as vigorous as some of the other Virginia creepers, but quite vigorous enough to cover a garden wall or fence in a couple of years.
Approx. height and spread after 5 years: 2.5 × 1.5 m (8 × 5 ft). *After 10 years*: 5 × 3 m (16 × 10 ft) C.

Good climbers and wall shrubs for sun

Actinidia kolomikta This is a superb foliage plant, with large, heart-shaped leaves that start out green but quickly assume bold splashes of cream and pink on the lower portion.
Approx. height and spread: 3 × 4 m (9× 12 ft) T.

Trumpet vine (*Campsis radicans*) The trumpet vine needs a well-protected sunny wall to do well, but its dramatic, large orange-red trumpet flowers, produced from August to October, make it worth taking the chance. It has also attractive, lush green foliage, not unlike that of wisteria.
Approx. height and spread: 4.5 × 6 m (14 × 18 ft) C.

Clematis There are so many different varieties that like their heads in the sun and their roots in shade that it's possible to have one in flower practically the whole year round. In winter, there's the evergreen fern-leafed clematis (*C. balearica*) with creamy-white bell-shaped flowers. In spring, there is *C. alpina* with blue and white or pink nodding flowers and in late spring/early summer, *C. macropetala*, similar to *C. alpina* although its pink, blue or white flowers are semi-double and larger. Throughout the summer there are any number of large-flowered hybrids in shades of pink, mauve, lavender blue, purple and wine red, while in late summer there are the *C. viticellas*, with small single or double white, wine-red or rich purple flowers, or *C. orientalis*, the orange peel clematis, which has grey-green foliage, and nodding yellow cup-shaped flowers in September and October, which are followed by fluffy silvery seedheads lasting into the winter.

Since many types of clematis are best pruned back each year, it's most useful to know the amount of growth they'll make in one season. *Large-flowered hybrids*: 2 to 5 m (6 to 16 ft). *Small-flowered species*: 3 to 7 m (10 to 23 ft) T.

Moroccan broom (*Cytisus battandieri*) This fast-growing shrub has attractive large silvery leaves, and plumes of bright yellow flowers which smell of sweet, ripe pineapple. It dislikes both very acid and very alkaline soils but will grow happily in ordinary and even poor, dry soils.
Approx. height and spread after 5 years: 45. × 2 m (14 × 6 ft). *After 10 years*: 6.5 × 4 m (25 × 12 ft) W.

Chilean glory flower (*Eccremocarpus scaber*) This climber, which produces masses of orange-red tubular flowers from August to October, is only completely hardy in the mildest areas of the country. Everywhere else, it will get cut down to the ground by the first hard frost, but don't despair – pile some strawy manure or composted straw over the roots to protect them through the winter and, in all but the hardest winters, it will shoot again in spring. Alternatively, if you collect seed in the autumn, it's very easy to raise new plants that way in the spring.
Approx. height and spread (in one season): 3 m+ (10 ft+) T.

Jasmine (*Jasminum officinale*) Its small white flowers have one of the strongest, sweetest fragrancces of all, particularly in the evening, which makes it an especially good choice for a wall that gets the afternoon and evening sun. It is a particularly untidy grower, though, so you'll need to treat it with a firm hand or, better still, grow it over an arch, an arbour, or even a shed, where its untidiness won't matter. There is a pink-flowered variety, *J.o. stephanense*, and a lovely one with cream-variegated leaves, 'Argenteovariegatum', though you'd probably only find it in specialist nurseries.
Approx. height and spread: 9 m (30 ft) T.

Honeysuckle (*Lonicera*) Like clematis, most honeysuckles are happiest with their heads in the sun and their roots in the shade. For a long flowering period, plant both *L. periclymenum* 'Belgica', the 'Early Dutch' honeysuckle, which has sweetly scented, pale rose-purple and yellow flowers in early summer, and often again in early autumn, and *L.p.* 'Serotina', the Late Dutch honeysuckle, with darker red and paler yellow flowers which are produced from mid-summer to mid-autumn. For brighter flowers, though, without any scent, try *L.* × *brownii* 'Fuchsioides', which has brilliant orange-scarlet flowers in late spring and again in late summer.
Approx. height and spread: 4.5 × 6 m (15 × 20 ft) T.

Passionflower (*Passiflora caerulea*) Given a warm, sheltered spot, this will produce a succession of its large, intriguing white and purple flowers. The individual flowers are not long-lived, but so many of them are produced between June and September that it doesn't matter. In mild areas it is almost evergreen but a really hard frost will cut the growth to the ground. Protect the roots as you would the Chilean glory flower's and, after all but the coldest winters, it should produce new growth in spring.
Approx. height and spread (in mild areas): 4 × 3 m (13 × 9 ft) T.

Roses There are many climbers and ramblers to choose from, ranging from the simple, almost flat creamy-yellow flowers of 'Mermaid', to the elaborate, many-petalled, deep cerise-pink flowers of the thornless 'Zéphirine Drouhin'. Choose a repeat-flowering variety, that will flower more or less non-stop from June to October, or even later in a mild autumn, rather than one which flowers for only a few weeks in June. First-class varieties include the pinky-apricot 'Compassion', the deep rose-pink 'Aloha', the deep yellow 'Golden Showers', the white 'Climbing Iceberg', the pearly, blush pink 'New Dawn', 'Paul's Scarlet Climber' and 'Pink Perpetue', with clusters of double carmine-pink flowers. Roses make excellent hosts for clematis and you can really make the most of colour combinations – a blue clematis like 'Lasurstern' or 'Ascotiensis' would look marvellous with 'Golden Showers', while a red like 'Ville de Lyon' would make a dramatic contrast to 'Climbing Iceberg'.
Approx. height and spread: 2.5 × 4 m (8 × 12 ft) W.

Chilean potato tree (*Solanum crispum*) For a plant closely related to the common-or-garden potato, this scrambling wall shrub is very attractive, producing rounded clusters of small mauve flowers with prominent bright yellow stamens in abundance from June to October. Its long stems are sometimes killed by frosts in cold areas, but it takes a really severe winter to kill the plant altogether. Usually, it starts into growth again the following spring. It has a beautiful but even more tender relative, *S. jasminoides* 'Album', which produces clusters of pure white flowers with the same, prominent gold stamens. In a particularly sheltered spot, it's well worth the gamble.
Approx. height and spread: 5 × 5 m (16 × 16 ft) W.

Wisteria Although it is one of the loveliest of all climbing plants, with its huge pendulous trusses of violet-blue flowers in late spring and early summer, wisteria is really much too vigorous for a fence. It's much better growing against a high garden wall or a house. There is also a white variety, *Wisteria sinensis* 'Alba', while the less vigorous *W. floribunda* 'Macrobotrys' has trusses of lilac-blue flowers almost 1 m (3 ft) long!
Approx. height and spread: 20 m+ (66 ft+) (*W.* 'Macrobotrys' approx. 9 m (30 ft)) T.

Fruit

There's absolutely no reason why a strong, sunny fence should not play host to fruit trees like apples, pears, cherries, even peaches, or bushes like gooseberries, red- and white- but not black-currants. You'll need to choose trees specially trained to grow flat against walls – single-stemmed cordons, for instance, which grow at an angle of 45° to restrict the growth, espaliers which have tiers of branches growing horizontally, or fans. Although you can buy 'maiden' trees and start training them yourself from scratch, it's easier to buy two or three-year-old trees where training has been started.

Cordons should be planted about 75 cm (2 ft 6 in) apart and trained on horizontal wires attached to the fence at 60-cm (2-ft) intervals. Since the early training will have been done, all you have to do is prune the side shoots (those growing directly off the main stem) back to 7 cm (3 in) and the secondary shoots (those growing off the side shoots) back to 2.5 cm (1 in) each summer. In winter, prune back the main shoot by one third of the growth it made the previous summer. When the cordon has reached the top of the cane, prune the main shoot back to 7 cm (3 in) and the side shoots back to 2.5 cm (1 in) each summer from then on.

Espaliers should already have at least one horizontal tier when you buy them. Plant them 3 to 3.5 m (10 to 12 ft) apart. Tie those two branches to the lowest wire, and if the next tier is already part-trained on canes, with the two side branches at 45° to the main stem and the main stem itself going straight up, tie the canes to the next wire, 60 cm (2 ft) above the first. If it's not, then attach the two side branches and the main shoot to bamboo canes

This fan-trained morello cherry is ornamental as well as productive. It is best grown on a north-facing wall.

yourself and tie those to the wire in the same way. In the summer, on the lowest tier only, prune back the side shoots to 7 cm (3 in) and the secondary shoots to 2.5 cm (1 in). The following winter remove the canes from the second tier, and tie the branches down to the second wire. Remove the cane from the centre shoot and prune it back to 5 cm (2 in) above the third wire. In the spring tie two side shoots which will have formed to canes, and attach them at an angle of 45° to the third wire. Tie the main shoot to a cane and train it straight up. Cut out any other shoots that have formed above the second tier. Carry on until you have reached the height you want. When you reach it just train two side shoots horizontally and cut out the main shoot. After that, prune it every summer as you would a cordon.

Fans (peaches and nectarines)

If you buy a two- or three-year-old tree, the central shoot will already have been pruned away, and you could have four side shoots on each of the two main side branches (two above and two below) already being trained on canes. Plant them 3 to 3.5 m (10 to 12 ft) apart if you're planting more than one, and tie them on to horizontal wires 25 cm (10 in) apart. That summer choose side shoots 10 cm (4 in) apart to form the fruit-bearing spurs, remove the rest and rub out any unwanted buds. That winter cut back all the growth on the main framework branches by about half. The following summer, in order to encourage fruit production, allow each side shoot to produce four to six new leaves, then pinch out the tip. Allow it to produce one new shoot at its base and remove any other new growths. After the fruit has been picked, prune out the shoot that has borne it, and tie in the new shoot to bear fruit next year.

Fans (cherries and plums)

These are sometimes trained in a different way. Before the main central shoot has been pruned out, two side branches are trained horizontally, and in spring and summer, only new shoots growing *above* those branches are tied in to form the fan shape. Those growing below are removed. Some are now simply trained into a fan shape. (Ours is!) In the summer you should pinch out any shoots growing into or away from the wall and any that you don't need to form the fan shape. After the fruit has been picked, prune out any dead wood, and shorten by half the shoots you have pinched out.

Fruit bushes

Redcurrants, white currants and gooseberries can be grown as single cordons, growing straight up, double cordons growing in a U shape with two main stems trained 30 cm (1 ft) apart or triple cordons growing in a double U shape with three stems trained in the same way. Each bush should be planted so that its stems are 30 cm (1 ft) from its neighbour.

Front gardens

In a front garden, as a general rule, privacy is not so important, and so you need a lower fence just to keep out unwanted visitors and litter, and to mark your boundary. Besides, if you want to put up a fence, wall or even railings more than a metre high, you have to apply for planning permission. (There is no height restriction on hedges – they can be as tall as you like, although remember that a very high front hedge offers perfect cover for burglars.)

On some comparatively new housing estates, there are sometimes restrictive covenants which actually prevent you from putting up any kind of barrier in the front, so if none of your neighbours' gardens have one it's worth checking before you start.

Obviously a fence in the front garden is on show to the world at large, and, where possible, it should blend with the house. A low rustic picket fence or even a wattle fence would look fine outside a country cottage, but not so good outside a sixties house where a ranch-style fence, or even posts and chains, would look better. Posts and chains, either in metal or plastic for ease of maintenance, obviously don't give you much physical protection from wandering dogs or wind-blown litter, but they are relatively cheap and, combined with some dense planting, can be effective as a psychological barrier, marking out your territory.

As for the fence between your garden and the neighbours', you could use the same material as you've used along the front, or you could even use something like heavy duty trellis. Chain-link fencing is also a possibility, but, again, it's not very attractive so you should disguise it with plants as quickly as you can.

Walls

There's no doubt that one of the most attractive boundaries you can have is a weathered brick wall. It's the most solid boundary there is, and it offers not only the best protection but stored warmth as well so against it you can grow plants that might otherwise be too tender to survive.

If the garden has been neglected, then the chances are the wall will need work too. It may be unstable, and leaning, or even bowed in places. In that case, you'll need to get in a professional to advise and to tackle the work if major rebuilding is necessary. It may be, though, that the mortar between the bricks has crumbled and in a few places has allowed water to seep in, with the result that when it has frozen it has caused some bricks to 'spall' –

to crumble at the edges. If only a few individual bricks are affected, then you can get them out and replace them.

You'll need a brick bolster and a club hammer, plus stout gloves and safety goggles to protect your eyes from flying bits of brick and mortar. Chip away at the mortar around the damaged brick until the brick is loose, then wiggle it out. Brush inside the hole with a wire brush to remove all the debris, then spread stiff mortar on to the top, bottom and two ends of the replacement brick, slide it into place and then repoint. You may be lucky and find a few old bricks the right colour among the debris in your garden. If not, try the local demolition contractors. If you use bricks that are a completely different colour, they will stick out like sore thumbs and you may wind up having to paint the wall.

Repointing

To repoint a wall, you'll need a plugging chisel and club hammer, or, if you have an electric drill, a special masonry cutting disc, a pointing trowel, a large square piece of wood on which to mix the mortar, a hawk (a board with a handle to hold the mortar while you're working), a brush and a large sheet of polythene to catch the bits of mortar – old and new – when they fall.

It's best to work on roughly a square metre at a time. First of all, clean out the old mortar, either with the masonry disc on the electric drill or with the plugging chisel and hammer, and then brush the joints to remove any dust. Flick water over the bricks you're about to repoint to stop them absorbing moisture from the mortar and making it too dry to set properly. Mix up the mortar in the ratio 1 part lime, 1 part cement and 6 parts builders' sand. Always mix it by volume – by the bucketful ideally or, in the case of small quantities, children's seaside bucketfuls – so that the colour will always be the same. It's difficult to know how much to mix up at a time because you don't know how long the job will take you or how long the mortar will remain workable. It's probably better, although irritating, to err on the side of caution and make too little the first time so that you have to make some more, rather than make too much and find yourself rushing the job so that you can use up the excess mortar before it dries out.

Put a couple of large trowelfuls on your hawk and, starting at the top of the area you're working on, force mortar into, first, the vertical joints then the horizontal ones. Using the trowel, level the mortar roughly flush with the bricks as you go along. The simplest finish is to wait until the mortar is semi-dry and then rub along the joints with a piece of sacking until it is flush with the bricks. If you want a slightly recessed finish, find a small piece of wood with a rounded end (if all else fails, a couple of wooden lolly sticks glued together for extra strength would do the trick) and scrape it along each joint. When you've finished the area you're working on, brush it over with a soft brush to remove any excess mortar from the bricks.

Carry on until you've done the whole wall.

Painting the walls

You may find when you've finished repairing the wall that it doesn't look very good. It may be that it never looked very good in the first place – the bricks are dirty, perhaps, or stained or it's a dark back yard and the walls do little to lighten it. But before you paint it, do bear in mind that no external masonry paint, no matter how good, lasts for ever and the job will need re-doing every few years.

If you've decided that paint is the only answer, you need to think about colour. Obviously if the house walls are painted, it makes sense to use the same colour for both. White is the safest, and it certainly lightens a dark area, but it can be a bit cold and stark, so perhaps a warmer shade – cream, sandstone or magnolia or a very pale yellow or pink – might be a better bet. There is a wide range of exterior masonry paints available now, some for

A well-painted mural can be particularly effective in a tiny, shady city garden.

The 'trompe l'oeil' trellis on the shady patio adjoining our blank garden (right).

covering up fine cracks and poor surfaces, while others, based on solvents rather than water, will dry quickly even in cold, wet weather, so you can paint at any time of year.

If you have an artistic bent, or know a man who does, you can have a lot of fun with a mural in a small backyard which can be as simple or as complicated as your taste and talents allow. It could be anything from a climbing plant to a rural scene. You can also have a lot of fun with 'trompe l'oeil' effects, using specially treated outdoor mirrors on the wall, set at a very slight angle so that the reflection you get back isn't straight on. It can make the space look twice as large and if you surround the mirror with an arch and climbing plants it can suggest another garden through the archway in the wall. 'Vanishing' trellis, made to give a false perspective, can also be very effective on a brick wall, to lend distance, if not enchantment as it proved on the shady patio adjoining our blank garden. If you want to fix trellis above a brick wall – to give you a bit more privacy if it's quite low – then you'll either need to put posts into the ground at the base of the wall at 2 m (6 ft 6 in) intervals (you could use the spiked Metposts here rather than those that need concreting in, since they won't be carrying so much weight) and fix the trellis to those. Or you could use yet another kind of Metpost – those with a plate on the base that can be bolted to a hard surface – and bolt them to the top of the wall. It'll be a good bit cheaper, since you'll only have to buy very short posts, but it won't look very elegant, so the sooner you get climbing plants growing over them, the better.

Growing climbers

If you want to grow climbers on a painted wall, the best bet is to make panels of stout trellis, screw hinges on to them, and fix them to a wooden batten screwed on to the wall low down. Fix another batten to the wall just above the panel, and use metal hooks and eyes or clips to hold the panel in place. The climbers will then grow on, and through, the trellis, and when you need to repaint the wall you simply unfasten the hooks or clips at the top and swing the panel and climbers away from the wall. You could prop it up with a piece of timber, or even a heavy pair of steps while you get on with the painting.

If you want to grow climbers on an unpainted brick wall, then you can either make a wire framework (see p. 145) or use chicken wire. The only difference is that, first, you'll need to fix wooden battens to the wall, horizontally and vertically, to which the wires are attached. This lifts the wires away from the wall and not only allows twiners space to get behind them but it also allows air to circulate behind the plants and so helps prevent fungal diseases. If you're planning to grow just one climbing rose against the wall, say, then you could probably get away with knocking in a few lead-headed nails. These have a pliable flange of metal at the top which can be wrapped round the stem of a plant, or used to hold a plant tie in place.

CHAPTER 6

Trees

One of the real rewards of inheriting a mature garden is inheriting some mature trees. You can make a new garden look attractive and reasonably established with shrubs and herbaceous plants within three or four years, but trees take time. As they start to mature, they can give the garden its bones, they can help screen out not only ugly views but noise as well, and they can provide shade as well as having a vital ecological role to play.

While trees can be a real joy, the chances are, if the garden you've inherited is old and has been rather neglected, that at least some of the trees will be more of a curse than a blessing. They could be just too big now, taking up too much space, casting too much shade so that the patio is in shadow much of the day or you have large areas of the garden where not a lot will grow.

While there are some superb trees that are suitable for small gardens (see pp. 169–80), it must be said that the monkey puzzle, the weeping willow, forest trees like sycamores and oaks are not among them!

The trees may have been left unpruned too long, so that they have become overgrown and tangled, or they may have been pruned so badly that they are an ugly mess. They may also have been planted too close together so that they are growing into each other, or the larger one is taking so much of the light, nutrients and water that the smaller has become sickly and misshapen.

One of the most common problems is caused by trees growing too close to the house – and in the case of something like a fully mature weeping willow, planted in a clay soil, 'too close' could be as far as 38 m (125 ft) away!

Trees block out a lot of light, and can also be dangerous. Not only can their branches damage the structure in a storm, as the hurricanes of October 1987 and January 1990 demonstrated only too clearly, but their roots can do extensive – and expensive – damage to drains and to the foundations, particularly of houses built on clay soils.

Trees that need lots of water, willows and poplars in particular, suck so much moisture out of a clay soil – up to 100 gallons a day in the case of a mature poplar – that it shrinks, the foundations move and the visible results are large cracks in the house walls.

When it comes to decisions about your trees, though, it doesn't pay to be hasty. If you make a mistake in chopping down a tree, it could take twenty years or more to put it right! Try to visualise what your garden will look like without it, and what it may be screening.

You also need to consider the practical consequences of chopping down a tree. If you want to remove it because it's too close to the house and is causing damage, you could be doing more harm than good. If something that has been sucking huge quantities of moisture out of a clay soil and causing subsidence suddenly disappears, that moisture now remains in the soil, causing it to swell and leading to 'heave' – pressure against the structure, causing movement of the foundations and more cracks in the house walls. It seems in this situation that you're damned if you do and damned if you don't. The only answer is to reduce the size of the tree gradually, over a period of three or four years, to lessen its demand for water, giving the moisture level in the soil a chance to stabilise before finally taking the tree out.

This front garden is colourful but, already, very little light is getting in through the front windows and the weeping willow is nothing like fully grown yet. A prime example of the wrong tree in the wrong place.

Trees and the law

Before you prune so much as a twig, though, you need to know if all the trees in the area are covered by a Conservation Order or whether the individual tree has a Tree Preservation Order (TPO) on it. If so, it is an offence even to prune it, let alone chop it down without permission from the local planning authority. You could be fined a painfully large amount of money – up to £2,000 or twice the amenity value of the tree, whichever is the greater – if you don't get permission first. The person to ask is the tree officer who is usually to be found in the planning department at the local town hall.

You might think that a tree needs to be something rare and/or beauteous to behold to be given such protection, but no. Even that dreadful city weed, the sycamore, whose sole functions in life are to provide safe haven for every aphid in the district, suck every ounce of goodness and moisture out of the soil and reproduce itself so prolifically that it makes mustard-and-cress look like a slow and erratic germinator, can be accorded such status. The only types of trees that aren't covered are young trees, with trunks less than 7.5 cm (3 in) in diameter, measured at 1.5 m (4 ft 10 in) above the ground, and fruit trees being grown for fruit production, not purely for ornament. Shrubs aren't covered, either, so you can cut down a 6-m (20-ft) lilac with impunity.

A TPO or Conservation Order does *not* mean that the local authority assumes responsibility for the well-being and safety of your trees, though. If a branch comes crashing down on the neighbours' fence, or even their car, you are liable to pay for the damage. While you are allowed to do emergency work on trees – removing branches or indeed a whole tree if it's in a dangerous condition, for instance – without getting permission, it's in your own interest just to contact the planning department and let them know what you're going to do and why. Otherwise they could decide, after the event, that the work you carried out wasn't an emergency and you could be prosecuted.

Most local authorities aren't totally unreasonable, and even where trees aren't dangerous will grant permission for a limited amount of pruning, although most will want you to use a qualified tree surgeon to do the work.

DIY or call in the professionals?

While it's perfectly possible to do minor remedial pruning yourself (see p. 164), and to remove small trees, you're much better off calling in a professional for any major work on trees. Thinning the crown of a large mature tree to allow more light in, or reducing its height, is a very skilled job. Done well, it looks marvellous. Done badly, it looks dreadful and will do so for some years afterwards.

There's also the question of safety. Chain saws are very effective tools in the hands of a trained professional, but in the hands of an amateur they are potentially lethal.

If you have a lot of timber already lying in the garden that needs to be sawn up for logs or even just to be carted away, and you're prepared to put on all the safety gear necessary – the helmet, ear protectors, visor, gloves, ballistic trousers and so on – then you could hire a chain saw and the gear to do the job. A survey of tools from hire shops carried out by *Gardening from Which?* in November 1990 makes alarming reading, though. Many of the chain saws hired lacked safety features, like low-profile teeth, chain brakes, or chain catchers, in case the chain snaps, or tip guards. In some cases, untrained amateurs were given totally unsuitable, large, professional models, though in one case a shop actually refused to hire any chain saw to an investigator from *Which?* because they felt she was too inexperienced to use one safely. In other cases, no safety gear was offered with the saw.

To be honest, unless there really is a vast amount of sawing to be done, you'd be much safer doing it manually with a bow saw – and the exercise would do you good! Certainly, as an amateur, you shouldn't even *think* about climbing trees with a chain saw, or working from a ladder with one. It's much too dangerous.

You shouldn't think about working up a very tall tree, either, with any kind of saw. Professional tree surgeons not only have the skills of mountaineers, they also have all the proper harnesses and so on. But tree surgery, like any other business, has its fair share of cowboys – the sort of operators who appear on your doorstep after the gales asking if you've got any tree work to be done. Avoid them like the plague. It's not just a question of being ripped off. They can also be dangerous. Not only can they destroy trees they are meant to be pruning, they can cause a lot of damage in your own and neighbours' gardens – you'd be surprised what a mess a reasonably small branch falling from twenty feet up can make of a large greenhouse – or, worse, could cause themselves serious injury and, since they are unlikely to carry the insurance that all qualified tree surgeons carry, you will be liable as it's your tree.

It's not difficult to find a qualified tree surgeon. The tree officer in the planning department of your local authority will almost certainly have a list of those in your area or, if not, the Arboricultural Association* publishes a directory of approved consultants and contractors throughout the country and will be happy to send you a copy if you send them a large stamped addressed envelope.

Trees and neighbours

You may find that the problem tree that's casting too much shade or growing into another tree isn't actually in your garden but in your neighbours'. Assuming the tree isn't covered by a TPO and the whole area isn't covered by a Conservation Order, when of course the same rules as before would apply, the law allows you to cut back any branch overhanging your property to the boundary line. But obviously, if you start hacking at one side of a tree, not only is it going to look very ugly, but its health could suffer and it could even become unstable. It won't do much for the stability of the relationship with the neighbours either, so much better to discuss it with them, and if it's causing you more of a problem than it's causing them, offer to pay half of what it costs to sort it out.

Tree stumps

When you're thinking about having trees removed from the garden, you also need to think about what you're going to do with the stumps. (Or, of course, you might find there were already a few stumps left in the garden when you took it over.) Tree surgeons don't automatically include stump

---

* Ampfield House, Romsey, Hants SO51 9PA; Tel. 0794 68717

removal when they quote for felling a tree. It's an extra, and it can be quite a bit extra, too. You might think that you don't really need to bother about the stump, or indeed, you could get the tree surgeon to cut the tree off as close to ground level as possible, so that you don't have a stump to worry about. But either way you have problems. Visible stumps don't look very attractive, and both they and the ground-level kind will get in the way when you're replanting your border. More seriously, though, both can play host to honey fungus, which can spread vast distances under the soil and kill off other shrubs and trees in your – and your neighbours' – gardens. The best thing is to remove all tree stumps if you possibly can.

If the tree in question is relatively slender, then one easy solution is to get the tree surgeon to cut it down, leaving you with a stump about 2 m (6 ft) high. You then dig a trench around the stump, cutting through all the roots that you come across with an axe or, in the case of thinner roots, a spade. When you've cut through as many roots as you can see, ideally get someone else to stand on one side of the trunk, while you stand on the other, grasp it firmly and then rock it backwards and forwards between you as hard as you can. Eventually the remaining roots will snap and then you can lift the trunk out of the hole.

There are chemicals on sale called 'stump killers', but they literally do just that. They will kill the stump and make sure it doesn't start producing new growth. What they can't do is make it dissolve away as if by magic. Time and the natural rotting process will do that, but only very, very slowly. It could take as long as twenty years for a large hardwood stump to rot away. With bigger tree stumps, the best solution is to make sure the firm of tree surgeons you hire to remove your trees has a stump grinder. This is like a giant circular saw which squats astride the stump, reducing it to a pile of wood chippings as it bores its way 30 to 45 cm (1 ft to 1 ft 6 in) down into the ground until the stump has been demolished and only the roots remain. With most trees, this won't be a problem, but with some, like cherries, robinias, elms, white poplars, which are prone to throwing up suckers anyway, it can be. They will go on producing suckers along the length of the remaining roots, and you should treat them as you would any sucker (see p. 83). Since the tree's food supply all but vanished when the top growth was removed, the remains of the plant will soon be too weak to go on producing more growth. Alternatively, this time you could treat the suckers with glyphosate, since they are no longer attached to a tree that could be killed off in the process.

Most commercial stump grinders are actually quite large machines, attached to Land Rovers usually, so you need reasonably wide access – 1.2 to 2 m (4 to 6 ft) – to get them into your garden to do the job. If you live in a terraced house, with no rear access either, you have more of a problem. Robert Kennedy, the tree surgeon who worked on the trees in our Rugby gardens, solved the problem in one London garden by getting permission from the owners of the land on to which it backed to install a crane, and then lifted the stump grinder and Land Rover into the garden that way!

Dressed like a mountain climber, a professional tree surgeon can take down a large tree quickly and, more importantly, safely (right).

To you, from me. It's relatively easy to rock out a small tree stump, provided it's at least 1.5 to 2 m (4 to 6 ft) tall (below).

A stump grinder can quickly reduce large tree stumps to a pile of sawdust (above).

There is a very small stump grinder on the market called 'Little David', which can be transported in the boot of a car and carried through the house. It's obviously not as powerful as the larger models and can't grind down as deeply, but it's a great deal better than nothing. The more of a tree stump you can remove, the less remains for honey fungus to colonise.

Opinion differs as to whether it's worth drenching the soil around the stump with Armillatox to try to prevent honey fungus getting established. If the fungus is already in the tree, then it's a waste of time. If it isn't, then the chemical could keep it at bay for as long as it remains in the soil, but of course it will eventually wash out of the soil and then the stump is open to attack.

Using timber

Rather than just letting the tree surgeon cart away all the timber that's been felled, it's worth thinking about ways in which you might be able to use it in the garden. A long straight trunk could be used to make rough garden furniture – chairs, stools or tables – or it could be sawn up into slices to make stepping stones, either set in grass in a woodland area or in gravel. The only problems with wooden stepping stones are that they don't last forever – ten to twenty years depending on the type of tree – and that they can become slippery in winter. To prevent that, either wire-brush the surface each autumn, or wrap each piece of wood in chicken wire, making sure it's

This simple timber seat is a very good way of using up felled tree trunks or large branches and looks attractive in a woodland setting (above).

Slices of tree trunk make attractive stepping stones, though it's a good idea to wrap them in chicken wire before you sink them into the ground, so that they won't become slippery in wet weather (right).

pulled tight across the top, before you set it into the ground. It prevents the surface from ever becoming slippery and it's almost invisible. Any long, straight, slender branches 2.5 cm (1 in) or so in diameter could be used as bean poles and any shorter, twiggy growths could be used to support French beans, peas, or even sweet peas. As for the rest, it's worth asking the tree surgeon when you book him if he has a heavy-duty shredder and, if so, how much would it cost to bring it along. With one of those, small and medium-sized branches can be reduced to a pile of wood chippings in no time, and can provide you with a valuable source of mulching material in the garden for a couple of years to come. If he hasn't got one, but you have access to a small shredder, then it's worth hanging on to the smaller prunings and shredding them yourself.

Seedlings and saplings

If you are unlucky enough to have inherited a neglected garden with a sycamore, an ash or a horse chestnut tree in it, not only do you have the parents and the problems *they* bring, you will also have large quantities of their offspring to deal with, in all sizes from this year's crop of seedlings a few inches high to quite large saplings. The only answer is to remove as many as you possibly can. You can usually get the smallest ones out with a hoe, but even young plants two or three years old can have developed strong root systems and will require a fair amount of pulling out. The next size up will have to be dug out, while the largest saplings will have to be dealt with like the small trees they are. Cut them down and either rock their stumps out (see p. 161) or winch them out (see p. 131).

Pruning trees

If you have neglected small ornamental trees or old fruit trees in your garden, you can prune them yourself. In the case of ornamental trees, the object of pruning is to remove any dead or diseased wood, any branches that may be crossing since they are liable to rub against each other, damaging the bark and allowing disease to penetrate, and any branch that is causing problems – being in the way of a new fence, for example, or of a choice shrub growing under the tree. Do remember, though, that the tree needs to be balanced in shape, and removing one branch for the sort of reasons we've mentioned may mean you'll need to remove another, simply to keep the balance right. If you have a variegated ornamental tree like *Acer negundo* 'Elegans' or 'Variegatum' or a variegated holly, you might find that some of the shoots have reverted to plain green. You should cut those out, too, otherwise the whole tree will eventually revert to plain green, too, Summer is the best time to prune out dead wood, since it's very easy to distinguish it from the live wood then. It's also the logical time to prune out any growth that has reverted on variegated deciduous trees, although with evergreens it's best done in late spring. The best time to do the rest of the pruning is in early spring before the tree starts into new growth.

You'll need secateurs, a sharp pruning saw (with a thin curved blade that is ideal for manoeuvring between branches) and a pair of stout gloves. You might also need a ladder, a piece of rope and a helper.

If you're going to remove large branches, you'll need to do it in stages. First of all, throw the rope over a strong branch *above* the one to be cut, and then tie the end to the lower branch. Give the other end of the rope to your helper on the ground, standing well clear of the branch in question, and get him or her to take up the slack. There are several reasons for this. First, you're making sure the branch doesn't just fall and tear the bark on the tree, which can allow infection in, and second, you can control precisely where the branch comes down and avoid damaging plants or even fences in the process.

Start sawing the branch about 30 cm (1 ft) from the point where it joins the tree, making sure of course that the rope is on the far side of the point where you're cutting from the tree. Before you finally saw through the branch, make sure your helper is actually taking its weight. Once the branch has been severed, your helper can lower it to the ground.

To remove the final section of the branch, make a cut underneath the branch, about a quarter of the way through the branch and about 1.25 cm (½ in) from its junction with the trunk. The reason for making this cut is to prevent the weight of the stump tearing the bark on the main trunk if it should break away before you've finished sawing. Then saw through the rest of the branch from the top, again about 1.25 cm (½ in) from the junction with the trunk. The reason for not cutting off a branch flush with the trunk is that the material which will form a callus and allow the tree to heal naturally is found at the very end of the branch where it joins the trunk, so by leaving on just a bit of the branch you encourage it to heal more quickly. Don't leave it any longer than that, though, as it could well rot and die back into the tree. In the past, the conventional wisdom was that you should smooth the wound with a pruning knife to encourage it to heal, but these days there's some evidence to suggest that rough wounds callus over more quickly.

Opinions also vary as to whether or not you should use a wound-sealing paint to prevent diseases getting into the wound. Our feeling is that if you do you run the risk of trapping disease under the sealant, so you're better off leaving wounds alone. Even with plum and cherry trees which are susceptible to a disease called silver leaf that enters through open wounds, the best means of prevention is to prune in the growing season when wounds will heal quickly and not to use a sealant.

Damaged trees

You may well find some of the old trees in the garden have been damaged over the years. The trunk may have been scarred by lawnmowers, for instance, or by being tied too tightly to a stake in its youth with a tie that was never adjusted as the trunk expanded. You may also find cavities in the trunk where stumps were left after branches were removed, and eventually died back into the tree, leaving a hole. To prevent the rot spreading any further, you should cut away any damaged bark and rotting wood with a sharp pruning knife until you get back to healthy wood. To kill off any remaining disease, you can either paint the area with a fungicide, or you can char it with a blowtorch. If it is a deep cavity, you are better off filling it in, otherwise water can collect inside it and the whole rotting process can start all over again. You can use concrete, but of course it's not flexible and may well crack eventually, allowing water to penetrate. On small wounds, you could use grafting wax, while for larger ones you could make up a mixture of sawdust and bitumen, and fill the cavity with that. One school of thought says that it's better not to fill cavities at all in case you trap disease inside them. Instead, just char the inside with a blowtorch, drill a drainage hole through the bottom and put in a piece of thin plastic tubing to drain the water out through the trunk.

Fruit trees

If you have old fruit trees in the garden which are still productive then, again, pruning is really just a matter of getting rid of dead or diseased wood and any crossing branches. If they have stopped fruiting, though, or are producing only a few small apples or pears, then something more dramatic is required.

It's worth remembering that fruit trees have only a limited productive life – around forty years or so. Once they've reached that age, you really are better off taking them out and starting again. It's also worth remembering that it will take three or four years to get a badly neglected tree back into good fruiting heart, so if patience isn't one of your virtues it's probably better to start afresh. On the bright side, though, there are lots of excellent new varieties around and new developments like dwarfing rootstocks will enable you to grow favourite old varieties in much less space than before.

If a fruit tree is at or nearing the end of its useful life, then it may be worth tidying it up a bit and leaving it in the short term while you plant another tree nearby that will eventually take its place. In our blank garden, one of the previous owners had done just that – planted a Victoria plum, on a dwarfing rootstock, behind a large old apple tree which will need to come out in a few years' time. The only problem was that the old tree was beginning to take too much light from the youngster, so, as well as pruning out the dead wood, we removed a couple of branches to allow more light in.

Apples

Rejuvenating an old apple tree will take at least three years – the shock to the plant's system would be devastating if you did everything that needed doing in one go. In the first winter, remove all the dead and diseased wood, those crossing other branches and then cut out some of the over-tall branches in the centre of the tree, cutting them as close to the crotch of the tree (the point at which all the main branches join the trunk) as possible. If that's not possible, cut them back to a lower branch that is stout enough to take over from it as a main branch. You will find very vigorous shoots growing from the wounds later in the summer. They're called 'water shoots' and are useless in that they will never bear fruit, so rub them out as soon as you see them appearing.

The tree will need feeding so, if it's growing in grass, clear a circle at least 2 m (6 ft 6 in) in diameter around it, loosen the surface of the soil with a fork and sprinkle on a handful of blood, fish and bonemeal per square metre if you're gardening organically, or Growmore if you're not, in spring. Mulch the soil with some well-rotted organic matter to conserve moisture and to stop weeds growing, but make sure the compost doesn't actually touch the trunk itself.

The following winter remove some more of the main branches and some of the overcrowded secondary ones as well. What you're aiming at is an open-centred tree with its main branches spaced about 60 cm (2 ft) apart, so bear that in mind as you prune. It's worth stepping away from the tree each time you remove a branch, just to see how it's looking. Feed it again that spring.

In the third winter remove a few more of the main branches and secondary branches, and feed the tree again in the spring.

If the problem is not so much that there are too many branches, but that there are too many spurs (the short stubby growths on the side shoots that actually carry the fruit), you should thin them out gradually, removing about half of the total over four winters. Aim to wind up with the spurs about 25 cm (10 in) apart. Again, feed the tree each spring.

Pears

Pears can be treated in much the same way, although it's worth remembering that they can stand being cut back harder than apples, and that as they produce fruiting spurs more easily, they will need more thinning out.

Plums and cherries

With plums and cherries, most pruning consists of removing dead and diseased wood and overcrowded branches in the centre of the trees. The main difference is that this should be done in the summer, not while the trees are dormant, so that the wounds heal quickly and so lessen the chance of infection by silver leaf, a disease which can kill the tree. Incidentally, if you inherit a tree with rather a lot of dead wood, and the foliage when it appears has a distinctly silvery colour, then chances are the tree is already diseased. Cut off part of a dead or dying branch. If there is a purple or brown stain in the wood, then it does have silver leaf. As soon as you see the symptoms, buy some Binab T pellets containing a parasitic fungus called *Trichoderma viride** and insert them into holes 5cm (2 in) deep in the trunk. In the summer, cut back all dead and infected growth to at least 15 cm (6 in) past the point where infection is visible. As an added precaution, you can paint the wounds with Binab T powder mixed to a paste, or spray them with a diluted mixture.

Fruit bushes

Blackcurrants

If you inherit some blackcurrant bushes, the first thing you need to know is how old they are, because any branches older than four years need to be cut right out. It's relatively easy to determine the age because the bark of each year's growth is a slightly different colour, so start at the tip of the branch and count the different coloured sections. If any branches have more than four sections, cut them out at ground level, give the bush a good feed – a couple of handfuls of blood, fish and bonemeal, or Growmore – and mulch it with well-rotted compost. You can do this in the winter, or you can wait to see if there is any fruit and prune immediately after you've picked it. If every branch appears to be more than four years old, you can prune the whole bush right back to ground level, feed and mulch it as before and in three years you'll have virtually a new bush.

If you have inherited several old blackcurrant bushes, deal with them in rotation. In the first year prune one of them (A) right back to the ground, and take out about a third of the old branches on the other two (B and C). Next year, cut B right back to the ground, prune out some more old wood on C and leave A alone. In the third year, cut C right back to the ground, leave B alone and prune out the wood on A that has borne fruit.

---

* From Henry Doubleday Research Centre, Ryton-on-Dunsmore, Coventry CV8 3LG.

If you discover some really fat, round buds on your blackcurrant bushes, that wither away in the spring, then they have big bud, a disease caused by microscopic mites, which also carry another serious disease called reversion virus which causes very poor cropping. It's impossible to cure, so the only answer is to dig them up and burn them. Again, to look on the bright side, it gives you the chance to replace them with new varieties, which are certified virus-free. 'Ben More' and 'Ben Lomond' both produce heavy crops of fruit, and if space is at a premium then a new variety called 'Ben Sarek', which only grows to about 90 cm (3 ft), as opposed to 1.5 m (5 ft), would be ideal.

Redcurrants, white currants and gooseberries

Redcurrants and white currants, strangely enough, should be treated like gooseberries, not like blackcurrants. With old neglected bushes, in early spring, cut out all the dead or diseased wood and branches that cross, or are overcrowded, with the object of opening up the centre of the bush and creating a goblet shape. Then cut back the previous season's growth on the main framework branches by a third. In the summer prune back the side shoots to two buds. If the bushes have been badly neglected, feed them twice in the first year with two handfuls of blood, fish and bonemeal or Growmore, once in March and again in June.

You may find you have inherited an old strawberry bed, as we did in our large neglected garden, and that the plants look pretty healthy. Chances are, though, that they will be infected with virus disease which will mean you'll get little or no fruit, so you're better off digging them all up and starting a new strawberry patch in a different part of the garden, making sure, of course, that the new plants you buy are certified virus-free. There are lots of good varieties, but 'Honeoye', 'Bounty', the new 'Pegasus', 'Elsanta' and the perpetual-fruiting 'Aromel' are all well worth growing.

Trees to plant

If you've cut down a tree, or several trees, in your garden, then you'll almost certainly want to plant a replacement or two, not just to add to the beauty of your garden, but to do your bit for the environment. What you must do, though, is be quite sure that you're not going to create the sort of problems you inherited for the people who may buy your house in ten, twenty or thirty years' time. The way to do that is, first, to make sure you plant trees for small gardens, and leave the forest giants like oaks and weeping willows to the owners of rolling acres! Second, make sure that you plant them in the right place, which is far enough away from the house not to block out all the light after a few years, and not to do damage. Don't forget, they must be far enough away from your neighbours' houses, too, because you are responsible for any damage your trees might do to their property.

The safe planting distance for trees depends to some extent on the type of soil you have – trees planted in clay oils which can shrink cause more problems than trees planted in sandy or chalky soils that don't shrink – but primarily on the depth of your foundations. Houses built before the 1950s tend to have shallower foundations – about 0.5 m (20 in) – which are more vulnerable to damage by tree roots than those built later with foundations of 1 m (3 ft) or more.

As a rough guide, if yours is an older house with shallow foundations, a safe planting distance is the same as the ultimate height of the tree, so the pretty ornamental crab, *Malus floribunda* (*not* on a dwarfing rootstock), should be planted 10 m (33 ft) from the house. In the case of big trees with dense canopies of leaves, like willows or poplars, it's one and a half times the ultimate height, so, given that a weeping willow can reach 25 m (82 ft), you shouldn't plant one within 38 m (125 ft) of the house. Incidentally, when you're calculating the distance from the house, include any extensions that were added later – a porch, conservatory or garage, especially as they are likely to be built on shallower foundations than the house itself.

If yours is a more modern house with foundations of 1 m (3 ft 3 in), the safe planting distance is 0.75 times the ultimate height of the tree, so a *Malus floribunda* should be 7.5 m (25 ft) from the house while a willow should be planted × 1.25 its ultimate height from the house – 31 m (103 ft). If your house has very deep foundations – 1.5 m (5 ft) or so – then the safe planting distances are half its ultimate height – 5 m (16 ft) – in the case of the *Malus* and the same distance as its ultimate height – 25 m (82 ft) – for the willow.

In the list of trees suitable for small gardens that follows we have given the safe planting distance for older houses with shallower foundations (SF) and for more modern houses with deeper foundations (DF), both on clay soils. These distances do err on the side of caution, and you are very unlikely to have any problems in your lifetime with trees you plant closer to the house. But spare a thought for the new gardeners of the mid-twenty-first century!

Maples (Acer)

Paperbark maple (*Acer griseum*) A near-perfect tree for a small garden, because it has so many good qualities – attractive orange-buff foliage in spring, glorious red and scarlet autumn colour and, in winter, on wood that's at least three years old, the orange-brown bark peels away to reveal the new cinnamon-coloured bark beneath. Added to which, its ascending branches and rather open habit allow light to reach plants growing beneath it. It's also very slow-growing.

Many Japanese maples like this one, Acer palmatum *'Linearilobum', have stunning autumn foliage and are ideal trees for very small gardens (left).*

*The golden Indian bean tree (*Catalpa bignonioides *'Aurea') can be damaged by frosts or high winds, so it's best grown in a sheltered, sunny spot (right).*

Approx. height and spread after five years: 2 × 1.2 m (6 × 4 ft). *After 20 years:* 6 × 3 m (20 × 10 ft).
Safe planting distance: SF 7 to 10 m (23 to 33 ft). DF 5 to 7 m (16 to 23 ft).

***Acer negundo* 'Flamingo'** This acer has leaves which are pink when they open and then turn green and white with a pink flush which gradually fades as the leaves mature. The brightest and most attractive colouring is on new growth, so ideally the tree should be pruned every year, but since it can be quite difficult to prune something 4 to 5 m (13 to 16 ft) tall, it is certainly easier to grow as a shrub. Many nurseries supply it in both forms.
Average approx. height and spread (unpruned) after five years: 3 × 2 m (10 × 6 ft). *After 20 years:* 6 × 5 m (20 × 16 ft).
Safe planting distance: SF 7 to 10 m (23 to 33 ft). DF 5 to 7 m (16 to 23 ft).

***Acer pseudoplatanus* 'Brilliantissimum'** A very slow-growing tree with stunning spring foliage opening deep shrimp-pink, becoming paler flesh pink, then creamy-yellow, and then pale green before assuming its summer mid-green. The downside is that it's rather dull the rest of the year.
Approx. height and spread after five years: 2.5 m × 1.5 m (8 ×5 ft). *After 20 years:* 4.5 × 3.5 m (14 ft 6 in × 12 ft).
Safe planting distance: SF 3 to 5 m (10 to 16 ft). DF 3 to 5 m (10 to 16 ft).

*Birch (*Betula*)*

The native British silver birch, while very beautiful, looks best in groups and few gardens have the sort of space needed.

Himalayan birch (*Betula jacquemontii*) This tree has such dazzling white stems under its brown, peeling bark that it looks as though it's been whitewashed. It has good autumn colour, catkins in winter and its bare twiggy branches are also attractive against the sky.
Approx. height and spread after five years: 6 × 1.5 m (20 × 5 ft). *After 20 years:* 12 × 5 m (39 × 16 ft).
Safe planting distance: SF 15 to 20 m (50 to 65 ft). DF 10 to 15 m (33 to 50 ft).

Purple-leaved birch (*Betula pendula* 'Purpurea') Smaller than the rest of the family, this tree has bright purple leaves in spring, slowly fading to green throughout the summer. It has purple catkins in winter.
Approx. height and spread after five years: 4 × 1 m (13 × 3ft 3 in). *After 20 years:* 8 × 2 m (26 × 6 ft 6in).
Safe planting distance: SF 7 to 10 m (23 to 33 ft). DF 5 to 7 m (16 to 23 ft).

Golden Indian bean tree (*Catalpa bignonioides* 'Aurea') This small tree, which is eventually as wide as it is high, has the most beautiful large, golden velvety heart-shaped leaves which have a coppery tinge when they first unfurl. It needs a deep rich slightly acid soil to do really well.
Approx. height and spread after five years: 1.5 × 1.5 m (5 × 5 ft). *After 20 years:* 4 × 4 m (13 × 13 ft).
Safe planting distance: SF 5 to 7 m (16 to 23 ft). DF 3 to 5 m (10 to 16 ft).

Weeping cotoneaster (*Cotoneaster* 'Hybridus Pendulus') A truly mini semi-evergreen tree for a very small space, it has masses of small white flowers in spring followed by bunches of small red fruits in autumn and winter. Ideal for a tiny garden or a container.
Approx. height and spread after five years: 2.5 × 1.2 m (8 × 4 ft). *After 20 years:* 3 × 4 m (10 × 13 ft).
Safe planting distance: SF 2 to 3 m (6 ft 6 in to 10 ft). DF 2 to 3 m (6 ft 6 in to 10 ft).

Flowering thorn (*Crataegus oxyacantha* 'Paul's Double Scarlet' or 'Coccinea Plena') A small, round-headed tree with dark pinky-red double

flowers in late spring and early autumn and a few small red berries in the autumn. Less widely available although very attractive is the double pink-flowered variety *C. o.* 'Rosea Plena'.
Approx. height and spread after five years: 4 × 1.2 m (13 × 4 ft). *After 20 years:* 6 × 6 m (20 × 20 ft).
Safe planting distance: SF 5 to 7 m (16 to 23 ft). DF 3 to 5 m (10 to 16 ft).

Golden honey locust (*Gleditsia triacanthos* 'Sunburst') Perhaps the best golden foliage tree there is, with feathery foliage that is bright gold when it first appears. It is prone to wind damage so does best in a sheltered spot.
Approx. height and spread after five years: 3 × 1.5 m (10 × 5 ft). *After 20 years:* 7 × 5 m (23 × 16 ft).
Safe planting distance: SF 10 to 15 m (33 to 50 ft). DF 7 to 10 m (23 to 33 ft).

Golden chain tree (*Laburnum* × *watereri* 'Vossii') This beautiful tree has masses of bright golden flowers hanging down in long bunches in May and June, and its sharply ascending branches mean that you can usually grow plants underneath since they will get plenty of light. The only drawback with laburnum is that every part of it – not just the seeds – is poisonous, so it's not a tree to choose if you have young children.
Approx. height and spread and spread after five years: 4 × 2 m (13 × 6 ft). *After 20 years:* 7 × 5 m (23 × 16 ft).
Safe planting distance: SF 7 to 10 m (23 to 33 ft). DF 5 to 7 m (16 to 23 ft).

*Ornamental crab apples (*Malus*)*

You really are spoilt for choice here because so many varieties of ornamental crab are excellent for small gardens, with masses of flowers in spring, in some cases attractively coloured foliages, and brightly coloured fruits in autumn. For a really small tree, choose one grafted onto a dwarfing rootstock.

Japanese crab (*Malus floribunda*) A wonderful sight in spring, when it has masses of deep red buds, newly opened pale pink flowers, and more mature blush-white ones all at the same time. It has a semi-weeping habit, and branches on mature specimens can almost reach the ground. In autumn it has small, cherry-like fruits.
Approx. height and spread after five years: 4 × 1.5 m (13 × 5 ft). *After 20 years:* 8 × 6 m (26 × 20 ft).
Safe planting distance: SF 5 to 7 m (16 to 23 ft). DF 3 to 5 m (10 to 15 ft).

Malus hupehensis This small tree flowers abundantly in spring, and as a bonus its white flowers, which are pink in bud, are scented. In autumn it has small yellow fruits flushed with red.
Approx. height and spread after five years: 3 × 1.2 m (10 × 4 ft). *After 20 years:* 6 × 4 m (20 × 13 ft).
Safe planting distance: SF 7 to 10 m (23 to 33 ft). DF 5 to 7 m (16 to 23 ft).

This crab apple, Malus floribunda, *is a picture in spring with its masses of red buds, opening into pink flowers which fade to white.*

Malus sargentii One of the smaller crabs, it has masses of scented white flowers (tinted yellow in bud) with golden stamens. In autumn it has bright red, currant-like fruits, and its leaves turn yellow.
Approx. height and spread after five years: 1.5 m × 70 cm (5 ×2 ft). *After 20 years:* 5 × 2 m (16 × 6 ft).
Safe planting distance: SF 3 to 5 m (10 to 16 ft). DF 3 to 5 m (10 to 16 ft).

Malus 'Golden Hornet' White flowers are followed by bright yellow fruits in autumn. For some reason, birds prefer red and orange fruits to yellow, so these usually get left alone until well into the winter. It's also useful as a pollinator for apple trees.

Malus 'John Downie' This has a more upright habit than 'Golden Hornet', has pink-budded white flowers and plenty of large orange fruits flushed with red which are the best for making jelly or wine.
Approx. height and spread after five years: 4 × 1.5 m (13 × 5 ft). *After 20 years:* 8 × 6 m (26 × 20 ft).
Safe planting distance: SF 7 to 10 m (23 to 33 ft). DF 5 to 7 m (16 to 23 ft).

Coloured foliage

***Malus* 'Profusion'** As well as its coppery-crimson young foliage which slowly turns green through the summer, it also has purplish-red flowers which fade to pink, and oxblood red fruits.

***Malus* 'Royalty'** Considered by some to be the best purple-leaved form, since its wine-coloured foliage keeps its glossiness until it falls. It has large mid-pink flowers and wine-red fruits.
Approx. height and spread after five years: 4 × 1.5 m (13 × 5 ft). *After 20 years:* 8 × 6 m (26 × 20 ft).
Safe planting distance: SF 7 to 20 m (23 to 33 ft). DF 5 to 7 m (16 to 23 ft).

***Malus* 'Red Jade'** A small, weeping crab, with bright green leaves, which turn yellow in autumn, and blush-white flowers, followed by small, bright red fruits.
Approx. height and spread over five years: 2 × 1.5 m (6 × 5 ft). *After 20 years:* 3 × 5 m (10 × 16 ft).
Safe planting distance: SF 3 to 5 m (10 to 16 ft). DF 3 to 5 m (10 to 16 ft).

*Flowering cherries, plums and almonds (*Prunus*)*

This species offers an even wider choice than the ornamental crabs, although you need to stop yourself being seduced by some of the spectacular, double-flowered varieties and make sure you choose one that has something to offer after the blossom has gone.

Some breeders are now offering Japanese flowering cherries grafted on to dwarfing rootstocks, which means the final height and spread of the tree is reduced. Instead of *P.* 'Taoyoma Zakura' ending up at 7 × 7 m (23 × 23 ft) after twenty years, for example, it will only reach about 5 × 5 m (16 × 16 ft). It's worth checking with the garden centre before you buy as to which sort of rootstock your tree is grafted on to.

Purple-leaved plum (*Prunus cerasifera* 'Nigra') This small tree is best in spring when the new blood-red foliage provides a dramatic contrast to the pale pink flowers which appear at the same time, or even sometimes slightly before it. The foliage gradually darkens to purple through the summer.
Approx. height and spread after five years: 3 × 1.5 m (10 × 5 ft). *After 20 years:* 8 × 4 m (26 × 16 ft).
Safe planting distance: SF 7 to 10 m (23 to 33 ft). DF 5 to 7 m (16 to 23 ft).

Prunus 'Accolade' A superb small tree with a graceful, open, spreading habit and in early April clusters of deep pink buds open into semi-double, pendulous, light pink flowers up to 4 cm (1.5 in) across, with fringed petals. It goes on flowering for weeks.
Approx. height and spread after five years: 3.5 × 3 m (12 × 10 ft). *After 20 years:* 8 × 8 m (26 × 26 ft).
Safe planting distance: SF 5 to 7 m (16 to 23 ft). DF 3 to 5 m (10 to 16 ft).

'Yoshino cherry' (*Prunus* × *yedoensis*) This makes a graceful small tree with arching branches and masses of almond-scented, blush-white flowers in late March/early April. It also has good autumn colour.
Height and spread after five years: 3 × 2 m (10 × 6 ft). *After 20 years:* 7 × 5 m (23 × 16 ft).
Safe planting distance: SF 7 to 10 m (23 to 33 ft). DF 5 to 7 m (16 to 23 ft).

Sargent's cherry (*Prunus sargentii*) This eventually makes a rather flat-topped tree which offers a long season of interest. It has masses of single pink flowers in early spring, followed by new leaves which are coppery red when they first appear, turning green in summer, then, as early as September in some areas, turning brilliant vermilion and scarlet.
Approx. height and spread after five years: 3.5 × 2.5 m (12 × 8 ft). *After 20 years:* 9 × 10 m (30 × 33 ft).
Safe planting distance: SF 10 to 15 m (33 to 50 ft). DF 7 to 10 m (23 to 33 ft).

Korean hill cherry 'Autumn Glory' (*Prunus serrulata pubescens*) This tree also scores heavily on several counts, with bronzed-tinged new foliage, single white flowers, and handsome autumn tints – deep purples and reds. It forms a spreading, dome-shaped tree, and in winter its somewhat twisted stems make a delicate tracery against the sky.
Approx. height and spread after five years: 2.5 × 2 m (8 × 6 ft). *After 20 years:* 8 × 9 m (26 × 30 ft).
Safe planting distance: SF 10 to 15 m (33 to 50 ft). DF 7 to 10 m (23 to 33 ft).

Tibetan cherry (*Prunus serrula*) Although this has masses of small white flowers in May its main claim to fame is its superb, mahogany-coloured bark which peels away to reveal a patina as smooth and polished as superb antique furniture. It takes between five and ten years for this to develop.
Approx. height and spread after five years: 4 × 2 m (13 × 6 ft). *After 20 years:* 7 × 4 m (23 × 13 ft).
Safe planting distance: SF 10 to 15 m (33 to 50 ft). DF 7 to 10 m (23 to 33 ft).

Autumn cherry (*Prunus subhirtella* 'Autumnalis') This small tree produces semi-double white flowers on bare stems from November intermittently right through the winter to April, depending on the weather. A really cold snap can delay the flowers, but a spell of mild weather will bring them out. It also has good golden autumn colour, too. There is also an attractive variety with pink flowers, *P. s.* 'Autumnalis Rosea'.

Approx. height and spread after five years: 1.5 × 2 m (5 × 6 ft). *After 20 years:* 7 × 7 m (24 × 24 ft).
Safe planting distance: SF 7 to 10 m (23 to 33 ft). DF 5 to 7 m (16 to 23 ft).

*Japanese flowering cherries (*Prunus serrulata*)*

Lombardy cherry (*Prunus serrulata* 'Amanogawa') This tall, narrow tree has pale candy-pink flowers in spring and its foliage turns gold and flame in autumn. It's a very popular choice for small gardens because it is so narrow.
Approx. height and spread after five years: 3 × 1 m (10 × 3 ft). *After 20 years:* 6 × 2.2 m (20 × 7 ft).
Safe planting distance: SF 7 to 10 m (23 to 33 ft). DF 5 to 7 m (16 to 23 ft).

***Prunus* 'Shirotae' or 'Mount Fuji'** This very attractive tree has fragrant single or semi-double pure white flowers, and fresh light green leaves, with distinctive fringed edges. It forms a wide-spreading tree, and in mature specimens some of the horizontal branches may touch the ground.
Approx. height and spread after five years: 3.5 × 2.5 m (12 × 8 ft). *After 20 years:* 8 × 8 m (25 × 25 ft).
Safe planting distance: SF 7 to 10 m (23 to 33 ft). DF 5 to 7 m (16 to 23 ft).

Great white cherry (*Prunus* 'Tai Haku') produces single pure white flowers up to 5 cm (2 in) across, which are set off by the coppery-red young foliage in mid-spring. The leaves, which are exceptionally large, turn first green, then red and gold in autumn.
Approx. height and spread after five years: 3.5 × 2.5 m (12 × 8 ft). *After 20 years:* 7 × 7 m (23 × 23 ft).
Safe planting distance: SF 5 to 7 m (16 to 23 ft). DF 3 to 5 m (10 to 16 ft).

Weeping cherries

***Prunus* × *yedoensis* 'Shidare Yoshino'** This tree has masses of pale pink flowers, fading to white, on branches that weep to the ground in early spring. *Prunus* × *yedoensis* 'Ivensii' has fragrant snow-white flowers and a similar habit. These forms are not so easy to find as Cheal's weeping cherry (*P.* 'Kiku-shidare Sakura' or *P. subhirtella* 'Pendula') but specialist nurseries have them and they are well worth the extra effort involved in finding them.
Approx. height and spread after five years: 3 × 3 m (10 × 10 ft). *After 20 years:* 5 × 6 m (16 × 20 ft).
Safe planting distance: SF 5 to 7 m (16 to 23 ft). DF 3 to 5 m (10 to 16 ft).

Some Japanese flowering cherries, like Prunus serrulata *'Shirotae', are very suitable for small gardens.*

*Ornamental pear (*Pyrus*)*

Snow pear (*Pyrus nivalis*) This takes its common name not only from the white flowers which it produces in abundance in spring, but also from the white 'wool' which covers the young leaves and shoots appearing at the same time. The foliage then becomes silver-grey. It's not very widely available, but most good specialist nurseries stock it.
Approx. height and spread after five years: 3 × 2 m (10 × 6 m). *After 20 years:* 7 × 5 m (23 × 16 ft).
Safe planting distance: SF 7 to 10 m (23 to 33 ft). DF 5 to 7 m (16 to 23 ft).

Weeping willow-leaved pear (*Pyrus salicifolia* 'Pendula') Its long, silvery, willow-like leaves are also covered in a silky-white down until early summer. It does have small white flowers in April, but it is grown primarily for the dense mound of silvery foliage it eventually forms.
Approx. height and spread after five years: 2.5 × 2 m (8 × 6 ft). *After 20 years:* 4 × 3 m (13 × 10 ft).
Safe planting distance: SF 7 to 10 m (23 to 33 ft). DF 5 to 7 m (16 to 23 ft).

Golden false acacia (*Robinia pseudoacacia* 'Frisia') Its feathery golden foliage is late to appear in spring, but is well worth waiting for. It's quite slow-growing, but it does eventually form a large tree, nearly 12 m (40 ft) high, so it's not the right tree for a very small garden. The other problem with it is that its branches are rather brittle and snap easily, so only plant it in a spot sheltered from strong winds.
Approx. height and spread after five years: 3 × 2 m (10 × 6 ft). *After 20 years:* 12 × 6 m (39 × 20 ft).
Safe planting distance: SF 15 to 20 m (50 to 65 ft). DF 10 to 15 m (33 to 50 ft).

*The beautiful weeping willow-leaved pear (*Pyrus salicifolia *'Pendula') makes a superb specimen tree, or, as here, an arch.*

Rowan, mountain ash and whitebeams (Sorbus)

Another family with many members which really earn their keep in small gardens, since they can boast flowers, pretty foliage, good autumn colour and berries.

Mountain ash (*Sorbus aucuparia* 'Joseph Rock') This has clusters of small white flowers in spring, and fresh green feathery foliage which turns copper and gold in autumn when its yellow berries appear. Although it is a pyramid shape when young, its branches become more steeply ascending with age and it finally forms a tight, neat head. *S.* 'Embley' has superb autumn colour.
Approx. height and spread after five years: 2.5 × 1.5 m (8 × 5 ft). *After 20 years:* 10 × 5 m (33 × 16 ft).
Safe planting distance: SF 7 to 10 m (23 to 33 ft). DF 5 to 7 m (16 to 23 ft).

Kashmir mountain ash (*Sorbus cashmiriana*) A graceful little tree, with very pale pink flowers in spring, and beautiful fern-like foliage which turns red in autumn. Its hanging clusters of pearl-white berries stay on the tree until well into the winter.
Approx. height and spread after five years: 2 × 2 m (6 × 6 ft). *After 20 years:* 4 × 4 m (13 × 13 ft).

Sorbus vilmorinii This makes a slightly larger tree than *cashmiriana*, but has similar white flowers in spring and delicate ferny foliage which turns purplish-red in autumn. Its berries, which hang in clusters, start out a rosy red, then fade slowly to pink, blush-white and finally white.
Approx. height and spread after five years: 2.5 × 1.5 m (8 × 5 ft). *After 20 years:* 6 × 3 m (20 × 10 ft).
Safe planting distance (for both): SF 5 to 7 m (16 to 23 ft). DF 3 to 5 m (10 to 16 ft).

Sorbus sargentiana This tree is superb in the autumn and winter when its large and attractive leaves, up to 30 cm (1 ft) long, take on brilliant orange and scarlet tints. It also has bright red fruits which are then replaced by large crimson buds, sticky like a horse-chestnut's, on pale creamy-green stems.
Height and spread after five years: 2.5 × 1.5 m (8 × 5 ft). *After 20 years:* 6 × 3 m (20 × 10 ft).
Safe planting distance: SF 7 to 10 m (23 to 33 ft). DF 5 to 7 m (16 to 23 ft).

Whitebeam (*Sorbus aria* 'Lutescens') A picture in the spring when it has white flowers and new silvery foliage covered in creamy down. The leaves turn grey-green on top and grey-green below, which creates an attractive effect when the wind disturbs them. It sometimes has orange-red berries in autumn. If you can find its near relative, *S.* 'Mitchellii', snap it up. Its leaves are twice the size and quite dramatic in spring.
Approx. height and spread after five years: 3 × 2 m (10 × 6 ft). *After 20 years:* 12 × 8 m (39 × 26 ft).
Safe planting distance: SF 10 to 15 m (33 to 50 ft). DF 7 to 10 m (23 to 33 ft).

You shouldn't plant trees like Norway maple (*Acer platanoides*), sycamore (*Acer pseudoplatanus*), horse chestnut (*Aesculus hippocastanum*), ash (*Fraxinus*), beech (*Fagus sylvatica*), oak (*Quercus robur*), or lime (*Tilia*), within 25 m (80 ft) of any house – yours or the neighbours' – while poplars and weeping willow (*Salix alba* 'Tristis' and *S.* × *chrysocoma*) shouldn't be planted within 38 m (125 ft). However, given the wide range of beautiful trees suitable for average-sized and small gardens, why should you want to?

Planting a tree

You can plant container-grown trees at any time of the year, provided the ground isn't waterlogged, frozen or bone dry. Autumn is a particularly good time because the soil is still warm, there's unlikely to be a prolonged dry spell (and copious watering is the secret of success when it comes to planting trees and shrubs), and once their leaves have fallen most plants put their energies into a final spurt of root growth before closing down, so to speak, for the winter. The only disadvantage of autumn planting is that a prolonged spell of really cold winter weather can kill off a few less hardy plants while they are still not properly established, so trees that are slightly tender, like the golden honey locust, are best left to the spring.

Planting container-grown trees

By the time you've got round to buying your trees, you will already have prepared your border by digging it over, clearing it of weeds, and improving the soil in whichever ways are necessary (see Chapter 2). It can't be stressed too strongly that you must never simply dig a hole in uncultivated ground, throw in a bit of organic matter and plant your tree in that. On a clay soil, the hole will act as a sump, drawing water from the land around, so you will be planting your tree in cold, waterlogged soil. If you're lucky, the tree will just be very slow to start in growth. If you're not, the roots will be deprived of air and so drown, or will rot away. Either way, the tree will die.

Before you actually start digging your hole, give the tree a thorough soaking while it's still in its container. Not only will it be easier to remove the pot when the time comes, but you are also making sure the roots and the soil around them are really moist before you plant the tree, something that's much more difficult to do once they're in the ground.

Dig a hole slightly bigger than the container. Check that it is deep enough by putting the container in the hole, then laying a bamboo cane, or even your spade, across it. If the cane rests on the soil both sides *and* the top of the container touches it, then the hole is deep enough.

If your soil is low on organic matter, add a few spadefuls of well-rotted manure or composted straw and a couple of handfuls of blood, fish and bonemeal or rose fertiliser if you're not an organic gardener to the pile of soil you've dug out. Then remove the tree carefully from its pot. If it's in a thin black polythene one, cut the polythene off with a sharp knife. If it's in a rigid plastic pot and you've watered it thoroughly beforehand, then it should lift out fairly easily. If not, try gently squeezing the sides of the pot just to loosen the soil. If all else fails, you'll have to cut the pot away, using a Stanley knife or something similar.

Put the rootball into the hole and make sure that the tree is facing the right way. Many trees have a pretty obvious front if you look at the shape, so make sure that's facing the point from which you'll be looking at it most often. Then start carefully shovelling in the soil. When you've filled the hole, firm the soil with the ball of your foot. What you're trying to do is to get rid of any large air pockets, in which the roots would dry out and die, without compressing the soil too much, so go gently.

It's a very good idea to use the surplus soil to build a low retaining wall, a couple of inches high and about 60 cm (2 ft) in diameter, around the tree. When you give it a thorough soaking, that wall will help keep the water where you want it – directly over the rootball – and stop it flowing all over the border.

Staking

Almost all new trees need staking, but recent research has shown that short stakes – reaching only one-third of the way up the trunk – are more efficient than the traditional, much longer ones. Allowing the top of the tree to sway about in the wind, it seems, thickens the base of the trunk and helps strengthen the root system.

You'll need two stakes of 5 × 5 cm (2 × 2 in) timber. To work out their length, measure the tree's trunk and divide by three (to give one-third its length) and add 45 cm (1 ft 6 in) to hammer into the ground.

Hammer them in just outside the rootball on either side, then nail a crosspiece between them. Nail a special plastic tree tie, which has a collar to prevent it chafing the trunk, to the crosspiece to stop it slipping and buckle it round the tree. Check it now and again to make sure it hasn't become too tight. If you really are on a tight budget, you could use a nylon stocking, tied in a figure of eight, to attach the tree to the stake, but whatever you do don't use wire or nylon twine, which will cut into the tree as it grows and either kill it outright or allow diseases in.

Alternatively, you can use just one stake, the same length, and hammer it diagonally into the ground behind the tree and close to the trunk. Then use a tree tie in the same way.

Planting evergreens

Evergreens, like conifers, are best planted in September or left until April or even May. They are almost always supplied either in containers (in which case plant them as you would any container-grown tree) or 'rootballed', which means they have been dug up with a good ball of soil around the roots, which is then wrapped in sacking for delivery. Leave the sacking round the roots until the moment you are ready to plant. Not only does it protect the roots from damage, but as you'll need to keep the soil well watered, the sacking stops it washing away from the roots. When you have dug the correct-sized hole, place the rootball, sacking and all, in the hole and cut away as much of the sacking as you can easily reach. What's left underneath the rootball will soon rot away in the soil. Then finish planting in the same way as before.

Planting bare-rooted trees

These must be planted while they are dormant – between November and March – when the soil isn't waterlogged or frozen, although autumn is probably the ideal time for the reasons given above.

The most important thing to remember when you're dealing with bare-rooted trees is that the roots must never dry out. The very small roots which take up essential nutrients, as well as water, will die if they're exposed to the sun or to drying winds for any length of time. That means if the trees arrive at a time when you can't plant them right away, you must 'heel them in'.

Dig a trench of about a spade's depth, throwing the soil forward. Lay the plants in the trench with the roots at the bottom and the trunk leaning away from you, on to the soil you've thrown forward. Then cover the roots by digging another trench behind the first and throwing the soil forward on to them. On the day you're ready to plant, dig a hole roughly wide enough to take the roots when they are spread out and deep enough for the soil to be level with the soil-mark on the trunk of the tree, once it's planted. Then remove the tree from where you had heeled it in, and wrap the roots in wet sacking or an old wet towel. Check that the hole is wide enough to take the roots once they are well spread out, and that it's the right depth, by using a bamboo cane or a spade placed across the hole. The soil mark on the trunk should be level with the cane or spade.

Check the roots and if any are broken or damaged cut them back cleanly with a sharp knife or secateurs.

Cover the roots again with the wet sacking while you hammer a stake one-third the length of the trunk, plus 45 cm (1 ft 6 in) into the hole (see above). Place the tree in the hole, arranging the roots around the stake if need be, and then put in a little fine soil (mixed with blood, fish and bonemeal or rose fertiliser) over the roots. Hold the trunk of the tree firmly and jerk it up and down a few times, so that the soil settles in between the roots. Half-fill the hole and tread it firmly but gently down with the ball of your foot. Again, the object of the exercise is to eliminate large air pockets, but avoid compressing the soil too much. Refill the hole completely, and firm the soil with your foot.

Attach the trunk to the stake with a special tree tie, and mulch around the trunk with well-rotted compost or manure.

Caring for newly planted trees

It's a salutary fact that over *half* of all trees and shrubs planted die within the first year, which is not only deeply disappointing to new gardeners, but also very expensive. There's no doubt that the main reason for this horticultural slaughter is lack of water. People may think they've watered their plants diligently, but it is astonishing just how much water a tree or shrub needs. The odd bucketful now and again, or your standing there for five minutes with the hose, barely moistens the surface. It takes hours for soil to be saturated at the lower levels where the roots are, and if you only wet the surface thirsty roots will come looking for water there, and will be even more susceptible to damage from hot sun or drying winds.

Once you've planted your tree, run the hose gently on the rootball and leave it for several hours. If you've built a retaining wall of soil, obviously that will help keep the water where it's most needed. In warm weather, water every few days, and if there's been a light shower don't think that you needn't bother. Unless it's really poured down for an hour or two you'll still need to water your newly planted tree. Evergreens, particularly conifers, need special care when it comes to watering. Since they retain their leaves all year they lose water through them constantly, so unless they can replace it the leaves start to shrivel and turn brown. In dry weather their only source of water is you and the hosepipe. For the same reason, if you have conifers that you haven't got round to planting yet you'll need to protect them from frost. A rootball can freeze very easily in a plastic pot, and with the water turned to ice the plant can't take it up and suffers effectively from drought.

To protect them, dig the containers into the soil if it isn't frozen. If it is, or you have no space, stand the pots on a thick layer of newspaper to give the bottom some insulation. Heap something like bark or straw around the pot, or wrap it tightly in another thick layer of newspaper.

Calendar

No matter at what time of year you take over your garden, there are a number of jobs that you can be getting on with. Most construction work – putting up fences, laying paths, repointing walls and so on – can be done at almost any time of the year, and so can *de*struction – knocking down greenhouses, taking down fences, pulling out hedges, cutting down trees, digging out shrubs and so on. The two provisos for both construction work and horticulture are, first, don't undertake any work on the soil – or even walk on it – when it is waterlogged, and second, if soil is frozen, don't even try planting anything (very keen beginners have been known to pour bucketfuls of boiling water on to the soil to make it physically possible to plant. The soil freezes again soon after, and most of the plants die!) or walk on the grass, since you can do it a lot of damage.

January

Clear rubbish, debris from the garden, and dig out weeds. (Not much point in applying weedkiller now, as the weeds need to be growing strongly for it to be effective.)

Soil Dig over cleared ground that was heavily infested with weeds. Don't dig over borders where there is evidence of plants. You don't know what may come up in spring, and you could destroy what's there if you dig now.

Hedges Dig out any hedges that you are not going to keep. Prepare the ground ready for planting a new hedge (see p. 137). Plant bare-rooted deciduous hedging plants in a mild spell.

Clear out the bottom of any hedge you are going to keep, then mulch it with well-rotted farmyard manure, garden compost or composted straw.

Trees and shrubs Get a tree surgeon to look at trees that need work. Plant bare-rooted trees and shrubs in a mild spell.

February

Soil Carry on clearing rubbish, debris and weeds and dig over cleared ground, as in January.

Hedges As January, but you can also plant container-growing deciduous and evergreen hedging plants now. Feed established hedges with blood, fish and bonemeal, Growmore or rose fertiliser.

Trees and shrubs As February. Winter-prune fruit trees (not plums or cherries, though) if the weather is reasonably mild. Feed fruit bushes, like blackcurrants. Move any fibrous-rooted shrubs that need moving (see p. 84). Prune hard back those deciduous shrubs that flower from mid-summer on, like *Buddleia davidii* and *Lavatera thuringiaca* 'Barnsley' (see p. 75 for pruning guide) and late-flowering clematis.

March

Soil Carry on clearing as January, and improve the soil by adding well-rotted organic matter and, on heavy clay soils, coarse grit.

Now that you can see what bulbs and herbaceous plants you have, start clearing existing borders of weeds, although it's best to wait until next month to use weedkiller.

Hedges Bare-rooted deciduous plants must be planted by the end of this month. You can still plant container-grown kinds. Cut back overgrown hedges now (see p. 127) and feed. Prune informal hedges, like barberry (*Berberis*) and firethorn (*Pyracantha*) which have carried berries through the winter months.

Lawns Rake a lawn you are going to keep to remove the thatch, either by hand or with a scarifier. Once new grass is showing through, start to mow (see p. 54). Start cutting down very long grass now (see p. 44). If you are going to lay a new lawn on bare soil, turf it now, or prepare it for seeding later on.

Trees and shrubs Carry on planting bare-rooted and container-grown trees and shrubs. Prune roses, foliage shrubs like the smoke bush (*Cotinus coggygria*) and the golden cut-leaved elder (*Sambucus racemosa* 'Plumosa Aurea') to produce better colour. Also shrubs like dogwoods and some willows, grown for the colour of their winter stems. Although the conventional wisdom is that you shouldn't prune certain trees after March because they bleed, experienced tree surgeons will prune most kinds in summer too.

Other plants Dig up and heel in (see p. 38) bulbs that have finished flowering if you need to clear the ground around them or they are in the wrong place. If they are overgrown, divide them and replant. Lift, divide and replant herbaceous plants (see p. 87).

April

Soil Carry on clearing the ground and improving the soil. Now the weeds are growing strongly it's a good time to apply weedkiller.

Hedges Plant evergreens and container-grown deciduous plants, but be prepared to water in a dry spell. Prune informal spring-flowering hedges that don't have berries. Feed and mulch existing hedges.

Lawns Lawns that are beyond salvation should be killed off now with weedkiller and the ground rotavated, ready for turfing or sowing next month. Continue to turf or sow new lawns on bare soil. Start mowing existing lawns frequently, and carry out any restoration work that's needed (see p. 46).

Trees and shrubs Prune plums and cherries now. Prune spring-flowering shrubs like forsythia and flowering currant (*Ribes*) now.

Other plants Carry on lifting, dividing and replanting herbaceous plants, but only until the middle of the month.

Alpines and rock plants Clear out a weed-infested rockery now (see p. 104) and trim back any alpines that are spreading too far.

Pools Clear out an overgrown or leaking pool now, saving any plants worth saving and any fish. In a reasonably healthy, well-balanced pool, remove the early growths of blanket weed, and plant any new water plants.

May

Soil As April.

Hedges Keep newly planted hedges well watered and free of weeds. Trim established hedges, although conifers are best left until August.

Lawns You can still lay a new lawn now, although you must be prepared to water it regularly. Feed an established lawn.

Trees and shrubs Prune any late-spring flowering shrubs, like *Kerria japonica* and bridal wreath (*Spiraea arguta*). Prune early-flowering clematis like *C. montana* only if they have filled their allotted space. Tie in new growth of climbers.

Other plants Stake any tall-growing herbaceous plants, like delphiniums, before they grow too large. Remove any dead bulb foliage. Put out containers – tubs, baskets and so on – at the end of the month. Keep well watered in milder areas.

Ponds Thin out overgrown plants, remove any blanket weed and any excess duckweed. Empty and repair existing ponds.

Alpines and rock plants Clear out a weed-infested rockery now (see p. 104) and trim back any alpines that are spreading too far.

June

Soil As April.

Hedges Trim existing hedges that weren't trimmed in May, although again conifers are best left until August.

Lawns You can still lay turf or sow seed, but obviously the hotter and drier the weather the riskier it becomes, especially if there's a chance of a hosepipe and sprinkler ban. Cut established lawns twice a week if possible, and feed again at the end of the month. Kill off grass that is beyond salvation. Cut down long grass.

Trees and shrubs Prune early summer-flowering shrubs like weigela and mock orange (*Philadelphus*) once flowering is over.

Other plants Remove faded flower spikes from herbaceous plants.

Ponds Top up if necessary in dry weather, and keep a constant guard against blanket weed. Drain and repair a leaking pond.

Alpines and rock plants As May.

July

Soil As April.

Lawns As June, except that they don't need feeding again.

Trees and shrubs Cut back shrubs that have finished flowering. Start taking semi-ripe cuttings of shrubs like berberis, ceanothus, choisya, hebe, potentilla, spiraea, syringa, weigela and so on.

Other plants Plant autumn-flowering bulbs, like autumn crocus, colchicums, hardy cyclamen now.

Alpines and rock plants As May.

August

Soil As April.

Hedges Trim conifer hedges now (see p. 139).

Lawns As July.

Trees and shrubs Prune rambler roses. Continue to take half-ripe cuttings from shrubs.

Other plants Carry on planting autumn-flowering bulbs in the first part of the month, and daffodils and narcissi in the second half. Begin to lift, divide and transplant herbaceous plants.

Alpines and rock plants Take cuttings of alpines like aubrietias.

Ponds As June.

September

Soil Carry on clearing the ground, but weedkillers are now less effective because the weeds are growing less vigorously.

Hedges Probably the best time to plant container-grown evergreen hedging plants. Weed and generally clear out the bottom of an established hedge.

Lawns Probably the best time to sow a lawn from seed, while the soil is still warm, and there's likely to be some rain. Good for turfing, too. Cut an established lawn less often and towards the end of the month rake out the accumulated dead thatch. This is about the last time you can cut long grass and expect it to survive.

Trees and shrubs Prune trained apple trees, peaches, nectarines, blackcurrants, gooseberries and plums. Plant evergreen shrubs, or move established ones.

Other plants Plant spring-flowering bulbs (except tulips). Cut down the dead growth of herbaceous plants, and continue to lift, divide and plant.

Ponds Clean up the pool, and cover it with wire netting or mesh to prevent it from being clogged with autumn leaves. Although you can drain and repair a leaking pond now, you shouldn't replant it until the spring.

October

Soil Carry on clearing the ground, but don't apply weedkiller. Dig over what ground you can, especially if you have heavy soil, to let the frost break it down, and kill soil pests.

Hedges Start planting bare-rooted plants.

Lawns Give an established lawn its last cut of the season, then put the mower in for a service. Much better than waiting until the mad scramble in March. You can still lay turf and also sow seed but only if the weather is mild. Leave long grass now until the spring.

Trees and shrubs Plant container-grown and bare-rooted trees and shrubs once the leaves have fallen. Take hardwood cuttings from shrubs like dogwood (*Cornus alba*), mock orange (*Philadelphus*) and willow (*Salix*). Prune blackcurrants if you haven't already.

Other plants Remove dead growth of herbaceous plants and have a general tidy-up before the winter. Carry on lifting, dividing and replanting. Plant tulips and lilies late in the month.

November

Soil As October. Rake up dead leaves and store them in a wire-netting bin to rot down into leaf mould, the best soil conditioner there is.

Hedges As October.

Trees and shrubs Plant container-grown and bare-rooted trees and shrubs. Winter-prune bush apples and pears. Winter-prune deciduous shrubs, removing dead or diseased wood or branches that cross.

Alpines and rock plants Remove all fallen leaves from on top of alpines, otherwise these plants will rot. Many hate wet conditions, so protect them with small sheets of glass or perspex, fixed with metal clips.

December

Soil As November.

Hedges As October.

Trees and shrubs Carry on planting when conditions allow. Move any shrubs that are in the wrong place. Finish winter pruning of trees, fruit trees and shrubs, although not if frost is threatened. Protect tender plants with straw or bracken.

Other plants Protect slightly tender herbaceous plants, like *Gunnera manicata* or *Nerine*, even if they die right away in winter, either with straw, weighted down with soil, or with their own dead foliage.

Index

Figures in **bold** refer to pages with illustrations.